PENGUIN BOOKS

BOHEMIANS, BOOTLEGGERS, FLAPPERS & SWELLS

Graydon Carter is the editor of *Vanity Fair*. The American edition of *Vanity Fair* was launched by the publisher Condé Nast in 1913. Under the stewardship of editor Frank Crowninshield, who assigned most of the pieces in this volume, the magazine was a literary and visual treasure of the Jazz Age and featured an imcomparable slate of writers through 1936, when it was folded into *Vogue* as a casualty of the Great Depression. *Vanity Fair* was revived in 1983. Carter has been its editor since 1992.

David Friend, a writer, editor, producer, curator, and formerly *Life* magazine's director of photography, is *Vanity Fair's* editor of creative development.

BOHEMIANS, BOOTLEGGERS, FLAPPERS, AND SWELLS

THE BEST OF EARLY *VANITY FAIR*

INTRODUCTION BY **GRAYDON CARTER**

EDITED BY

GRAYDON CARTER

WITH **DAVID FRIEND**

PENGUIN PRESS

PENGUIN BOOKS
An imprint of Penguin Random House LLC
375 Hudson Street
New York, New York 10014
penguin.com

First published in the United States of America by Penguin Press,
a member of Penguin Group (USA) LLC, 2014
Published in Penguin Books 2015

THE LIBRARY OF CONGRESS HAS CATALOGED THE HARDCOVER EDITION AS FOLLOWS:
Bohemians, bootleggers, flappers, and swells: the best of early Vanity fair /
introduction by Graydon Carter; edited by David Friend.
pages cm
ISBN 978-1-59420-598-9 (hc.)
ISBN 978-0-14-312790-1 (pbk.)
1. American literature—20th century.   2. Literature, Modern—20th century.   3. United States—
Civilization—20th century—Literary collections.   I. Friend, David, 1955– editor.   II. Carter, Graydon.
III. Vanity fair (New York, N.Y.)
PS536.B595 2014
810.8'0052—dc23
2014009783

Printed in the United States of America
3 5 7 9 10 8 6 4

Designed by Gretchen Achilles

CONTENTS

1920s

1930s

VANITY FAIR AND THE BIRTH
OF THE NEW

GRAYDON CARTER

When the dreariness, the madness, and, oh, the sheer tackiness of modern life get to you, isn't it tempting to imagine a different life in a different place and period? The places and periods I go to in my mind—and I have no rational explanation for this—are invariably set in big cities in the last century: San Francisco in the sixties, Paris in the fifties, London between the wars, Los Angeles in the thirties. And for the purposes of this introduction: the New York of the twenties. New York back in those days was the fizzy incubator of the Jazz Age and the Roaring Twenties. It was the big room: Jimmy Walker was mayor; Wall Street and bootlegging were booming; jazz, modern art, and talkies were the rage; everyone—from statesmen to sandhogs—was trying to get their head around the latest theories of Freud and Einstein; and the bible for the smart set was *Vanity Fair*.

It was *the* modern magazine during that early incarnation, from 1913 to 1936. And everybody, but everybody, wrote for it, including, in no particular order, P. G. Wodehouse, Alexander Woollcott, F. Scott Fitzgerald, T. S. Eliot, e. e. cummings, Noël Coward, Gertrude Stein, A. A. Milne, Stephen Leacock, Thomas Mann, Djuna Barnes, Bertrand Russell, Aldous Huxley, Langston Hughes, Sherwood Anderson, Walter Lippmann, Carl Sandburg, Theodore Dreiser, Colette, John Maynard Keynes, Ford Madox Ford, Clarence Darrow, Janet Flanner, Paul Gallico, Dalton Trumbo,

William Saroyan, Thomas Wolfe, Walter Winchell, and Douglas Fairbanks (both Sr. and Jr.).

They were drawn to *Vanity Fair* by a decent word rate and by the magazine's editor, Frank Crowninshield. He was known as Crownie to his intimates, who recognized him for his skills as a cultural clairvoyant and a taste maker. He helped launch the seminal Armory Show in 1913, which introduced avant-garde painting to America, and was a founding trustee of the Museum of Modern Art. He would also play a significant role in the birth of what came to be known as café society, cohosting small get-togethers with Condé Nast, the publisher of *Vanity Fair* and *Vogue*. Their parties brought together the era's brightest minds, talents, and wits, and were staged at the thirty-room penthouse apartment at 1040 Park Avenue that Crowninshield and Nast shared. (Same-sex domesticity was not uncommon back then.)

For twenty-two roller-coaster years, Crowninshield reveled in his singular cultural perch atop the masthead of what became the quintessential Jazz Age magazine. His *Vanity Fair* brimmed with groundbreaking photography and bold illustration and design. But just as important—in ample evidence here—were its sparkling essays, commentary, profiles, poetry, and fiction from many of the most forward-thinking writers of the day. Some contributors were public intellectuals (Huxley, Russell, H. L. Mencken). Others were experts in what was then experimental art and music (Clive Bell, Roger Fry, Gertrude Stein, George Jean Nathan, Virgil Thompson, Tristan Tzara, Carl Van Vechten, Erik Satie, and Jean Cocteau). Still others, such as Fitzgerald, Anita Loos, John Emerson, and Donald Ogden Stewart, would go west to seek their fortune in the movie trade.

The offices of the magazine in those days—first on fabled West Forty-fourth Street and later in the new Graybar Building, adjacent to Grand Central Terminal—reflected its editor's eclectic tastes. Crowninshield, who had a soft spot for sleight of hand, kept a deck of cards ready for the amusement of staffers or for guests who would often pop in—Harry

Houdini, say, or Charlie Chaplin. Editorial lunches with his three rising staff members, Dorothy Parker, Robert Benchley, and Robert Sherwood, consisted of eggs Benedict, kippered herring, chocolate éclairs, and *café spécial*.

According to Condé Nast's biographer Caroline Seebohm, Crownie would run the office "with the greatest informality. Actresses, models, photographers, and writers were always milling about in the reception room, under the impression that he had invited them to a personal interview. (He often had.)" On many Saturday nights, Crowninshield could be found gambling in the basement of a brownstone on East Thirty-seventh Street, where friends like Woollcott would place wagers on tiny mechanical horses that would zip around a tabletop racetrack, the random victor determined by what they called a "chance machine."

Crowninshield both sought and attracted excellence. The senior editors who would pass through *Vanity Fair*'s doors were a storied lot: not only Parker, Benchley, and Sherwood, but also Edmund Wilson, Edna St. Vincent Millay, and Clare Boothe Brokaw, a brash, young dynamo who would eventually sleep her way through much of the masthead. (She also wrote the play *The Women*, married Henry Luce, and became a congresswoman and a U.S. ambassador to Italy.)

The magazine regularly predicted which cultural forces would leave a lasting mark. (To that end, I recommend the stories in this volume on Picasso, Chaplin, James Joyce, W. Somerset Maugham, Joan Crawford, Cole Porter, and Babe Ruth.) They took the pulse of the period—in real time—with an unrivaled sense of taste. The writing in *Vanity Fair* pushed boundaries with its muscular and often experimental prose. In examining the daunting shape of things to come, the magazine's writers wrote about men's rites and women's rights, the intrusive media and exclusive bastions of the well-to-do. They questioned our destructive fascination with the entertainment industry and our addiction to organized sports. They used satire to criticize ostentation, Prohibition, marital duplicity, and the grinding new "publicity machine." Social historian Cleveland Amory would later observe that the magazine was "as accurate a social barometer of its time as exists." The finest pieces in the Jazz Age *Vanity Fair*, seventy-two of which are collected here, focus more often than not on how Americans, especially New Yorkers, in confronting the Machine Age, radical art, urbanization, Communism, Fascism, globalization (epitomized by a World War), and the battle of the sexes, were coping with the growing pains of a new phenomenon: *modern* life.

To the reader: For historical accuracy, these articles, stories, and poems retain the spellings and punctuation that appeared at the time of their initial publication in *Vanity Fair*.

1910s

THE PHYSICAL CULTURE PERIL

P. G. WODEHOUSE

FROM MAY 1914

Physical culture is in the air just now. Where, a few years ago, the average man sprang from bed to bath and from bath to breakfast-table, he now postpones his onslaught on the boiled egg for a matter of fifteen minutes. These fifteen minutes he devotes to a series of bendings and stretchings which in the course of time are guaranteed to turn him into a demi-god. The advertisement pages of the magazines are congested with portraits of stern-looking, semi-nude individuals with bulging muscles and fifty-inch chests, who urge the reader to write to them for an illustrated booklet. Weedy persons, hitherto in the Chippendale class, are developing all sort of unsuspected thews, and the moderately muscular citizen (provided he has written for and obtained the small illustrated booklet) begins to have grave doubts as to whether he will be able, if he goes on at this rate, to get the sleeves of his overcoat over his biceps.

To the superficial thinker this is all very splendid. The vapid and irreflective observer looks with approval on the growing band of village blacksmiths in our midst. But you and I, reader, shake our heads. We are uneasy. We go deeper into the matter, and we are not happy in our minds. We realize that all this physical improvement must have its effect on the soul.

* * *

A man who does anything regularly is practically certain to become a bore. Man is by nature so irregular that, if he takes a cold bath every day or keeps a diary every day or does physical exercises every day, he is sure to be too proud of himself to keep quiet about it. He cannot help gloating over the weaker vessels who turn on the hot tap, forget to enter anything after January the fifth, and shirk the matutinal development of their sinews. He will drag the subject into any conversation in which he happens to be engaged. And especially is this so as regards physical culture.

The monotony of doing these exercises every morning is so appalling that it is practically an impossibility not to boast of having gone through with them. Many a man who has been completely reticent on the topic of his business successes and his social achievements has become a mere babbler after completing a month of physical culture without missing a day. It is the same spirit which led Vikings in the old days to burst into song when they had succeeded in cleaving some tough foeman to the chine.

A gain, it is alleged by scientists that it is impossible for the physical culturist to keep himself from becoming hearty, especially at breakfast, in other words a pest. Take my own case. Once upon a time I was the most delightful person you ever met. I would totter in to breakfast of a morning with dull eyes, and sink wearily into a chair. There I would remain, silent and consequently inoffensive, the model breakfaster. No lively conversation from me. No quips. No cranks. No speeches beginning "I see by the paper that . . ." Nothing but silence, a soggy, soothing silence. If I wanted anything, I pointed. If spoken to, I grunted. You had to look at me to be sure that I was there. Those were the days when my nickname in the home was Little Sunshine.

Then one day some officious friend, who would not leave well alone, suggested that I should start those exercises which you see advertised everywhere. I weakly consented. I wrote for the small illustrated booklet. And now I am a different man. Little by little I have become just like that offensive young man you see in the advertisements of the give-you-new-life kind of medicines—the young man who stands by the bedside of his sleepy friend, and says, "What! Still in bed, old man! Why, I have been out with the hounds a good two hours. Nothing tires me since I tried Peabody and Finklestein's Liquid Radium." At breakfast I am hearty and talkative. Throughout the day I breeze about with my chest expanded, a nuisance to all whom I encounter. I slap backs. My handshake is like the bite of a horse.

Naturally, this has lost me a great many friends. But far worse has been the effect on my moral fiber. Before, I was modest. Now, I despise practically everybody except professional pugilists. I meet some great philosopher, and, instead of looking with reverence at his nobby forehead, I merely feel that, if he tried to touch his toes thirty times without bending his knees, he would be in the hospital for a week. An eminent divine is to me simply a man who would have a pretty thin time if he tried to lie on his back and wave his legs fifteen times in the air without stopping. . . .

There is another danger. I heard, or read, somewhere of a mild and inoffensive man to whom Nature, in her blind way, had given a wonderful right-hand punch. Whenever he got into an argument, he could not help feeling that there the punch was and it would be a pity to waste it. The knowledge that he possessed that superb hay-maker was a perpetual menace to him. He went through life a haunted man. Am I to become like him? Already, after doing these exercises for a few weeks, I have a waist-line of the consistency of fairly stale bread. In time it must infallibly become like iron. There is a rudimentary muscle growing behind my right shoulder-blade. It looks like an orange and is getting larger every day. About this time next year, I shall be a sort of human bomb. I will do my very best to control myself, but suppose a momentary irritation gets the better of me and I let myself go! It does not bear thinking of.

* * *

Brooding tensely over this state of things, I have, I think, hit on a remedy. What is required is a system of spiritual exercises which shall methodically develop the soul so that it keeps pace with the muscles and the self-esteem.

Let us say that you open with that exercise where you put your feet under the chest of drawers and sit up suddenly. Well, under my new system, instead of thinking of the effect of this maneuver on the abdominal muscles, you concentrate your mind on some such formula as, "I must remember that I have not yet subscribed to the model farm for tuberculous cows."

Having completed this exercise, you stand erect and swing the arms from left to right and from right to left without moving the lower half of the body. As you do this, say to yourself, "This, I know, is where I get the steel-and-indiarubber results on my deltoids, but I must not forget that there are hundreds of men whose confining work in the sweat shops has entirely deprived them of opportunities to contract eugenic marriages."

This treatment, you will find, induces a humble frame of mind admirably calculated to counterbalance the sinful pride engendered by your physical exercises.

Space forbids a complete list of these spiritual culture exercises, but I am now preparing a small illustrated booklet, particulars of which will be found in the advertising pages. An accompanying portrait shows me standing with my hands behind my head and with large, vulgar muscles standing out all over me. But there is a vast difference, which you will discover when you look at my face. I am not wearing the offensively preoccupied expression of most physical-culture advertisements. You will notice a rapt, seraphic expression in the eyes and a soft and spiritual suggestion of humility about the mouth.

AUGUST STRINDBERG

GEORG BRANDES

FROM OCTOBER 1914

S trindberg was the most brilliant author of modern Sweden, and one of the most gifted I have ever known. Ibsen, in speaking of him, once said: "Here is a greater man than I."

But Strindberg was a wholly abnormal type, mentally. A man so eccentric that, except for his masterly writings, I should have called him insane.

But let me begin by saying a word as to his physical appearance! His strongly modeled forehead clashed strangely with the vulgarity of his lower features. The forehead reminded one of Jupiter's; the mouth and chin of a Stockholm street urchin. He looked as though he sprang from irreconcilable races. The upper part of his face was that of the mental aristocrat,—the lower belonged to "the servant girl's son," as he called himself in his autobiography.

During a long acquaintance with him I was fortunate in being able to agree with him on fundamental principles and to find that minor differences of opinion never irritated him against me, nor caused the slightest break between us.

It was my fate to be present at many crucial moments in Strindberg's mental life. More than once I have seen him on the turn-rail, as it were, which changed the entire direction of his spiritual and mental locomotive. And each time I have been able to remark how deep and sincere were

his changes, even if they contained a trace of the theatrical in their outward expressions.

I saw Strindberg for the first time during a short stay which he made in
Denmark. I remember his first visit to me very clearly, because he made
several rather odd remarks to me. After the usual greetings had been
exchanged I asked him if he had any friends or relatives in the little town
of Roskilde, for I had seen by the papers that he had spent a good deal of
time there.

"Indeed not," he replied. "I visited Roskilde on account of the Bistrup
Insane Asylum, which, as you know, is located there. I wanted the director
to give me a certificate as to my sanity. I have an idea my relatives are
plotting to trap me."

"And what did the doctor say?" I asked.

"He said he could not give me a certificate off hand, but that he
undoubtedly could do so if I would remain there under observation for a
few weeks."

I then realized that I was dealing with an original temperament.
Strindberg continued:

"I suppose you know that my tragic and ridiculous marriage has been
broken off?"

"I did not even know you were married," I replied. "I am thoroughly
familiar with your books, but I know nothing whatever of your private
life."

Let me explain that Strindberg's hatred of women amounted almost to
a monomania. Many critics have attributed his violent antipathy to
them—an obsession which colored all of his work—to his first marriage,
which, as is well known, was most unhappy. But, like many women
haters—Schopenhauer, merely to quote an example—Strindberg was always under some strong feminine influence.

At about this time he asked me to direct the rehearsals of his play "The
Father" at the Casino Theatre in Copenhagen. A few days later, as I was

trying to explain the play to the actors, who were used to plays dealing with more frivolous subjects, Strindberg tapped me on the shoulder and said:

"Listen! Is 1500 kr. too much to pay here for an apartment of six rooms and a kitchen?"

"But why in the world do you want six rooms, you, a single man!"

"I am not single! I have a wife and three children with me."

"You must excuse me, but did you not say the other day that your marriage had been broken off?"

"In a measure, yes! I sent Madame Strindberg away as my wife, but I have retained her as my mistress."

"Excuse me, but such a thing is impossible. By all the laws of this country under such circumstances, she immediately becomes your wife again. You may safely embark on such a venture with any other woman in the world but not with your wife."

One November night in the year 1896, I witnessed a crisis in Strindberg's life. I had been out, and found his card on my desk as I returned. He was passing through Copenhagen, he had written, and did not wish to leave the city without seeing me. And he asked me to meet him in some quiet place, as he had brought no good clothes with him.

From this note I gathered that he must have grown more peculiar than ever. When I reached his hotel I learned that he had already gone to bed.

"He sent for me himself," I said.

The door of his room was open. He was in bed, fast asleep. As I touched him on the shoulder he awoke and said:

"I took a sleeping powder. I felt sure you wouldn't come."

But he got up and dressed himself quickly, and it turned out that he was much better dressed than I. While dressing, he said:

"Did you know that my existence was predicted, long ago, by Balzac?"

"Where?"

"In 'Seraphitus-Seraphita.'" He searched for the book in his valise, opened it and pointed to the words: 'Once again the light shall come the North.' "There! you see, Balzac refers to me."

I said, to tease him a little: "How do you know Balzac didn't allude to Ibsen?"

"Oh, no, he meant *me*, there isn't a doubt about it."

Balzac's book had made a strong impression on him on account of its touches of Swedenborgianism.

We went to a restaurant and ordered some wine. Strindberg grew excited as he talked.

"You're out of touch with the reigning intellectual movements," he said. "We're living in an age of occultism. Occultists rule the life and literature of our day. Everything else is out of date."

He spoke with much admiration of the newer occultists and with real reverence of Joseph Pelladan who, at the time, still called himself Sar and Mage. He also spoke of the Marquis of Guita, about whom his friend Maurice Barres had written a book. I told him that I had been following with interest the discussion between Huysmans and Guita. Huysmans— then living in Lyons—accused Guita—residing in Paris—of having willed him acute pains in the chest by means of black magic. Guita retorted that he dealt with white magic only, not black, and described his proceedings. To this Huysmans replied that he had seen the ingredients of black magic in a closet in Guita's home.

This remark excited Strindberg violently. "Is it possible," he asked, "that Huysmans had the same experience as I? I've been suffering, too, from a pain in the chest which a man in Stockholm caused me during my stay in Paris."

"Who was he?"

"My one time benefactor, who tried to punish me for my recent ingratitude."

Then, without transition: "You have an enemy. A newspaper enemy. I want to do something for you. Let me kill your enemy."

"You're very kind. But I should prefer not."

"But no one would know about it."

"So all criminals think. Besides, don't you feel it would be rather unjust to kill a man on account of an unkind newspaper article?"

"Well, let's not kill him. We'll simply blind him."

"I still have my doubts. However, how would you go about it?"

"If you will give me the man's photograph, I will, with my magic, blind him by driving a needle through his eyes."

"In that case, you could easily deprive me of my eyesight, too, if you wished?"

"Hardly. It must be done with hatred."

"Granted, but if a man who hates me tears my picture into pieces, will I fall to the ground in bleeding bits?"

This remark seemed to put him out, and he did not answer me.

He continued, however, to explain in detail the intricacies of magic— black and white—and he dwelt particularly on the evils of black magic when exercised by criminal hands.

The restaurant closed, and we began to walk up and down along the water-front.

At one time Strindberg was greatly interested in alchemy. He even claimed to have obtained gold in small quantities.

He once gave me a copy of his book, "Inferno." All through it there runs the mortal fear of persecution. The book shows that he felt that a special interest attached to his every movement, and that supernatural powers were forever busied with him, now warning him, now punishing him, now guiding him and never allowing him to get out of their reach. In Paris, for instance, he felt this distinctly. Strindberg lived in constant fear of being murdered by a Polish writer for having loved the latter's wife before she met her husband. A Norwegian artist—a friend of the Pole—met

Strindberg, and, probably in order to play a joke on him, told him that the dreaded man was expected in Paris.

"Is he coming to kill me?" asked Strindberg.

"Of course. Be on your guard."

Strindberg wished, however, more details, and decided to look the artist up, but he dared not approach the house. A few days later he screwed up his courage and went to call on him. At the door he saw a little girl on the doorstep. In her hand she held a playing card. It was the ten of spades.

"The ten of spades," he shouted. "There is foul play in this house," he muttered, and hastily left the place.

In "Inferno" Strindberg thought that he had finally found the explanation of many of the mysteries of Swedenborg's spirit world. The book closes with Strindberg's longing to seek solace in the Catholic Church. Swedenborg had prejudiced him against Protestantism, explaining that it was treason against the Mother Church. The growth of the Catholic Church in America, England and Scandinavia seemed to him to prove the decisive triumph of Catholicism over Protestantism and the Greek Church. And he concludes the book by confessing that he has sought to be admitted to a Belgian monastery.

Later on, however, Strindberg publicly declared that he never wished to seek consolation in the Catholic Church.

THE WORLD'S NEW ART CENTRE

FREDERICK JAMES GREGG

FROM JANUARY 1915

New York is now, for the time being at least—the art capital of the world, that is to say, the commercial art centre, where paintings and sculptures are viewed, discussed and purchased and exchanged.

Many predictions had been made, from time to time, as to when this state of affairs would come about. For years the drift of "old masters" has been Westward. Dr. Bode of Berlin, and other experts, had talked about the danger represented by the American buyer as competitor, in the open market, with the public galleries of Europe, limited as the latter were by slender resources and the niggardliness of parliaments. The London National Gallery and the Louvre have envied and feared the mighty resources of our Metropolitan Museum, which enabled it, at any moment, to pounce on whatever might emerge from private ownership—whether it was a newly discovered Rembrandt or a hitherto unsuspected collection of Chinese porcelains. So, while England, or France, was appealing to the patriotic to subscribe in order that some treasure might be kept from making the Atlantic voyage, word would come suddenly that the worst had happened, and that the dreadful Americans had scored again, thanks to the Rogers bequest or the alertness of some private benefactor.

The Great War—which has affected everything and everybody—hastened what prophets regarded as inevitable. Paris, London, Berlin and

Petrograd, having the grim necessity of national self-preservation to attend to, simply went out of business as far as "art" was concerned.

The young painters and sculptors, like the young men in the picture-shops, are with the Colors. The exhibitions are all off. Hundreds of studios are locked up, and the cafés where the quarrelsome geniuses took their meals, and their ease, are but sad and quiet resorts of the casual and careless sightseer.

This is where technically neutral New York arose to her opportunity. For a while everything was up in the air, like Wall Street. But through patience and perseverance the tangle was straightened out. So the six weeks' Matisse exhibition, planned to take place in the Montross Galleries in January, has become an assured fixture, and the set of exhibitions of the men of the younger French school at the Carroll Galleries will occur in the winter months just as if Europe, instead of being convulsed from one end to the other, were wrapped in profound peace. It is to be hoped that not many of the paintings will have to be hung with the customary purple.

New York will see, at the Matisse show, what the most discussed of all the Moderns regards as his most important, because most significant, work.

In the ultra Modern exhibition, at the Carroll Galleries, will be seen the work of Gleizes, Jacques Villon; Derain, painter of the "Fenêtre sur Parc;" Redon, of the humming flowers; Chabaud, of the "Flock Leaving the Barn;" de Segonzac, Dufy, de la Fresnaye, Moreau, Marcel Duchamp, who staggered New York with his "Nude Descending the Stairs;" Rouault, Picasso in his successive "red," "blue," and "cubist" periods; de Vlaminck, Signac, Seurat, and Duchamp-Villon. There will also be total strangers to us like Vera, Valtet, Ribemont-Desseignes, Mare, Sala and Jacques Bon. In addition, the veteran impressionist master Renoir will make his bow to the public as a sculptor, with a figure in the round and a plaque.

One striking thing about the "new men" is the way in which they change from one medium to another, as Picasso and Jacques Villon with their etchings, Dufy with his wood engravings, Vera with his wood cuts and Mare with his book bindings. Perhaps, as far as our own artists are concerned, one result of the display of the creations of these Frenchmen will be to cause them to show what they have been doing in unexpected directions. The wood carvings of Arthur Davies and the wood engravings of Walt Kuhn would astonish most of those who are not familiar with the very private activities of these two artists.

There has been more quarreling about Henri Matisse than about any other individualist of our epoch. If Matisse were not convinced of his genius, he might well be reassured on the subject by listening to the shouts of "Impostor!" "Rogue!" "Knave!" with which he is greeted by those who don't like him. But this solid artist, who looks more like a professor of biology than a painter, is quite undisturbed by such popular clamor. If it is dishonest to paint without regard to the rules, he is content to be considered dishonest. But—great virtue in your "but"—nobody knows where your blessed rules are to be found, not even the learned creatures who talk so much about them.

Matisse does not care whether or not they call him a charlatan. He considers his art perfectly sincere and simple. Take his method of etching a portrait. Days are taken up in observation of his subject. Then he sets to work rather elaborately. The result is put aside. The second attack shows still less detail. In the final effort—that for which the rest was but preparation—every non-essential has been eliminated—nothing is left but something which suggests rather the qualities than the externals of his model. In a word—even if such a comparison is dangerous—Matisse develops a work from the heterogeneous to the homogeneous, from the complex to the baldly simple.

He has obtained less recognition at home than abroad, though Marcel Sembat, the present Minister of Public Works, and, since the death of Jaures, the chief socialist leader, is an ardent collector of his works. On the occasion of his first exhibition at Vollard's, the preface of the catalogue was written by no less official a person than Roger Marx, the editor of the

"Gazette des Beaux Arts." The fact that the dealer wanted to give greater prominence to the critic than to the painter caused a disturbance which had true farce-comedy features, but Matisse won—on points.

The following proves nothing. But facts which are inconclusive, logically, are often interesting. Many of the Rembrandts, for instance, now in the Altman collection—which is the most gorgeous possession of our Metropolitan Museum—were, some years ago, the property of Alphonse Kann. He got tired of "old brown varnish"—people will get tired of everything, no matter how classical—and to-day he buys only Matisses. One of his proudest possessions is the nude, "with the blue leg," a painting which, shown in the International Exhibition of 1913, surprised New York, disgusted Chicago and horrified Boston. Still M. Kann, if he felt it necessary to defend himself from the sneers of the scornful, might point out that Matisse is safely enshrined, through his drawings in the French Museums; that, other drawings, in spite of the notorious and aggressive conservatism of the Kaiser, are in the Print Cabinet at Berlin, and that he is more sought after by German collectors than any of the other "new" Frenchmen. Two characteristic paintings of prime importance, which will be seen in the Montross exhibition are the "Woman at a Desk" and "The Gold-fish." These are the property of a Moscow collector. As, owing to the war, it was impossible to send them to their owner, Mr. Matisse decided, after some urging, to allow them to come to America, provided they didn't go further West than New York.

Soon after the war broke out Matisse lost all trace of his mother, his brother and his brother's family, who lived at his birthplace, Le Cateau, in the Nord. For months he could not work. He went to his country home, from which he was recalled to Paris to make selections for his New York exhibition. This took his mind off his family troubles. By this time he is probably in active service, for, in spite of his rheumatism, he was determined to get to the war. If he envies a soul in the world it is the painter Derain who went out in the artillery, was wounded, returned to Paris, and has now gone back to the trenches.

ARE ODD WOMEN REALLY ODD?

HYMAN STRUNSKY

FROM JUNE 1915

An odd creature has lately made its appearance on the horizon of man's world. Scientists have craned their necks in the effort to determine its species, and psychologists have offered many conflicting explanations of its nature.

Was it man or was it woman?

Was it brute or was it human? Was it—What?

Inasmuch as it stood erect and glided with ease and in a spirit of independence, it suggested man; but it lacked man's salient characteristics and coarser habits. Its shape and beauty—the clearness of the skin and the softness of the eyes—were decidedly womanly, but it lacked woman's love of frills, her thirst for gossip, and her aptitude for useless occupations.

There was nothing about it to suggest the brute. It did not profane nor debauch; it did not utter coarse oaths, nor did it resort to violence. It was not human, in the sentimental meaning of the word. It did not cry nor did it whimper; it did not pout nor did it frown; it did not cuddle with weakness, or even crouch with fear.

Close observation, careful scrutiny and much wrangling, established the fact that the creature was a woman, after all, but an odd one! Gissing even wrote a book about her and called it "Odd Women." Other authors followed him. H. G. Wells, for instance. G. B. Shaw, May Sinclair, W. L. George and a hundred lesser literary lights have all taken a shy at the "Odd" woman.

Especially does she appear odd to Madame X., the old fashioned woman, who has been slumbering under the impression that there was nothing at all odd about her own type of womanhood. Mrs. X. finds it a bit disturbing.

Woman's historical position does not invite critical analysis. The fact is that men have not been treating her fairly. We very chivalrously called our wife our "better half," but always regarded her as an inferior and kept her in strict subordination.

She was not a partner to the man, but an auxiliary, she was an extension to man, man, the gigantic structure; the centre of the universe. When we spoke of her "virtues," we usually meant such of her character-istics as were pleasing and gratifying to us. Obedience, self-sacrifice, beauty, fidelity, tenderness, and affection, were qualifications highly valued,—because of their contributive share to the general happiness of husbands.

She was not master of herself. Her body belonged to her husband, her heart to her children, her mind to her home. Her sex was her sole means of subsistence. From the arms of an indulgent father she passed on to the shoulders of a supporting husband. Her function was to breed children and to amuse men. Whether poor or rich she was in a state of depend-ence. When poor she was a slave in a hovel; when rich she was an inmate of a glorified Doll's House.

Marriage was her only trade, and like all other trades it was subject to the fluctuations caused by the law of supply and demand. The supply happened to overlap the demand and the market suffered a slump. Wise and knowing parents took charge of the matrimonial arrangements of their children. In these arrangements matters of convenience figured more prominently than questions of the heart. Love was too delicate a substance to attract the parent eye. Sexual selection, a biological play of emotion and passion—on which depends the make-up of posterity—was crowded out by "practical" considerations. The daughter was not to obey

her instincts, but her parents. Disobedience meant—for the daughter—
celibacy, and celibacy meant economic dependence.

The odd woman has odd notions about marriage, the oddest of which
is that she thinks it is largely her own affair. To her, marriage is more
than the privilege to indulge in dutiful submission. It is a matter of instinct in which her womanhood is involved, and unless she can have it
beautifully she will not have it at all.

She is willing to give her labor and strength in exchange for a livelihood but she draws the line on the surrender of her soul. To obey parents
is noble, but the will of the parent is the voice of the past and marriage is
the demand of the future. The nuptial tie is not to mean the shackling of
hearts, and a child is not to be the offspring of a business transaction. If
celibacy threatens to lead to economic dependence then she will simply
accept other trades as a means of subsistence.

She has at last found these other trades. Marriage is now not her only
means of support.

She has discovered that there are other vocations besides being a wife.
She has become a worker; a useful member of society; a fellow citizen in
an industrial democracy. She is not the inferior but the equal of man.
With him she enters the workshop, the library, the college. She writes
books and edits magazines. She practices law and medicine. She paints
pictures and takes photographs. She is a chemist, a geologist, a biologist,
a stenographer, a decorator, a designer. She is a manufacturer. She owns
farms and runs hotels. She is a lecturer and an actress. She is a teacher.
She is a buyer. She is—odd!

Extremely odd—when judged by Madame X., whose frailties and
weaknesses have heretofore constituted our standard of womanhood. We
do not shrug our shoulders in deprecation at Madame X., who sleeps late,
eats much, plays often and works seldom. We do not think it wrong of her
to spend her best hours in the occult devices of the boudoir, where mani-
curists and masters of tonsorial art are mustering her faculties to the

requirements of her social functions, and repairing, with color and cream, the ravages of Habit and Time.

Madame X. regards the odd women with amazement because they are different; because they rise early, play little, work much, make money, and are seldom idle.

Whether the odd woman is in business, or in a profession, she is beginning to earn a high salary and to stoop to no man in economic independence. She lives in a comfortable apartment and has a small place in the country. When her parents, or friends, are in need she assists them without suffering the humiliation of wheedling the money from her husband. Her contributions to charity are not the cause of "scenes" at breakfast. She is capable, efficient, and able to stand on her own feet. She is not a passive, but an active, member of society. Life is to her—what it should be to all women—a busy and strenuous experience.

Not long ago, in New York, two "odd" women—an authoress and a painter—were discussing Madame X. The authoress was describing to the painter a routine day in Madame X.'s life: Her pleasures, her dresses, her auction parties, her dances, her gossip, at luncheons, her race-meets and her susceptible admirers.

The authoress paused in her recital:

"And is that *really* her life?" asked the painter. "What an *odd* woman she must be."

NEW YORK WOMEN WHO EARN $50,000 A YEAR

ANNE O'HAGAN

FROM AUGUST 1915

t is more than probable that, during the months of June and July, the Commissioner of Internal Revenue for New York has become convinced that the earning capacity of New York women is a fairly good reason for giving them the suffrage—in November. Perhaps, some day, he will let the world know to how many of the checks, sent by women in payment of their income tax, was attached one of those specially printed little blanks, which the suffragists have circulated so widely, reading: "I pay this tax under protest, in obedience to a law in the making of which I had no voice."

A few weeks ago, the editor of this magazine [Frank Crowninshield] stated, in a widely contradicted address, that he knew, personally, a dozen women in New York who were earning over $50,000 a year by their own talents or industry. He said that he also knew fifty more who were earning $10,000 a year, or over. His statement was widely ridiculed and challenged, by many newspapers, and space writers, and by a host of conservative persons (whose social ideas had ceased to develop at the end of President Hayes's administration, or thereabouts). They sought to convince the editor that the clever—and presumably beautiful—ladies had a little deceived him.

* * *

This writer has just completed a limited investigation into the question of the earnings of successful New York women. And she is quite convinced that without any exploring of New York's by-ways, the editor's statement was, in reality, a mild one.

Take for example, the playwrights.

Miss Jean Webster is a modest woman and wouldn't for worlds make anarchists and bomb-throwers of the envious rest of us by telling exactly what she earns. But she does permit herself to say that from $500.00 to $700.00 a week is what "Daddy-Long-Legs," in the hands of a single company, nets her as the author of it. Well, there have been several companies playing "Daddy-Long-Legs" for the greater part of the past year. There are, in addition, royalties on the moving picture rights of it, royalties upon it in book form, princely prices for other work, a serial and several short stories from her pen—and other side issues to swell the youthful playwright's income, during the past year, to a figure a little over $50,000.

Since we began with playwrights let us go on with them.

There is "Twin Beds" continuing for Margaret Mayo—Mrs. Edgar Selwyn—the beneficent work of endowment which her first farce, "Baby Mine" began for her, a few years ago. Mrs. Selwyn has had several $50,000 years, and more are in store for her.

Then—but not in the $50,000 class—there is Eleanor Gates, whose "Poor Little Rich Girl" not only gave great delight to New York's jaded public, a winter ago, but made her a comfortably rich little girl herself. And then there is Rachel Crothers. Or consider the case of Kate Douglas Wiggin—whose "Rebecca of Sunnybrook Farm" laid a neat fortune in her lap when it went upon the boards, after following as a book, the filial example of "The Birds' Christmas Carol" and the Penelope stories in laying treasures of love and admiration there. And if Mrs. Francis Hodgson Burnett, down at her place on Long Island, fails to feel the financial security of a steel magnate, with "Sara Crewe" and "Little Lord Fauntleroy" and the "Dawn of a To-morrow" defying time and change—but the thing is unthinkable.

A nd since we are speaking of the stage, what of the actresses? In what golden chariots may they not ride during the period of their prosperity, and ever after, if they are but wise and thrifty! That printed slip of defiance to the income tax commissioner seems tame when one considers what Miss Maude Adams or Miss Ethel Barrymore might say—or Laurette Taylor, or Ruth Chatterton, or Billie Burke, or Jane Cowl, or Frances Starr, or Margaret Illington, or Margaret Anglin, or Dorothy Donnelly or Chrystal Herne, or many, many less resplendent twinklers in the theatrical sky.

And the vaudeville favorites! There are, literally, a dozen of them who earn more than ten thousand dollars, like Gertrude Hoffmann, or Beatrice Herford, or Nora Bayes, or Nazimova, or Calve, for instance. Chief among them is Eva Tanguay whose salary is somewhere between $50,000 and $75,000 a year.

As for the film actresses, they are out of the Arabian Nights, no less! Think of the Mary Pickfords of $100,000 a year, and Marguerite Clarks at over $50,000 and the Mary Fullers, Lottie Briscoes, Pearl Whites, Anita Stewarts, Ruth Rowlands, Irene Fenwicks, Marie Doros, Pauline Fredericks, and many others at salaries which take one's breath away.

Marie Doro, more or less of a novice on the films, has recently received an offer by a responsible firm—of $100,000 a year. She has earned within the past year, by acting and movies, as much as $4,000 in ten days.

M iss Geraldine Farrar is acting for the "movies" for two months this summer at a fabulous salary. Next winter she will receive $2,500 a performance for singing in opera or concert. This says nothing of her royalties on phonograph records. Think of Lucrezia Bori and Miss Ober, and the other opera singers. One of the impresarios, who has managed many concert and opera singers, furnishes a careful estimate of the incomes of only a few of them thus: Alma Gluck, $75,000 a year; Schumann-Heink, $85,000; Emmy Destinn, $50,000; Julia Culp, $20,000; Frances Alda, $25,000; Gadski, $30,000; Fremstad, $30,000; Caroline Hudson Alexander, $10,000. These sums only represent the earnings of ordinary concert work; what would be added to them by including the fees and royalties from records made for the talking machine companies, one's dazed mathematical faculties fail to compute. Through the making of records, even the comparatively modest incomes of violinists, like Kathleen Parlow's and Maude Powell's ten-to-fifteen-thousand dollars-a-year, are greatly increased.

Alma Gluck, during the past twelve months, has probably earned more money than any woman alive. She is, today, the most popular singer in the phonograph. Her total income, from concerts and records, has considerably exceeded $120,000.

Before we leave the stage and turn to the more prosaic occupations in which women are laying up wealth, let us look at the dancers! How much do women like Mrs. Vernon Castle, or Pavlowa, make? It has been carefully computed that Mrs. Castle and her husband have earned more than $110,000 during the past twelve months. Following after Mrs. Castle are Joan Sawyer and Florence Walton, and Bessie Clayton and a half dozen others.

And then there are the women writers! There are many of these who earn $10,000 a year even without help from the dramatization of their work. Fannie Hurst is one of the authoresses among those present at any gambol on Mt. Croesus of ten-thousand-dollar women. Take Elizabeth Jordan, editor and writer. Consider Gertrude Atherton—she is a New Yorker now—and those strong, colorful novels of hers. And Edna Ferber, and Kathleen Norris, and Mrs. Riggs, and Gene Stratton Porter and a dozen others. Take even the woman publicist, who does not expect to rank financially with those writers whose function is primarily to amuse; she, also (Miss Ida Tarbell, for instance) does not find ten thousand a year a goal at all impossible of attainment.

And the ladies who illustrate. If May Wilson Preston, one of those rare human beings who may claim to be a satirist and a humorist with the pencil, demanded, instead of the beggarly ten or fifteen thousand dollars which she now earns, a hundred thousand a year, it would not be her admiring public which would demur or call her claim too large!

Then there's Helen Dryden, who does covers, and fashion pictures, and who designs costumes for Mr. Dillingham. And there is Rose O'Neill Wilson, the mother of all the Kewpies. Once the Kewpie pictures and dolls were the whole Kewpie family. But now, with factories turning out Kewpie dolls, Kewpie dishes, boxes, jewelry, candy, clocks, clothes, postcards, toys—and with Mrs. Wilson receiving royalties on every one of them, it is safe to say that she has long ago passed the $50,000 mark.

And the artists and portrait painters! What about Cecilia Beaux and Mrs. Rand and Miss Emmet, and others like unto them? And the sculptors, like Mrs. Whitney and Evelyn Longman! Ten thousand dollars a year would be meagre pay for them.

But all these women—the conservative man is likely to object—have unusual talents—genius; an afflatus apart from the gift of mere industry. But we are ready for him. We beg him to look at the heads of schools, business enterprises, of cigarette factories, of decorating establishments, of dressmaking houses.

What does he say to the schools in New York like those built up by Mrs. Finch (now Mrs. Cosgrave), by Miss Clara Spence, Miss Chapin, Miss Marie Bowen, Miss Rutz-Rees, and many more? That schools like these earn multiples of $10,000 a year cannot be denied.

And what will the conservative man say to women like Miss Belle Greene, who is officially the librarian of the late J. Pierpont Morgan's library, but who was also his able lieutenant in all the work pertaining to his various collections?

And what about Mrs. M. E. Alexander, the pioneer woman in the New York real estate business, of whom it is recorded that she put through, for her employer, a $90,000 deal during the first two months (and the last) of her apprenticeship? Mrs. Alexander, after that pleasant demonstration of her fitness for the business she had chosen, went into it for herself!

And then there are the dressmakers and milliners—to call them by names too prosaic for their bewildering products. What is to be said of Lucille, Louise, Simcox, Mollie O'Hara, McNally, Farquharson & Wheelock (both women), Van Smith, the Fox Sisters, and a score of others like unto them who have proved themselves not only designers and saleswomen, but labor-managers as well? One of them, Mrs. Simcox, spoke for them all when she smilingly declared that a woman in her line of business would consider herself a failure if she were not clearing more than ten thousand a year.

What about play brokers and managers, like Miss Elizabeth Marbury? How many times does the gentleman with views on the financial inability of women think that that hard-working lady multiples our figure of $10,000 a year? And there are others in her profession, like Miss Alice Kauser, who forge along at a not too great distance behind.

Consider the growing horde of women decorators. Miss Elsie de Wolfe would think it a poor year if she did not clear $50,000 in profits. There are half a dozen more New York women—like Miss Swift, or Mrs. Rand, for instance, who are treading upon one another's heels in achieving success in the same profession.

A little over a year ago a building was in course of construction upon Fifth Avenue. A woman had taken the land on forty-two years' lease, and she was putting up the building. She was putting it up with earnings from her tea-rooms. It was only twelve years ago that Miss Ida L. Freese came to New York from Ohio, with no business training. To-day she runs her building, tea-rooms, a photographic studio and a farm, whence come the vegetables used in her restaurants.

When your true conservative smokes one of "Brennig's Own" cigarettes does he realize that it is a woman's enterprise which places it between his lips? Mrs. Brennig's annual income—derived from her cigarettes—is one which has long ago tripled our modest $10,000 minimum.

When the reader eats "Mary Elizabeth's" candy, or takes luncheon in "Mary Elizabeth's" luncheon rooms, does he realize that twelve or fourteen years ago Mary Elizabeth Evans, a schoolgirl in Syracuse, began to put up home-made candies to help the family purse?

Even to the women who do not manage enterprises of their own, but who are valuable cogs in the great wheels of other people's enterprises, ten thousand a year is no such unattainable goal. Mrs. Ray Wilner Sundelson, manager of an agency of the Equitable Life Insurance Company, is one of the highest salaried women in New York. She and fifteen thousand dollars a year have long been happily acquainted. And the management of a few department stores admit the presence of one or two women in their employ who qualify for this list—women buyers, department managers, advertising managers, and the like.

And there you are. In shop-keeping, hotel managing, teaching of singing and dancing, song writing, and in other branches of New York's varied life, there are dozens of other women who earn, through their own talents or industry, at least $10,000 a year.

And we are only fifteen years advanced into the new century.

What will they earn when this century of marvels—with its great opportunities for women—draws to its close?

ANY PORCH

DOROTHY ROTHSCHILD (PARKER)

FROM SEPTEMBER 1915

Dorothy Parker's first published poem

"I'm reading that new thing of Locke's—
    So whimsical, isn't he? Yes—"
"My dear, have you seen those new smocks?
    They're nightgowns—no more, and no less."

"I don't call Mrs. Brown *bad*,
    She's *un*-moral, dear, not *im*moral—"
"Well, really, it makes me so mad
    To think what I paid for that coral!"

"My husband says, often, 'Elise,
    You feel things too deeply, you do—'"
"Yes, forty a month, if you please,
    Oh, servants impose on *me*, too."

"I don't want the vote for myself,
    But women with property, dear—"
"I think the poor girl's on the shelf,
    She's talking about her 'career.'"

"This war's such a frightful affair,
      I know for a fact, that in France—"
"I love Mrs. Castle's bobbed hair;
      They say that *he* taught her to dance."

"I've heard I was psychic, before,
      To think that you saw it,—how funny—"
"Why, he must be sixty, or more,
      I told you she'd marry for money!"

"I really look thinner, you say?
      I've lost all my hips? Oh, you're *sweet*—"
"Imagine the city to-day!
      Humidity's *much* worse than heat!"

"You never could guess, from my face,
      The bundle of nerves that I am—"
"If you had led off with your ace,
      They'd never have gotten that slam."

"So she's got the children? That's true;
      The fault was most certainly his—"
"You know the de Peysters? You *do*?
      My *dear*, what a small world this is!"

FOOTBALL AND THE NEW RULES

WALTER CAMP

FROM SEPTEMBER 1915

With the actual preliminary football games of this season upon us, lovers of the game feel the necessity of becoming posted on the most important alterations in the rules. Spectators are not the only ones interested in this, for there are a great many players and some coaches who are by no means sure of even the most important changes.

The first addition to the machinery of the game which spectators will notice is the office of field judge. Last year this official was optional, but now he is obligatory. Moreover, the new rules have given the position of Field Judge a real significance by placing the watch of the time-keeper in his hands, with the idea that the linesman who kept time last year should concentrate his attention on the line-up during scrimmage. It is hoped that this new division of labor will make it easier for the officials to detect and penalize "off-side" play. Another rule, conceived with the idea of making things easier for the officials, and also to do away with the usual confusion in the last period of the game, is that which prevents the resubstitution of a player except at the beginning of a period. Last year everyone found it more or less annoying when, just before the end of the game, coaches sent in a whole army of substitutes. Aside from distracting the interest of the spectator, this indiscriminate mobilization on the side lines frequently resulted in the presence of a great number of non-combatants on the field of action when the ball was actually in play—an exceedingly confusing thing for the officials. Along these same lines the committee passed a note deprecating the custom of putting in substitutes for the purpose of conveying information to the team. The general practise of numbering the players was also recommended.

With regard to the conduct of the individual player, the penalty for unsportsmanlike conduct was changed from disqualification to a fifteen-yard setback, but flagrant misconduct is still punishable by disqualification. While this may seem to be too much power in the hands of the man with the whistle, it really ought to work out for the best interests of the game. Frequently, last year, when there was a reasonable doubt as to the actual intention of a player to willfully break the rules, the official was forced to let the offense go unpunished rather than inflict the drastic penalty of disqualification. Under the new ruling he can placate his conscience by compromising on the fifteen-yard penalty.

Before the rules were changed last year, running into the full-back in any way, intentionally or unintentionally, was penalized. Last season "roughing" the full-back was a "penal offense." This year the rule has been clearly divided into two parts. Running into the full-back is penalized by a fifteen-yard set-back, but "roughing" the full-back not only penalizes the offending team fifteen yards, but in addition, disqualifies the player committing the offense.

A rule which has been added in order to do away with unnecessary delay is that which instructs the referee always to bring the ball out fifteen yards, when it goes out of bounds, unless the captain of the side in possession of the ball requests a lesser distance.

This year's rules ring the curfew knell on the practise which started last year of intentionally throwing the ball out of bounds. The old rule provided that when a forward pass went out of bounds it went over to the team not in possession of the ball, at the spot where it crossed the side line. This made it possible for a team, on its opponent's forty-five yard line (though not in a convenient position to make a field goal) to signal for a forward pass and throw the ball out of bounds somewhere near their opponent's five-yard line. As a forward pass can naturally be executed more accurately than a kick, the result was that the opposing team, forced to put the ball into play at this point, and denied the chance which they would have had to run back the ball if it had been kicked, found itself in an uncomfortable position. This seemed to give an unfair advantage to the team making the pass. So it has been ruled that a forward pass which goes out of bounds, whether it touches a player or not, is an incompleted pass. In other words, the ball comes back to the line of scrimmage and counts as a down on the first, second and third tries. On the fourth try, it goes over to the opposing team on the line of scrimmage.

Another addition to the rules specifies that the interference will no longer be permitted to bowl over the secondary offense after the whistle blows. This practise was greatly abused last year. A half-back, on the defense, seeing the play stop in the line, would relax, when suddenly he would be struck from the side or from behind by a member of the interference who had been detailed to cross over from one side of the line and take the secondary defense. This was not only dangerous to the players, but frequently, in the more important games, came very near resulting in bad feeling. The interference, under the new rules, must stop when the whistle blows, and no man, either on the offense or defense, can run into a player after the referee has blown his whistle.

Another bad trick practised by the interference last year was for them to drop before a player, and throw their legs at him so that their feet and lower leg would strike the player across the body or thighs. This has resulted in several injuries. There is already a rule providing that if a player strikes his opponent below the knee with his lower leg it is "tripping." The ruling now reads that a player who strikes another with his lower leg above the knee costs his side a penalty of fifteen yards.

One other play has been legislated against. In this play the center would start to pass the ball back, hold it for a fraction of a second, and then snap it to another lineman, who would come around and carry it. This year, when the center makes the motion to snap the ball back, he must actually let it go.

One other rule has been most properly altered—the rule relating to a player touching a forward pass. Last year this rule was altogether too severe. When two men were both eligible to receive the pass, and one of them touched the ball, the second player had to keep his hands off it or be penalized. This seemed somewhat unjust, and the rule has been altered so that a case of this sort is simply an incompleted forward pass, with the loss of a down, but no penalty to the second player.

To be letter-perfect in these rules, and at the same time to have the sharpness of vision, the rapidity of thought, and the clearness of purpose necessary to rule under them, is the task of the football official.

Naturally men of this caliber are hard to find and the universally high quality of American football officials is due largely to the efforts of one man. That man is Dr. James A. Babbitt of Haverford. He is chairman of the committee on officials, and in this capacity handles the machinery necessary for the appointment of thousands of officials for the games played in the Fall. He is backed by a committee, but all the details of the work are due to the energy and tact of this one man.

When the great upheaval came several years ago and the rules were radically revised, it was not entirely the effect of this revision which brought about a marked improvement in the game. A large proportion of this improvement came from the more careful selection of officials. Three of these officials have been in the last year or two made an adjunct of the Rules Committee, in order that this Committee may, during its considerations, refer to them from time to time, and ascertain what difficulties were found in the code of the previous year.

The three officials working with the Rules Committee are Nathan A. Tufts of Brown, Wm. M. Morice of the University of Pennsylvania, and Wm. S. Langford of Trinity—all of them thoroughly experienced in the handling and conduct of big games. The Central Board of Officials is made up of E. K. Hall of Dartmouth, Percy Haughton of Harvard, Parke H. Davis of Princeton, A. A. Stagg of Chicago, C. W. Savage of Oberlin, Harris G. Cope of the University of the South, and [this] writer. These men assist Dr. Babbitt as far as possible.

WAR SCENES ACROSS THE CANADIAN BORDER

STEPHEN LEACOCK

FROM OCTOBER 1915

I n Canada we are at war. Eighty thousand Canadian soldiers have crossed the ocean for the front. Some sixty-five thousand more are enlisted for Overseas Service and are training in military camps in Canada. At Valcartier beside Quebec, at Niagara and elsewhere there are wide tented cities of Canadian soldiers. The streets of our great towns are filled with men in khaki. Across the leading thoroughfares are broad white streamers that mark recruiting places,—for the fiftieth, the sixtieth, the one hundredth, and soon, no doubt, the one hundred and fiftieth battalion of the Expeditionary Force of the Dominion. About fifteen to twenty battalions,—an army division of forty thousand men,—are already on the fighting line. The others follow in a steady stream, that moves more strongly with every month and shows no ending. The regiments are filled as fast as their formation is announced. The mingled elements of which our Commonwealth is made up are reflected in them. There are French regiments from Old Canada speaking their own tongue, Highland regiments,—like that of Montreal, all honor to it, that fought at Langemarck,—troops of horse from the West, and Irish Rangers so called, after the Irish fashion, because they have never ranged and never been in Ireland. In single troop ships and in little fleets they move across the ocean. One great flotilla that sailed a year ago carrying the men of the first Valcartier camp was the largest military force that has ever, in all the world's history, crossed the Atlantic Ocean. The forces that sailed with Cortes or Pizarro, or that came under Burgoyne or Admiral Howe, do not compare with it.

All this is being done among us with but little parade, or outward show. There is no need now for the tin glory of the militia camp. The people of Canada have reached the stage when their eyes can look through the mere pomp and circumstance of war and see the hard reality behind it. They have counted their dead. They are counting them every day with each fresh list of "casualties" that the telegraph brings from Ottawa. In the first year of the war Canada lost,—dead, wounded and missing,—10,870 men. From Halifax to Vancouver there is no village but has its name inscribed upon the roll of glory. You may see the record of it running in every country newspaper in Canada. "Killed in action in France, Such and Such a One, of Pleasant Vale, Ontario," with the battalion and the regimental number. There is in it all the humble pathos of personal obscurity lifted a moment to the light. Without the war this man might have been moving among the yellow sheaves of wheat to the clicking of the reaper in an August harvest field, in some lost corner of Ontario. There is much in it that will bear thinking of.

Yet with the growing losses and the increasing sternness of the conflict the recruiting and the mustering under arms move only the faster. There is no turning back. There is no thought of peace. As some one said, the other day: "There are no Jane Addamses, thank God, among our women." The spirit of Canada is rising to meet the danger as the sea bird rises before the blackening storm.

Those of us in Canada who can look back in retrospect for twenty-five or thirty years over the shifting surface of our politics, can see in what is happening the realization of our final destiny. In the past we scarcely knew what we were or what we meant to be; a "nation" seemed too large, a "colony" too small. In our debating societies young men argued the question "Shall Canada be Independent?" with such feeble warmth as they might; an imaginary tyranny was denounced with mimic rage; a benevolent chairman, perhaps, declared with a smile that the affirmative had won and Canada was declared "independent" with polite applause: after which the whole audience rose and sang "God Save the Queen" so lustily that "Independence" was blasted out of existence. But beyond the walls of the debating room independence never went.

Independence! What British people ever really wanted it? The full measure of independence needed by free men was acquired for the whole lot of us,—your people of the United States and our people of the British Dominions,—somewhere about the time of the Magna Carta. Our ancestors obtained it by means of yew-tree bows and quarter-staffs and a few lusty cracks over the head given to upstart princes who misunderstood Saxon freedom. Your so-called War of Independence was not really independence at all. It was a row: a first class family row: it sticks in my mind, as a professor, that Benjamin Franklin said that before 1776 he "had heard no one speak of independence, either drunk or sober." But the quarrel,—chiefly through the stupidity of a German King,—was mismanaged and the two communities separated, each being just as independent as before, no more and no less. Since then they have run along side by side, each vastly superior, and each imitating the other. You copied our House of Commons. We stole your Senate. You invented a President, but in less than no time, we turned out the same article, imitated to a nicety, as a Prime Minister. Our separation is not so very great after all. And some day, I truly believe it, our diplomats will come together round a big table, fill themselves up with grape juice and, in the mad exhilaration of it, sign a compact that shall reunite America and England.

Small wonder then that with such a native kinship we in Canada often talked of annexation, or joining in with the United States. Every time in the last hundred years of history that we felt surly against England we spoke of annexation. There was a time (it was in 1849) when all the notables of Montreal signed a document asking for it. We might have had it, too, long ago, but for the attitude of the people of England. "Glorious," they said, "a grand idea." Cobden grew rhetorical about a great republic from the Polar seas to Mexico; Gladstone said farewell to us in Greek, and Disraeli called us millstones and began to untie us from his neck. This was more than we could stand. We stayed where we were.

But in any case annexation proved impossible on larger grounds. As a mere matter of kingship and high diplomacy it might have been arranged. But it ran against such higher realities as your tariff and ours, the price of hay in Cahoga county, your bacon and our butter. We didn't object to your institutions. We were afraid of your cattle on the hoof. These things are the bed rock of politics.

So we have stayed on in the British Empire, wondering what we were to be, till now suddenly, with the first shock of war, we know. That is the supreme meaning of the war to us. The rush to arms in Canada is the glad cry of a people that have found themselves.

We are free men, we in Canada, and our kinsfolk in Australia and South Africa. There is no compulsion on us. England has never asked, and never will, a single soldier or a single sovereign from the dominions overseas. And England now may draw from them, if need be, their men in thousands, their money in millions, till all are gone. This is the spirit of the British empire. We know now the full meaning of our motto *Imperium et Libertas.*

Let those who have ruled and misruled Germany these fifty years under the name of empire reflect upon it. Buckle yourself tight, O German officer, driving your Silesian peasants to the cannon mouth: clap down your pointed helmet on your skull and scowl your fiercest as you multiply your wanton deeds against the helpless. Empire you have, made as you wanted it, of Blood and Iron, but freedom, that should give it power and meaning, never.

This is the war of the free peoples against the peoples still in chains.

England and France and Italy are free and answer to the people's will. Russia, in the very travail of the war, is born into democracy. In Germany and Austria and under the banner of the Turk, the old tyranny that mankind has fought since the first dawn of freedom stands for its last fight. Who, that believes in humanity or God, can doubt the end?

ARE THE RICH HAPPY?

STEPHEN LEACOCK

FROM DECEMBER 1915

L et me admit at the outset that I write this article without adequate material. I have never known, I have never seen, any rich people. Very often I have thought that I had found them. But it turned out that it was not so. They were not rich at all. They were quite poor. They were hard-up. They were pushed for money. They didn't know where to turn for ten thousand dollars.

In all the cases that I have examined this same error has crept in. I had often imagined, from the fact of people keeping fifteen servants, that they were rich. I had supposed that because a woman rode down town in a limousine to buy a fifty dollar hat, she must be well to do. Not at all. All these people turn out on examination not to be rich. They are cramped. They say it themselves. Pinched, I think is the word they use. When I see a glittering group of eight people in a stage box at the opera, I know that they are all pinched. The fact that they ride home in a limousine has nothing to do with it.

A friend of mine who has ten thousand dollars a year told me the other day with a sigh that he found it quite impossible to keep up with the rich. On his income he couldn't do it. A family that I know who have twenty thousand a year have told me the same thing. They can't keep up with the rich. There is no use in trying. A man that I respect very much who has an income of fifty thousand dollars a year from his law practice has told me with the greatest frankness that he finds it absolutely impossible to keep up with the rich. He says it is better to face the brutal fact of being poor. He says he can only give me a plain meal—what he calls a home dinner—it takes three men and two women to serve it—and he begs me to put up with it.

As far as I remember, I have never met Mr. Carnegie. But I know that if I did he would tell me that he found it quite impossible to keep up with Mr. Rockefeller. No doubt Mr. Rockefeller feels the same.

On the other hand there are, and there must be rich people somewhere. I run across traces of them all the time. The janitor in the building where I work has told me that he has a rich cousin in England, who is in the South Western Railway and gets ten pounds a week. He says the railway wouldn't know what to do without him. In the same way the lady who washes at my house has a rich uncle. He lives in Winnipeg and owns his own house, clear, and has two girls at the high school.

But these are only reported cases of richness. I cannot vouch for them myself.

When I speak therefore of rich people and discuss whether they are happy, it is understood that I am merely drawing my conclusions from the people that I see and know.

My judgment is that the rich undergo cruel trials and bitter tragedies of which the poor know nothing.

In the first place I find that the rich suffer perpetually from money troubles. The poor sit snugly at home while sterling exchange falls ten points in a day. Do they care? Not a bit. An adverse balance of trade washes over the nation like a flood. Who have to mop it up? The rich. Call money rushes up to a hundred per cent, and the poor can still sit and laugh at a ten cent moving picture show and forget it.

But the rich are troubled by money all the time.

I know a man, for example—his name is Spugg—whose private bank account was overdrawn last month twenty thousand dollars. He told me so at dinner at his club, with apologies for feeling out of sorts. He said it was bothering him. He said he thought it rather unfair of his bank to have called his attention to it. I could sympathize, in a sort of way, with his feelings. My own account was overdrawn twenty cents at the time. I knew that if the bank began calling in overdrafts it might be my turn next. Spugg said he supposed he'd have to telephone his secretary in the morning to sell some bonds and cover it. It seemed an awful thing to have to do. Poor people are never driven to this sort of thing. I have known cases of their having to sell a little furniture, perhaps, but imagine having to sell the very bonds out of one's desk. There's a bitterness about it that the poor can never know.

With this same man, Mr. Spugg, I have often talked of the problem of wealth. He is a self-made man and he has told me again and again that the wealth he has accumulated is a mere burden to him. He says that he was much happier when he had only the plain simple things of life. Often as I sit at dinner with him over a meal of nine courses, he tells me how much he would prefer a plain bit of boiled pork, with a little mashed turnip. He says that if he had his way he would make his dinner out of a couple of sausages, fried with a bit of bread. I forget what it is that stands in his way. I have seen Spugg put aside his glass of champagne,—or his glass after he had drunk his champagne,—with an expression of something like contempt. He says that he remembers a running creek at the back of his father's farm where he used to lie at full length upon the grass and drink his fill. Champagne, he says, never tasted like that. I have suggested that he should lie on his stomach on the floor of the club and drink a saucerful of soda water. But he won't.

I know well that my friend Spugg would be glad to be rid of his wealth altogether, if such a thing were possible. Till I understood about these things, I always imagined that wealth could be given away. It appears that it can not. It is a burden that one must carry. Wealth, if one has enough of it, becomes a form of social service. One regards it as a means of doing good to the world, of helping to brighten the lives of others, in a word, a solemn trust. Spugg has often talked with me so long and so late on this topic,—the duty of brightening the lives of others,—that the waiter who held blue flames for his cigarettes fell asleep against a door post, and the chauffeur outside froze to the seat of his motor.

Spugg's wealth, I say, he regards as a solemn trust. I have often asked him why he didn't give it, for example, to a college. But he tells me that unfortunately he is not a college man. I have called his attention to the need of further pensions for college professors; after all that Mr. Carnegie and others have done, there are still thousands and thousands of old professors of thirty-five and even forty, working away day after day and getting nothing but what they earn themselves, and with no provision beyond the age of eighty-five. But Mr. Spugg says that these men are the nation's heroes. Their work is its own reward.

But after all, Mr. Spugg's troubles,—for he is a single man with no ties,—are in a sense selfish. It is perhaps in the homes,—or more properly in the residences, of the rich that the great silent tragedies are being enacted every day,—tragedies of unbelievable grimness of which the fortunate poor know and can know nothing.

I saw such a case only a few nights ago at the house of the Ashcroft-Fowlers, where I was dining. As we went in to dinner, Mrs. Ashcroft-Fowler said in a quiet aside to her husband, "Has Meadows spoken?" He shook his head rather gloomily and answered, "No, he has said nothing yet."

I saw them exchange a glance of quiet sympathy and mutual help, like people in trouble, who love one another.

They were old friends and my heart beat for them. All through the dinner as Meadows,—he was their butler,—poured out the wine with each course, I could feel that some great trouble was impending over my friends.

After Mrs. Ashcroft-Fowler had risen and left us, and we were alone over our port wine, I drew my chair near to Fowler's and I said, "My dear

Fowler, I'm an old friend and you'll excuse me if I seem to be taking a liberty. But I can see that you and your wife are in trouble."

"Yes," he said very sadly and quietly, "we are."

"Excuse me," I said. "Tell me,—for it makes a thing easier if one talks about it,—is it anything about Meadows?"

"Yes," he said, "it is about Meadows."

There was silence for a moment but I knew already what Fowler was going to say. I could feel it coming.

"Meadows," he said presently, constraining himself to speak with as little emotion as possible, "is leaving us."

"Poor old chap!" I said, taking his hand.

"It's hard, isn't it," he said. "Franklin left last winter,—no fault of ours, we did everything we could,—and now Meadows."

There was almost a sob in his voice.

"He hasn't spoken definitely as yet," Fowler went on, "but we know there's hardly any chance of his staying."

"Does he give any reason?" I asked.

"Nothing specific," said Fowler. "It's just a sheer case of incompatibility. Meadows doesn't like us."

He put his hand over his face and was silent.

I left very quietly a little later, without going up to the drawing room. A few days afterwards I heard that Meadows had gone. The Ashcroft-Fowlers, I am told, are giving up in despair. They are going to take a little suite of ten rooms and four baths in the Grand Palaver Hotel, and do their best to rough it there for the winter.

Yet one must not draw a picture of the rich in colors altogether gloomy. There are cases among them of genuine, light-hearted happiness.

I have observed that this is especially the case among those of the rich who have the good fortune to get ruined, absolutely and completely ruined.

AN AFGHAN IN AMERICA

SYYED SHAYKH ACHMED ABDULLAH

FROM FEBRUARY 1916

My father's wireless was a shock to me: "Expect me New York Monday. Steamship *Afghanistan*." I am a Moslem. Islam is said to teach two things at least to its followers: Utter resignation to Fate, and respect for one's parents. But, somehow, when I read that telegram I felt that both of these painfully acquired virtues were slipping away from me.

My father had never before been to America. He had been educated in Europe in the good old days when it was still fashionable for Afghan princes and Hindu Rajahs to know the difference between the teachings of Spencer and those of Comte, and to prefer a hirsute German professor's latest philosophic extravaganzas to the ancient, solid wisdom of the Vedas and of Moslem doctors. He knew the old Europe well: The London of Gladstone and Disraeli, the Paris of Cora Pearl, Madame Paiva, and the July Monarchy. I, on the other hand, had America to thank for whatever Occidentalizing I had experienced. And I liked America. Liked the zip of it. Also the bang. Mostly the bang. And then I liked *her*. So I felt nervous. For my father would surely sneer at her. All elderly Orientals sneer. And then I would lose my temper. All young Orientals lose their tempers.

Then I decided that I would not lose my temper. Not at all. For my father remits promptly, vastly, and regularly. He also remits between-times. He can be counted upon in the hour of need. In Afghanistan he is the head of a large corporation. He is the corporation itself . . . a business organization which makes a specialty of helping itself to the lands and goods of other weaker chiefs and tribes. Also I had to think of *her*.

"Her" was a widow. She was older than I. I had been warned against her. Her hair was dangerous. In fact, everything was in her favor. I wanted to marry her . . . at times. She shone, socially. She shone like the planet Khizr. So did her sisters.

So did all of her family.

They were, in fact, a constellation. She used bistre-brown face powder which smelt distressingly of red Jamaican jessamine. Her hair mated Ysabel; it also was every-day mouse-color. More mouse than Ysabel.

I liked her house. Some day I meant to live in it. The second floor was charming. It combined a nuance of Florentine distinction with all the latest American creature comforts. So I decided that the second floor would do for my private apartments . . . after our . . . yes . . . after our . . .

The first ball of the season was to be given two days after my father's arrival. "Her" was giving it. My father arrived at his hotel in New York in due course of time, and went to the ball with me. I told him that it was given in his honor. I lied to him. (I studied the art of lying in Kashmere, the home of deceits.) I do not think that my father believed me. (He, I forgot to say, had also studied the art of deceit in Kashmere.)

Of course I danced with "her" . . . my hostess. For she could dance. The rhythm of her lithe body reminded me of Petrarch twanging his melancholy lute in the gardens of Vaucluse. And, as we swung together to the cadences of the latest Argentine tango, I was mentally composing verses to her in my native Persian. I am somewhat of a poet in my own modest way. One started like this:

Thy feet are like twin blossoms scampering in the wind of desire;
Thy throat is the soft throat of the passionate kokila-bird . . .

and so on. Never mind. The dance was over. I returned to my father who
had been watching us with the sneering expression of a cross-grained
Buddha.

"I saw you dancing," he said.

"I am fairly good at it, don't you think?" My father lit a cigarette.

"When I was your age I lived in Kabul," he said. "I did not dance with
women. I had women dance for me . . . *for* me," he repeated, with a rising
accent. "And I paid 'em out of hand. Now there was one little Nautch girl:
my cousin sent her to me as a Ramazzan present. Her name was
Khaizr'an . . ."

It is not good for the old to shock the young. I pointed at the crowd.

"Over there, father, is a man who has just made a million dollars out
of Standard Copper . . . all in a week . . . and the little chap talking to
him . . . that's the man who made such a furore last year at Newport. He
gave a dinner party at which the farmyard animals were represented by
the guests, and . . ."

My father interrupted me. My country is a strange, barbaric country.
There the old can interrupt the young.

"When I was your age I did not bother about financial affairs.
By the way, my son," he drew pencil and paper from his pocket. "What's
the name of the stock you spoke about? Standard Copper? Still going
up? Thanks. Yes . . . we didn't bother about sordid financial details.
We left that to Hindu bankers. Also to Armenians. Also to Greeks. Also
to pigs."

Then he began reminiscing again. He told me anecdotes of the friends
of his youth in Paris. I could not stop him. He spoke of M. de Montalem-
bert, M. de Falloux, Mgr. Dupanloup, about Jules Simon, whom he
hated . . . and then he spoke at length about the old Duke de Broglie.

I tried to change the conversation. The only Falloux I knew was a
shirtmaker on the Boulevard des Italiens who had invented a soft-rolling

cuff, and the only Dupanloup I had ever met was not a Monsignor of the Church. On the contrary, she lived in the Rue Nouvelle.

The hostess came up to us. She was very beautiful, as I have explained. She smiled at my father . . . and, by the red pig's bristles!, the old warhorse smiled back at her.

He turned to me.

"Being in an alien land I must conform to alien customs. I shall dance with her."

He danced with her the rest of the evening. He did several new steps . . .

He also drank forbidden spirits. Many of them.

I had great difficulty in putting him to bed. He was babbling about dancing, about forbidden spirits. He murmured that an Asian gentleman should observe the customs of alien lands.

"Yes," he muttered as I got him into his bed, and he looked at me with a stern expression, "it is good and just. Labid considered it right. And Mahommad el-Darmini, the great sage, specially recommended spirits in alien lands. Tell the wallah to call me early. The mouse-haired woman has asked me to lunch . . ."

In the morning he addressed me:

"Tell me, my son. You know this great land and its quaint customs. In writing a little note to a mouse-haired woman, would it be thought graceful to employ the beautiful Afghan term of endearment, 'Blood of my Liver'? Or would it be better to use the charming Pukhtu, 'Wind of my Nostrils'?"

THE ART OF BEING A BOHEMIAN

ROBERT C. BENCHLEY

FROM MARCH 1916

Some day, when Fate has delayed your laundry and you have only one clean collar left, go down and take a try at being a Bohemian. You can do it. Hundreds of people, with no worse bringing up than you have had, are doing it, and, after it is all over, and you have had a cold shower, you'll feel ever so much better for it. Your own home life will seem cheerier and brighter and you won't mind the hearth and fireside half so much.

All that you have got to do is, after the day's work is done (the day's work may consist in thumbing a wad of clay into futuristic representations, writing liberated verse, or selling life insurance) to gather with the crowd in some so-called restaurant that has boxes for tables in the front parlor and a bunch of gutta-percha grapes suspended from the ceiling. Then you must toast the proprietor in *eau de quinine* and of course call him by his first name. (*Any* first name will do.) That's practically all there is to Bohemia. The distinction lies in the length of time you can stick it out. If you do it for one night only, you call it "slumming." If you have a good digestion and stick out a winter at it, you call it living the wild, free life of Bohemia.

The charm of Bohemia lies, not so much in its delights (as practiced in this country) as in the alluring things which have been said of it in its native climes. From the *Quarter Latin* of Paris we have had wafted to us triolets and sketches, operas and novels, all fragrant with the long-haired, happy abandon of the French artist, who lives in a garret and eats, to all intents and purposes, nothing at all, but who simply can't sing long or hard enough about Love and Mimi, and the Stars, and the pale, gray fountain in the Parc Monceau.

It is a free life, they would have us know, and one filled with incomparably tender memories.

You will notice, though, that most encomiums on Bohemia are "tender memories" and done in the past tenses. "Those were happy, golden days," or "Long ago, when Love and We were young." Seldom do we get a scented iambic about Bohemia to the effect that the writer is going over to Tony's place *to-night* to eat onion soup and spaghetti *au gratin*. Like the measles, which are so delightful in retrospect because we remember only the period of convalescence and its accompanying chicken and jellies, Bohemia seems to be a state which grows dearer the farther away you get from it.

However, no one will deny (and even if any one did, it wouldn't make the slightest difference to me, because this is the nub of my whole story, and if I should concede a point here there would be no use sending it to the editor at all) that the lure of New York's Bohemia is an importation from Montmartre, in Paris, and that the unshaven Frenchman in his corduroy jacket and black tam-o'-shanter, is the artist's drawing for those Americans who come to New York from Waterbury, Conn., or from Erie, Pa., resolved to be Bohemians even if they choke in the attempt. Indeed, the Bohemia of New York has the imitative effect of high school theatricals—plenty of grease paint, properties and costumes—plenty of wonderful hand-painted scenery and all that sort of thing, but somehow, it is emotionally a trifle forced.

However, when the desire to be like a French Bohemian begins to form in your heart, you should make your way to Washington Square and pick a path around delightfully Parisian ash-cans and artistically soiled children until you come to any one of those old barracks which manage to elude the tenement-house law because they operate under the name of "studios." If possible there should be a line of washing hung out in a prominent place. A line of washing in Harlem is crass. In West Eighth Street it is the highest form of Art.

For proper Bohemian garb, any one of those books on the *ateliers* of Paris will furnish invaluable suggestions. If the New York clothing stores are not up (or down) to fitting you out, any costumer will be glad to assist you. Then, when you are properly clothed, and as soon as your studio (or store) has closed, or the packing-boxes are all stenciled, you must get the jolly girls and fellows all together, muss up their hair, and bohême. Some folks bohême in studios, and have their food brought in from an unpicturesque but convenient delicatessen shop. In such cases the great thing is to eat it by candle-light. Or it may be that you will want to dine at Musette's or "The Duke's" or "Phillipa's," preferably in some subterranean resort which is a remodeled residence of the Chester A. Arthur era, where a lubricated meal is served with something red in a bottle, as a premium, at a price that would buy a piece of beef-steak and a good glass of milk at Childs'.

Then, if it happens to be the special or gala night of the week at that particular restaurant, the evening is spent about the tables in just as jolly a revel as you can imagine—among young people who really need the sleep. The girls smoke, whether they like it or not, and the carefree lads all sing French songs (almost *in French*) and clink glasses, and play on a variety of instruments until you'd swear they were being paid for it.

So you see how simple it is to be a true Bohemian—if you can only give the time to it. Bohêming is a thing to be taken up seriously, like skating, and with constant practice and a little gritting of the teeth, you can in time come to be as care-free and unconventional as a Naiad in those art-photographs that they *will* insist on publishing in *Vanity Fair*.

The only trouble with this pitiless exposé of Bohemia is that I know practically nothing about the subject at all. I have only taken the most superficial glances into New York's Bohemia and for all I know it may be one of the most delightful and beneficial existences imaginable. It merely seemed to me like a good thing to write about, because the editor might, while reading it, think of a dashing illustration that could be made for it. You know the sort of thing. Men and women sitting on boxes, drinking *eau de quinine*, toasting people, and all that sort of thing. Indeed, the whole article might almost be condensed and made into a page of illustrations with only a very few snatches of the text retained as captions for the pictures. And, if I have been entirely in error in my estimate of Bohemia, maybe some *real, genuine* Bohemian will conduct me, some night, where the lights and good-fellowship are mellow and rich and where we may sit about a table and sing songs of Youth and Freedom, and Love, and Girls, like so many Francois Villons.

I think that in a way I'd like it. It would be picturesque, and then, after all, it does permit one to wear those wonderful shirts with soft collars and no cuffs.

WHY I HAVEN'T MARRIED

DOROTHY ROTHSCHILD (PARKER)

FROM OCTOBER 1916

I. RALPH, WHOSE PLACE WAS IN THE HOME

You see, this was the way it happened. The first one of them all was Ralph. His was one of those sweet, unsullied natures that believes everything it sees in the papers, and no matter what I said, he would gaze into my eyes and murmur "yes." He had positively cloying ideas about women. If any girl in his vicinity lit a cigarette, Ralph's eyes, behind their convex lenses, assumed the expression of a wounded doe's. He superfluously assisted me up and down curbs; he was always inserting needless cushions behind my back. He laboriously brought me a host of presents that I didn't want—friendship calendars, sixth-best sellers, and the kind of flowers that one puts in vases—but never wears. He had acquired a remarkable muscular development merely from helping me on with so many wraps and coats. His greatest fault was his lack of them.

I felt that life with Ralph would be a deep dream of peace, and I was just on the verge of giving him his answer and receiving his virginal kiss, when, in a flash of clairvoyance, I had a startlingly clear vision of the future. I seemed to see us—Ralph and me—settled down in an own-your-own bungalow in a twenty-minute suburb. I saw myself surrounded by a horde of wraps and sofa pillows. I saw us gathered around the lamp of a winter evening, reading aloud from "Hiawatha." I saw myself a member of the Society Opposed to Woman Suffrage . . . . . .

So I told Ralph that I wouldn't, just as gently as possible, and he went away to sob it out on his mother's shoulder.

II. MAXIMILIAN, TABLE D'HOTE SOCIALIST

Maximilian was the next disillusionment. He was an artist and had long nervous hands and a trick of impatiently tossing his hair out of his eyes. He capitalized the A in art. Together we plumbed the depths of Greenwich Village, seldom coming above Fourteenth Street for air. We dined in those how-*can*-they-do-it-for-fifty-cents table d'hôtes, where Maximilian and his little group of serious thinkers were wont to gather about dank bottles of sinister claret and flourish marked copies of "The Masses." I learned to make sweeping gestures with my bent-back thumb, to smile tolerantly at the mention of John Sargent; to use all the technical terms when I discussed Neo-Malthusianism. Maximilian made love in an impersonal sort of way. He called me "Comrade" and flung a casual arm across my shoulders whenever he happened to think of it.

But the end came. Maximilian painted my portrait. Chaperoned by an astounded aunt, I posed for him in an utterly inadequate bit of green gauze; posed until every muscle ached. Finally, one day, Maximilian flung his brush across the room—narrowly missing my aunt—threw himself into a chair, and wearily drew his hand across his eyes, murmuring, "It is done."

I stole around and looked over his shoulder at the canvas—and immediately Love went out of my life. Reader—are you by any chance a pool-player? Well, the only thing I can think of that the portrait resembled was what is known in pool circles as an "open break." I turned and fled from Max and Bohemia. I didn't know much about Art, but I knew what I didn't like.

III. JIM—OF BROADWAY

Perhaps it was only natural that the next one should be Jim. He was a thirty-third degree man about town. He could tell at a glance which one of the Dolly Sisters was Mrs. Harry Fox, and he could keep track of Nat Goodwin's marriages without calling in the aid of an expert accountant and a Burrowes adding machine. His peacock blue Rolls-Royce had worn a deep groove in Broadway and his checked suits kept just within the law about disturbing the public peace. Jim was a man of few words; his love-making consisted of but two phrases—"What are you going to have?" and "Where do we go from here?" I shall never forget the thrill of entering restaurant after restaurant with Jim and watching the headwaiters do everything but kiss him.

It was an idyll, while it lasted. We used to sit, a table's breadth apart, at cabarets, and shriek soft nothings at each other above the blare of the Nubian band, while waiters literally groveled at our feet. Jim gave me the deepest, truest love he had ever given a woman. In his affections I was rated third—first, and second, Haig and Haig; and then, third, me. I began to feel that life with him would be one long all-night cabaret, and I was just about to become the owner of the largest engagement ring in the city, when, one night we went to a dinner. Not a cabaret dinner, but one where two famous authors sat and ate with their forks, just like regular people. Everyone was properly stricken with awe—everyone, that is, but Jim. While the rest of us hung on the gloomy utterances of the authors, Jim loudly discussed (with a kindred spirit across the table) the certainty of "Hatrack's" winning the fourth race at Belmont Park, offering to back his conviction with a large quantity of coin of the realm, and urging that his friend either produce a similar amount of currency, or else desist from arguing. Under cover of the table, I kicked him into quietude. Presently a point was reached in the lofty-browed discourse whereon the two celebrities differed, and, as if going to the right source for information, they turned to Jim.

"Now what is *your* opinion of Baudelaire?" they inquired.

Jim looked up with that same perfectly-at-home air with which he entered the New Amsterdam theater on the first night of the Follies.

"I really can't say," he explained, affably, "I've never seen him get a good sweat-out in practise."

The silence that ensued seems still to crash in my ears . . .

IV. CYRIL, HERO OF THE SOCIAL REGISTER

Cyril, the next event, was almost *the* man. People are still shaking their heads over my idiocy in not taking him. You see, he had practically all the money in the world, and the plot of the Social Register was almost entirely written around his family. In spite of all that he was most amazingly intelligent. In fact he had such a disconcertingly remarkable memory that every time I said a clever thing, he remembered just who had written it. Cyril led a blameless life; whatever he did, one might rest assured was Being Done. His was a perfect day, from his cold shower at 11:30 to his appearance at the opera, exactly three-quarters of an hour late. The one religious rite in his life was his weekly pilgrimage to a sacred Mecca up the Hudson, to assist at the mystic ceremonies of the smartest week-end in America. His clothes—but who am I to write of them? It would require all the passionate lyricism of a Swinburne to do them justice. He made the debonair young gentlemen in the clothing advertisements look as if they'd been working on the railroad. Collars were named for him. What more can be said?

Yes, Cyril was faultless. I had almost decided to devote my life to living up to him, when, one terrible night I found a hideous flaw in him. It was at the opera. I remember that it was one of those awful German atrocities, and the stage was full of large, strong women, shouting "Yo ho" at each other. Relentless Fate directed my gaze to Cyril's left hand, as he sat there all unconscious in the box. And I saw it! Saw that his white glove, the glove of Cyril the impeccable, had split like that of a mere broker or bank clerk, split all the way around the thumb, the edges gaping like a hideous wound, and a part of his hand exposed in all its glaring nudity. I hid my eyes, but the sight had seared my brain. . . .

V. LORENZO, THE LIFE OF THE PARTY

Lorenzo was the next occurrence. Never have I seen anyone so bubbling over with good, clean fun. He specialized in parlor tricks. Give him but a length of string, three matches, and a lump of sugar, and he would be the life of the party for an entire evening. He had an uncanny habit of leaving the room for two minutes and, on his return, telling you exactly what card you had drawn from the pack. He had amassed a great repertoire of parlor anecdotes in Irish and negro dialects. It was he who wrote most of the jokes about the Lord car. It broke Lorenzo's heart to see people wasting their lives in mere conversation; he panted to gather them all in a big circle and play guessing-games. Nor did he care for one-steps, fox-trots, or such selfish dances; no, Lorenzo insisted on Paul Joneses and Virginia reels, so that all the people could get to know each other.

He did imitations, too, of bumble bees and roosters and fog-horns and of a man sawing wood. This last imitation had amazing touches of realism in it, especially when he came to the knot-holes. Lorenzo was not a fanatic on athletics; he didn't go in for golf or tennis, but he certainly played a rattling good game of parcheesi.

Life with Lorenzo might have been a continuous round of innocent little parlor tricks and yet—those tricks were the drawbacks to my happiness. I feared he might so perfect himself in his chosen art that I could never know at what moment he was going to reach over and take a guinea pig out of my hair, or remove the flags of all nations from my unsuspecting ears. The nervous strain would have been too great; and so we parted.

VI. BOB, SON OF BATTLE

Bob came next. I had always thought the American flag was the personal property of George M. Cohan until I met Bob and found that Mr. Cohan had ceded a half-interest in it to him. Bob was every inch a soldier, and you never could forget it. He wore his khaki uniform whenever it was possible (or even probable) and he always wore his chest well swelled out, the better to display his badge of honor—that awe-inspiring little bit of red ribbon that meant he kept his gun cleaner than any one else in his tent. The word "preparedness" was to him as a red flag to an anarchist. He lived but for the season at Plattsburg. He even carried the thing so far as to stand outside of a property tent, with all the persuasiveness of a Billy Sunday, exhorting the halt, the maimed, and the blind to enlist, like little men. He spoke tenderly and at great length of his horse, which, I gathered from his conversation, shared his pillow. He used to relate little anecdotes of its startlingly human intelligence. It walked, it ran, it neighed, it slept, it evinced a liking for oats. It even— yet some there are who say that dumb beasts have no souls—had been known to whisk away flies with its tail. Bob was a martial and God-fearing youth. I feel sure that every night before he went to bed he knelt down and asked General Leonard Wood to bless him and make him a good boy.

The thing was almost settled. You know there's something about a uniform—full or empty—and then those military weddings with crossed swords are always so picturesque. We were just going to announce it, when a cruel summons came for Bob to leave for Mexico with his troop. He left me, tenderly vowing to bring me back Carranza's head to put upon my mantelpiece—and then, while he was gone, Paul happened.

VII. PAUL, THE VANISHED DREAM

I cannot dwell on Paul, the last one. I have not yet fully recovered from him. He was the Ideal Husband—an English-tailored Greek God, just masterful enough to be entertaining, just wicked enough to be exciting, just clever enough to be a good audience. But, oh, he failed me! In a moment of absent-mindedness, he went and married a blonde and rounded person whose walk in life was the runway at the Winter Garden. I am just beginning to recuperate.

And these are the seven reasons why my mail is still being addressed to "Miss."

MEN: A HATE SONG

DOROTHY ROTHSCHILD (PARKER)

FROM FEBRUARY 1917

I hate men.
They irritate me.

I

There are the Serious Thinkers,—
There ought to be a law against them.
They see life, as through shell-rimmed glasses, darkly.
They are always drawing their weary hands
Across their wan brows.
They talk about Humanity
As if they had just invented it;
They have to keep helping it along.
They revel in strikes
And they are eternally getting up petitions.
They are doing a wonderful thing for the Great Unwashed,—
They are living right down among them.
They can hardly wait
For "The Masses" to appear on the newsstands,
And they read all those Russian novels,—
The sex best sellers.

II

There are the Cave Men,—
The Specimens of Red-Blooded Manhood.
They eat everything very rare,
They are scarcely ever out of their cold baths,
And they want everybody to feel their muscles.
They talk in loud voices,
Using short Anglo-Saxon words.
They go around raising windows,
And they slap people on the back,
And tell them what they need is exercise.
They are always just on the point of walking to San Francisco,
Or crossing the ocean in a sailboat,
Or going through Russia on a sled—
I wish to God they would!

III

And then there are the Sensitive Souls
Who do interior decorating, for Art's sake.
They always smell faintly of vanilla
And put drops of sandalwood on their cigarettes.
They are continually getting up costume balls
So that they can go
As something out of the "Arabian Nights."
They give studio teas
Where people sit around on cushions
And wish they hadn't come.
They look at a woman languorously, through half-closed eyes,
And tell her, in low, passionate tones,
What she ought to wear.
Color is everything to them,—everything;

The wrong shade of purple
Gives them a nervous breakdown.

IV
Then there are the ones
Who are Simply Steeped in Crime.
They tell you how they haven't been to bed
For four nights.
They frequent those dramas
Where the only good lines
Are those of the chorus.
They stagger from one cabaret to another,
And they give you the exact figures of their gambling debts.
They hint darkly at the terrible part
That alcohol plays in their lives.
And then they shake their heads
And say Heaven must decide what is going to become of them,—
I wish I were Heaven!

I hate men.
They irritate me.

THE SHIFTING NIGHT LIFE
OF NEW YORK

JAMES L. FORD

FROM FEBRUARY 1917

The crest of the so-called night life of New York has now reached as far north as 64th Street. Fifty years ago it had only stretched to 14th Street. Fifty blocks in fifty years! At that rate of progress the night life of New York will center, in another fifty years, around St. John's Cathedral and the district around Columbia College.

During the flash age that succeeded the Civil War in New York—an age that was the result of the thousands of newly made American fortunes—vulgarity, crime, and loose living overshadowed good taste and good breeding as it has never done before or since in the history of New York. That was a city that New Yorkers of to-day would find it hard to recognize. The profession of architecture was then about on a par with that of brick-laying. The newer parts of the town were composed of rows upon rows of "brown stone fronts," all precisely alike in appearance and construction, and as shallow and flimsy and perishable as the fortunes that had built them. The Tweed ring was in power and notorious thieves sat, unashamed, in the seats of the mighty. A gaping crowd every day delighted in gazing at Jim Fisk, as his four-in-hand brake, filled with bedizened women, paraded solemnly up and down the streets, usually followed by a well-known quack doctor of the time with no less than five horses hitched to his carriage.

* * *

Bank burglars, murderers, and gamblers fattened on the city. Crooks like Jimmie and Johnny Hope, "Sheeny Mike" Newman, "Reddy the Blacksmith," "Gentleman George" Howard, "Dutch Heinrichs," all of them men of the kind that, in better ordered communities, usually shun the light of day and walk only in darkness, daily decked themselves in fine raiment and joined the afternoon strollers on Broadway just below 14th Street.

From this carnival of vulgarity the fashionable society of the time of course held strictly aloof. They took their pleasures decorously, behind their own mahogany doors, at Delmonico's, at the theatre, or opera, and, once a year, at the Charity Ball, which was then held at the Academy of Music.

Near the Academy was a famous restaurant, known, in those days, as the Maison Dorée. It stood on the south side of Union Square, and opposite it was an Italian restaurant established in the fifties by Signor Moretti, for the purpose of supplying Mario and Grisi with their native food and, incidentally, to introduce chianti, maccaroni, spaghetti and other Italian delicacies to the American palate. Moretti's name still survives him on a restaurant signboard in West 35th Street.

It was in a theatre just west of 6th Avenue, afterwards rebuilt by Charles Fechter and now known as the Fourteenth Street (a motion picture house) that H. L. Bateman introduced French opéra bouffe to New York, with Tosté as his leading star. She appeared there in *"La Grand Duchesse," "La Belle Hélène,"* and in *"Orphée aux Enfers."* It was a very fashionable place of amusement then, and its first tier was composed of a circle of boxes for all the world as if Oscar Hammerstein had built it.

Above Union Square the streets were all dark at night, save in 23rd Street where Booth's Theatre—at the corner of Sixth Avenue—and the Grand Opera House—at the corner of Eighth Avenue—emitted their welcome beams of light. Further south was the theatrical district, for the Rialto was then stationed at Houston Street. There were also many places of amusement strung along Broadway, from Barnum's Museum, at Ann Street, to Lester Wallack's Theatre, at 13th Street. It was at Niblo's Garden— near Houston Street, on Broadway—that "The Black Crook" was given for the first time. I can still remember how it shocked the town, with its revelations of undraped women, and how it filled the house with the tired business men of that day, while the dust rose in clouds from the pulpit cushions on Sundays, for the clergy were all loud in their denunciation of the entertainment, and, incidentally, of infinite value in advertising it. Pauline Markham, as Stalacta, and Bonfanti, as the première danseuse—both of them still living in New York—appeared in the original cast of "The Black Crook." It was in celebration of the first named that Richard Grant White—the father of Stanford White—coined the phrases "Her voice is vocal velvet," and "She possesses the lost arms of the Venus of Milo."

Not far from Niblo's was the huge Olympic Theatre, where George L. Fox played "Humpty Dumpty" and burlesqued the "Hamlet" that Edwin Booth was giving for a hundred nights at the Winter Garden, which was then opposite Bond Street. The Winter Garden was on the site of what is now the Broadway Central Hotel, where Ed Stokes killed Jim Fisk—and next door to Pfaff's beer cellar, where Walt Whitman, Fitz James O'Brien, George Arnold, E. C. Stedman and other talented men were trying to create a bohemia such as Henri Murger, in Paris, loved to describe and write about. It was in Pfaff's that Henry Clapp dictated to Artemus Ward—who was then beginning his career as a lecturer—the famous reply of "Brandy and water," to the telegram that he had received from a western lecture manager: "What would you take for a hundred nights in California?" This brief answer did more to advertise Ward as a humorist in the then settled parts of the far west, than could have been accomplished by any amount of publicity and press work.

Strange as it may seem to the present generation, the basements of many reputable commercial buildings on Broadway were occupied by concert saloons in which men were served with drinks by short-skirted women, and, not infrequently, drugged and robbed. It was from these basements that the word "dive" was coined. The block between Bleecker and Houston Streets was known as "Murderers' Row," because of the frequent killings that took place there, while it was from a silent house, with heavily curtained windows, in East 14th Street, that Washington Nathan brought forth the frail witness who proved his alibi on the night his father was murdered in 23rd Street, just across the way from the Fifth Avenue Hotel.

The *jeunesse dorée* of that period did not disdain to seek amusement along the Bowery, which was filled with dives, concert halls, and variety shows, in many of which some of the sinister arts were practiced successfully—and without fear. Owney Geoghegan's "Old House at Home" was a favorite hang-out of professional beggars and desperadoes. Mr. Geoghegan's funeral, with two wives racing after the hearse all the way to Calvary, was a noteworthy event in the Bowery's social annals. There were respectable resorts there, too, including the Stadt, and Bowery Theatres, the Atlantic Garden, the Volks Garten, Tony Pastor's, and the Tivoli.

Harry Hill's picturesque dance house, situated at the northeast corner of Crosby and Houston Streets, and frequented by one kind of women and every sort of men, was one of the few resorts on the east side in which both life and pocketbook were rigorously safe-guarded by the proprietor. Harry Hill was a smooth-shaven Englishman of the old-fashioned sporting type, who had once driven a mail-coach in England, and who was brought to this country by Mr. Edward Woolsey of Astoria. Mr. Woolsey wanted him for a coachman, in which capacity he subsequently found employment with the Ironsides family in New London. Harry Hill's resort attracted men of every sort, including sailors, thieves, pugilists, revellers from distant cities and many gentlemen and aristocrats. Don Carlos, the

Spanish Pretender; the Grand Duke Alexis of Russia; the late Duke of
Marlborough, and Lord Mandeville, who afterward became the Duke of
Manchester, found much entertainment there. Weber and Fields, Pete
Dailey, W. J. Scanlan, Maggie Cline and Andrew Mack first appeared on
its little stage, and long before they became at all known to metropolitan
audiences. It was here that was held the first meeting of the Salvation
Army in New York, and it was here also that John L. Sullivan first put up
his fists in this city, in a fight with a pugilist named Steve Taylor, who had
been offered fifty dollars for standing in front of Sullivan for three
rounds—a feat which he failed to perform. Thomas A. Edison found in
Harry Hill one of his earliest friends; and it was at Hill's place that Edison's first electric light was installed. Hill remained at his old stand until
the early eighties when it was closed up by the police because he would
not pay them any more blackmail. It was to Harry Hill that the detectives
addressed their historic utterance: "This is an iron age, and everybody has
got to produce."

The flash age of the town ended in a single night, with the panic of
1873, and there followed a period of financial depression and enforced
economy that stilled much of the gaiety of the city and finally brought the
town down on its knees, in the dust and ashes of repentance—through the
great Moody and Sankey revivals.

During this period of depression, the doings of a so-called fast set in
New York society attracted a degree of popular attention that seems
strange to us now. This set was admirably satirized by Lawrence Olyphant
in "The Strange Adventures of Irene McGillicoddy," a book that seems to
us about as exciting as "Our Village," by Mrs. Gaskell. Having purified
itself in its revival exercises, New York soon began to regain its spirits.
Money flowed more freely and those forms of vice that are mis-named
pleasure entrenched themselves firmly in the region between 25th and
34th Streets—West of Broadway. It was this region that subsequently became known as The Tenderloin.

The Cremorne, the Buckingham, and the Argyle Rooms, all attracted visitors of the same class that had once frequented Harry Hill's and the other down town, Broadway resorts.

The late seventies found the theatrical Rialto at 14th Street, and it was on the sidewalks of Union Square that most of the theatrical business of the country was transacted. There, actors were engaged; companies booked, and dramatic printing ordered. Contracts were signed in the nearby hotels and saloons, and those who liked to gaze at actors on the stage, had ample opportunities for gratifying their longings. Then, very slowly, the Rialto drifted uptown, pausing at 26th Street, and then, with a brief stop at 35th, rushed on to "The roaring Forties."

In 1879, Augustin Daly, who had suffered many reverses in other houses, opened the theatre at 30th Street which still bears his name. He had chosen three young women of talent to arrest the public's attention. These were Catherine Lewis, Ada Rehan and Helen Blythe, and, curiously enough, it was in the last named star—now totally forgotten—that the manager placed his highest hopes. After many experiments in musical pieces, Mr. Daly devoted himself to German comedy, adapted to American needs, while at the same time Mr. A. M. Palmer presented French dramas at the Union Square and Mr. Lester Wallack gave English plays with a company exclusively British.

So that, until the close of the seventies the American dramatist was a wholly negligible quantity in our stage and it was not until Mr. Palmer presented "The Banker's Daughter," a play by Bronson Howard, and "My Partner," a drama by Bartley Campbell, that everybody began to take hope for the American drama. The first nights at the three theatres above alluded to soon became very fashionable events. At Harrigan and Hart's Theatre, many unforgettable local farces, at first enjoyed exclusively by the wise theatre-goers of the lower wards, finally attracted the more fashionable theatre-goers from uptown.

Fashion was far more staid, decorous, and conventional then than it is now. Only a few very daring hostesses were willing to "receive" actresses, not even such splendid artists, and women, as Sara Jewett, Adelaide Phillips, Clara Louise Kellogg and Christine Nilsson.

Mrs. [Lillie] Langtry, despite the fact that she brought letters from persons very high in English society, was cold-shouldered by everybody, while her subsequent affair with Frederick Gebhard caused the town to rock with a degree of feverish excitement that was conclusive proof of its lack of sophistication and its essential naïveté. The old-fashioned footlight illusion which divided the players from the audience, was then rigorously maintained, to the great benefit of the theatrical profession, which, in my opinion, has gained nothing and lost much through its general introduction into our best drawing-rooms.

The night life of New York now breaks, with a thunderous crash, on a cabaret and theatre district that stretches along Broadway as far as 64th Street, a distance of more than three miles from old Niblo's, where exactly fifty years ago, gaping crowds used to watch the spectacle of "The Black Crook."

To those New Yorkers who now spend an occasional evening in Longacre Square, and who can look back a half a century or so, the night life of the city, as it was fifty years ago, must seem in retrospect like the night life of a quiet and secluded little New England village.

ACTRESSES: A HATE SONG

DOROTHY ROTHSCHILD (PARKER)

FROM MAY 1917

I hate Actresses.
They get on my nerves.

There are the Adventuresses,
The Ladies with Lavender Pasts.
They wear gowns that show all their emotions,
And they simply can't stop undulating.
The only stage properties they require
Are a box of cigarettes and a package of compromising letters.
Their Big Scene invariably takes place in the hero's apartment.
They are always hanging around behind screens
And overhearing things about the heroine.
They go around clutching their temples
And saying, Would to God they were good—
Would to God they Were!

There are the Wronged Ones;
The Girls Whose Mothers Never Told Them.
In the first act they wear pink gingham sunbonnets
And believe implicitly in the stork.

In the third act they are clad in somber black
And know that there isn't any Santa Claus.
They are always going out into the night.
They faint a great deal,
And if anyone lets them get near the center of the stage
They immediately burst into hysterics.
They unfortunately never commit suicide until the last act—
It's always the audience that pays and pays and pays.

Then there are the Musical Comedy Stars;
The press-agent's livelihood.
They sing about love—in waltz time—
And they dance as if something were just about to break.
They end by appearing in a piece of court plaster
And an American flag,
And then the audience has to stand up.
The show isn't considered a success
Until they climb into a flower-wreathed swing,
And swing far out, over the orchestra—
O, that I might be there when the ropes break.

And there are the Emotional Ones;
The ones who say,
"I'll have two lumps of sugar in my tea, please,"
In exactly the same tones as they say
"Yes, it was I who murdered him."
They are forever tearing their hair—
I hope it hurts them.
They shriek at everything,
Usually at the hero,
And they hurl themselves on the floor at his feet
And say that they wish it were all over—
They said something.

Then there are the child Actresses
Who should be unseen and not heard.
They go around telling people about Heaven
As if they were special correspondents.
They are always climbing up on innocent bystanders
And asking them why they look so sad;
They eternally bring their fathers and mothers together,
Which is always an error of judgment.
They never fail to appear in their nightgowns
And then kneel down beside the orchestra leader,
And say their prayers to the spotlight man,—
I wish I were Commodore Gerry.

I hate Actresses.
They get on my nerves.

RELATIVES: A HATE SONG

DOROTHY ROTHSCHILD (PARKER)

FROM AUGUST 1917

I hate Relatives.
They cramp my style.

There are Aunts.
Even the best of us have them.
They are always dropping in for little visits,
And when you ask them to stay,
They take it seriously.
They never fail to tell you how badly you look;
And they relate little anecdotes
About friends of theirs who went into Declines.
Their conversation consists entirely of Insides;
They are never out of a Critical Condition.
They are always posing for X-Ray portraits
Of parts of their anatomy with names like parlor-cars.
They say the doctor tells them
That they have only one chance in a hundred,—
The odds aren't big enough.

Then there are In-Laws,
The Necessary Evils of Matrimony.
The only things they don't say about you

Are the ones they can't pronounce.
No matter what you do,
They know a better way to do it.
They are eternally searching your house for dust;
If they can't find any,
It is a wasted day.
They are always getting their feelings hurt
So that they can go around with martyred expressions
And say that you will appreciate them when they're gone,—
You certainly will.

There are Nephews;
They are the lowest form of animal life.
They are forever saying bright things
And there is no known force that can keep them
From reciting little pieces about Our Flag.
They have the real Keystone sense of humor,—
They are always firing things off in your ear,
Or pulling away the chair you are about to sit on.
Whenever you are striving to impress anyone,
They always appear
And try out the new words they learned from the ice-man,—
I wish the Government would draft all males under ten!

And then there are Husbands;
The White Woman's Burden.
They never notice when you wear anything new,—
You have to point it out.
They tell you about the deal they put through,
Or the approach they made,
And you are supposed to get all worked up.
They are always hanging around outside your door
And they are incessantly pulling out watches,

And saying, "Aren't you dressed yet?"
They were never known to be wrong;
Everything is always your fault.
And whenever you go out to have a good time,
You always meet them,—
I wish to Heaven somebody would alienate their affections.

I hate Relatives.
They cramp my style.

GEORGE JEAN NATHAN

THE EDITORS

FROM NOVEMBER 1917

One of the most amusing literary atrocities perpetrated in New York in many a day is a little pamphlet which has just made its appearance, entitled "Pistols for Two" (Alfred Knopf would, of course, be the publisher of it). It is the work of Owen Hatteras—if such a person really exists—and is made up of two brief biographies, the first of them a minced-meat life of George Jean Nathan, one of *Vanity Fair*'s most dauntless and debonair contributors (he invariably wears a cornflower—said to be artificial—as a boutonnière), the other a similarly chopped up biography of H. L. Mencken, a friend of Nathan's and, like Nathan, an incorrigible fellow of the literary stripe. Both of these desperate characters are devil-may-care reviewers, writers of pale lyrics, roisterers in type, bravos of the printed page. Mr. Hatteras's idea, as explained in his little scarlet pamphlet, is that biography as at present practiced is all wrong, Plutarch, all wrong. Who in the devil cares to know that a man was born, that he went to school, that he attended college, that he was married by a minister, that he had an illness, that he lived in Boston? Fatuous! Futile! Banal! No, none of that for the *soi disant* Mr. Hatteras. The really vital and important thing is, How does a man eat, What shirts does he wear, When does he wash, How often does he fall in love, How does he play? Put down these facts upon the printed page in any old order, in any old way, and let, whoever will, mess about among the debris and construct, from the scattered bits, a definite and symmetrical effigy.

So, here are a few of the more portentous facts concerning the life, diet, tooth powder, love affairs, and winter underwear of our sad, mad friend Nathan—the Pierrot of Broadway.

His boyhood ambition was to be an African explorer in a pith helmet; with plenty of room on the chest ribbon for medals to be bestowed upon him by the Crown Princess of Luxembourg.

He dislikes women over twenty-one, actors, cold weather, mayonnaise dressing, people who are always happy, hard chairs, invitations to dinner, invitations to serve on committees, railroad trips, public restaurants, rye whisky, chicken, daylight, men who do not wear waistcoats, the sight of a woman eating, the sound of a woman singing, small napkins, Maeterlinck, Tagore, Bataille, fried oysters, German soubrettes, French John Masons, American John Masons, tradesmen, poets, married women who think of leaving their husbands, professional anarchists of all kinds, ventilation, professional music lovers, men who tell how much money they have made, men who affect sudden friendships and then call him Georgie, women who affect sudden friendships and then call him Mr. Nathan, writing letters, receiving letters, talking over the telephone, and wearing a hat.

He never receives a woman caller save with his secretary in the room.

He can eat spinach only when it is chopped fine.

In his taste in girls, he runs to the demitasses. I have never heard of his showing any interest in a woman more than five feet in height, or weighing more than 105 pounds.

He never goes to weddings, and knows few persons who marry.

He drinks numerous cocktails (invariably the species known as "orange blossom," to which he has added two drops of Grenadine), a rich burgundy, and, now and then, a bit of brandy.

He has no use for women who are not sad at twilight.

He admires Max Beerbohm, Conrad, Dr. Lewellys Barker, Mozart, the Fifth and Ninth Symphonies and the songs in "Oh, Boy," sardines, ravioli, Havelock Ellis, chocolate cake, Molnar, Hauptmann, Royalton cigars, Anatole France, *Simplicissimus*, *E. W. Howe's Monthly*, an eiderdown blanket,

a hard pillow, a thick toothed comb, a stiff brush, Schnitzler, bitter al-
mond soap, George Ade, Richard Strauss, Pilsner, Huneker, and Florenz
Ziegfeld.

He wears the lightest weight underwear during the coldest winter.

He owns thirty-eight overcoats of all sorts and descriptions. Overcoats
are a fad with him. He has them from heavy Russian fur to the flimsiest
homespun. . . . He owns one with an Alpine hood attachment.

His telephone operator, at his apartment, has a list of five persons to
whom he will talk—so many and no more. He refuses to answer the telephone before five o'clock in the afternoon.

The living Americans who most interest him are Josephus Daniels
and Frank A. Munsey.

He never visits a house a second time in which he has encountered
dogs, cats, children, automatic pianos, grace before (or after) meals,
women authors, actors, *The New Republic,* or prints of the Mona Lisa.

He is not acquainted with a single clergyman, Congressman, general,
or reformer. He has never met any of the Vice-Presidents of the United
States.

He is free of adenoids.

His knee jerks are normal.

A newspaper interviewer once asked him if it was true that a certain
disgruntled theatrical manager had alluded to him as a "pinhead." "That,"
replied Nathan, "is, on the face of it, absurd. 'Pinhead' is a word of two
syllables."

He once observed that the reason the galleries of our theatres, as our
theatrical managers lament, are no longer filled with newsboys is that all
the newsboys are now theatrical managers.

He never writes love letters, and seldom reads them.

He cannot operate a motor car, cook anything, wind a dynamo, fix a
clock, guess the answer to a riddle, or milk a cow.

He regards camping out as the most terrible diversion invented by man.

For the last two years he has received weekly anonymous letters from
some woman in Bridgeport, Connecticut, who signs herself "L. G."

He takes a companion with him to the theatre only on rare occasions. He uses the extra seat sent him by the managers as a depository for his hat and overcoat.

He hasn't the slighted intention of ever getting married.

He gets squiffed about once in six weeks, usually in company with John Williams. He has a headache the next day.

He wears a No. 14½ collar and No. 7¼ hat. His favorite soup is Crême de Santé.

His valet's name is Osuka F. Takami. The latter has a penchant for polishing patent leather boots with sofa pillows.

He has never been in a Childs' restaurant.

He has been shot at three times, but never hit.

He likes chop suey, spaghetti, French pastry, horseradish sauce, Welsh rarebits, oysters *à la Dumas*, raw tomatoes, stuffed baked potatoes, green peppers, broiled lobster, halibut, mushrooms cooked with caraway seeds, and chipped beef.

His favorite hospitals are the Johns Hopkins, in Baltimore, and Galen Hall, in Atlantic City. Whenever he is ill he goes to one or the other of these hospitals.

Since 1901 he has loved seventeen different girls, and still remembers the names of all of them, and their preferences in literature, food, and wines. Of the seventeen, fourteen are happily married, one has been married and divorced, and the rest have gone West.

He wears pongee pajamas.

He knew Evelyn Nesbit when she was a baby.

He wears low, Byronic collars and rather gaudy neckties.

He is on good terms with but two members of his family.

He uses Calox tooth powder, Colgate's shaving soap, a double strength witch hazel, a Gillette razor, and Kitchell's Horse Liniment. He has never taken quinine, Peruna, Piso's Cough Syrup, Sanatogen, asperin [*original spelling*], morphine, opium, or castor oil.

He gets a cinder in his eye twice a day, on an average.

He believes that George Bickel is the funniest comedian on the

American stage, that Arnold Daly is the best actor, that Margaret Ellington is the best actress.

His usual pulse is 71 a minute. After drinking it rises to 85.

His favorite name for girls is Helen.

He has never visited the battlefield of Gettysburg.

FROM LEFT TO RIGHT IN THE MOVIES

DOUGLAS FAIRBANKS

FROM JANUARY 1918

A classified list of Who's Who on the screen:

First of all, there's the movie heroine. She is invariably one of those excruciatingly sweet young things who once saw Mary Pickford and has never been herself since. She walks with the approved Lilian Gish movement, at a pace which would seem to indicate that she is always on her way to a fire. She never sits, in the accepted sense of the word,—she merely takes a running jump at a chair and lands girlishly on all fours, then draws her knees up on a level with her chin and clasps her hands vivaciously around them. Her hair is always worn in curls—it's the unwritten law of the movies that all heroines, without regard to age, race, color or creed, must wear their hair in curls. So far as movie heroines are concerned, there is no other coiffure.

High white shoes, also, are extremely prevalent among heroines, but these, while important, are not absolutely essential.

The heroine is a marvel of versatility—her press agent says so himself. Versatility, in the movies, means starting the picture (in bare feet and a gingham dress torn in all the interesting places), as little Bessie, the Sunshine of Poverty Alley; in being adopted by a doting millionaire somewhere in the third reel; and playing the last thousand feet of the picture all Luciled up like a Century showgirl.

* * *

The heroine is the reason for the hero's introduction into the scenario. If it weren't for the crying need of someone to play opposite the heroine, all movie heroes would still be running elevators.

The hero is always a dark person with highly polished hair, which is worn in much the same style that Mrs. Vernon Castle wears hers. His taste in clothing runs to belted coats, gracefully plaited across the back—the model popularly known as the 'Varsity, a snappy style for young men and men who want to stay young. He uses those soft felt hats with the college hat-bands—the kind that the owner gets all the girls at the seashore to write their names on, as a souvenir of the two weeks' vacation.

These hats are always selected at least a size and a quarter too small, and are worn rolled dashingly up in back and pulled rakishly down to shade the eyes. The hat is on no account removed in the house, save to register that Mother has just passed away. Sport shirts are worn always, and neckties are worn never. White tennis shoes invariably complete the hero's costume, except when he is wearing his evening clothes with the jet buttons.

In that event, however, he always retains his white socks.

The hero's film life may be an eventful one, but there is always a pleasing element of certainty about it. No matter how wrong he may be in, there is the thrill of knowing that everything will be right for him eventually—that, after several fierce hand-to-hand struggles, which the villain evidently doesn't care much about winning, he will always end the reel with one arm around the heroine and the other pointing towards the great West, where their future lies—where the men may not take water with their whiskey, but they're square with their women. Upon this touching scene, the film fades slowly into darkness, and then follows the announcement of next week's attractions, in brilliant colors.

*   *   *

The villain is the third figure from the left. He may be one of two kinds—eastern or western. If he's the former, he wears a furlined overcoat, always open, and he owns one of those apartments with nude ladies holding bunches of grapes which light up. This shows that he is a man of wealth and artistic inclinations.

If he's a Westerner, however, he wears the usual Buffalo Bills, and he cheats at cards so cleverly that no one can detect him: no one, that is, but the audience.

Whether eastern or western, the villain is never without a big black cigar. On the screen a big black cigar always indicates villainy; on the stage, it means an impersonation of General Grant.

Mothers are also important figures in the screen world. The mother wears the conventional black and a becoming gray wig. She plays one of those watchful waiting parts—she never gives up hope that, maybe, Jim will get out of jail in time for Christmas. Mothers, in the movies, are never very well. They are always suffering uncomplainingly and they usually die at great length. In fact, it's considered rather unsportsmanlike for a mother to be still alive at the end of the picture.

The chee-ild is the lowest form of film life. The movie chee-ild is always a small blonde, who once overheard somebody say, "Isn't she cute?" and has tried to live up to it ever since. The little dear has the prettiest way of looking right into the camera every few minutes, just to be sure that she isn't missing anything that may be going on.

Of course, any Social Register of the movies cannot fail to include the director, the man behind the megaphone. He is a serious, tortoise-shell-glassed gentleman, who is always just on the point of revolutionizing the silent drama. His favorite indoor sport is giving out interviews, in which he may be quoted as saying "Motion pictures" (he always calls them "motion pictures," for publication) "are still in their infancy. It is but a matter of time when we shall have a universal screen language." These interviews are always illustrated with one of those shadowy photographs with the highlights on the brow, and are published in the magazine sections of the Sunday papers, under the title "Movies as a Fine Art."

Comedians and vampires are, of course, well-known movie figures, but they really couldn't be included in any perfectly nice left-to-right Social Register.

Their work is far too rough.

This concludes the evening's performance. Those who haven't seen all of the first show may remain for the second. Kindly pass out quietly, to the left. If you liked the show, please tell your friends,—if you didn't, don't tell the management.

EXCURSIONS INTO HUNLAND

LIEUT. E. M. ROBERTS, R. F. C.

FROM MARCH 1918

Roberts, formerly of the 10th Canadian Battalion, was a young American aviator who flew twenty-two months in Britain's Royal Flying Corps during World War I. The term "Hun" was used in Allied propaganda as a way to characterize members of the German military as barbaric.

My first turn of service at the front as a pilot consisted of patrol work for three days running. It was an uneventful start. On the fourth day I went up again on patrol about three o'clock in the afternoon and got to 20,000 feet. I was looking for Huns up there but found none. Since it was very cold I decided to go down a way, and shut off my power.

At the level of 18,000 feet, I found myself sweeping along a very large peak of cloud. Intending to spoil its pretty formation I dived into it and coming out on the other side found myself alongside of a Hun plane of the Albatross type.

I had no intimation at all that a Hun was present, and I guess he was in the same position concerning me. I suppose he was as much surprised as I was when he saw me emerging from the cloud. That he was surprised was indicated by his failure to open fire upon me. Neither of us could shoot at the other for the reason that the guns of the machine we were flying were fixed to the plane, so that the machine itself has to be pointed at the enemy in order to fire. We were so close together that this could not be done without our ramming one another, which both of us had to avoid if we did not wish to crash to the earth together.

The Hun waved at me, and I waved at him. We found ourselves in a very peculiar situation. I was so close to him that I could see with the naked eye every detail of his machine. I could also see his face quite clearly.

There was something off in our position. I had to smile at the thought that we were so close together and yet dared not harm one another. The Hun also smiled. Then I reached down to feel the handle of my pressure reservoir to make sure that it was in its proper place; for I knew that one of us would soon have to make a break.

I had never before met a Hun at such close quarters in the air, and although we flew parallel to one another for only a few minutes, the time seemed like a week. I remembered some of the tactics told me by several of the older and best fighters of the corps, and was wondering how I could employ them.

Finally an idea occurred to me. Two machines flying at the same height are not necessarily on exactly the same level. I was flying between the Hun and his own lines, and had fuel for another hour and a quarter anyway. I wanted to make sure of this bird, but decided to play a waiting game. We continued our flight side by side.

After a while, however, much sooner than I expected, the Hun started to get restless and began to manoeuvre for position. Like myself he was utilizing the veriest fraction of every little opportunity in his endeavor to outmanoeuvre his antagonist. Finally, the Hun thought he had gotten the lead.

I noticed he was going down a little, evidently for the purpose of shooting me from underneath. I was not quite sure as yet that such was really his intention; but the man was quick. Before I knew what had happened he had managed to put five shots into my machine. But all of them missed me.

I manoeuvred into an offensive position as quickly as I could, and before the Hun could fire again I had my machine gun pelting him. My judgment must have been fairly good. The Hun began to spin earthward. I followed to finish him, keeping in mind, meanwhile that it is an old game in flying to let the other man think you are hit. This bit of strategy will often afford the opportunity to get into a position that will give you the drop on your antagonist. The ruse is also sometimes used to get out of a fight when in trouble with gun jamb, or when bothered by a defective motor.

I discovered soon that this precaution was not necessary, for the Hun kept spinning right to the ground. He landed with a crash. A few minutes later I landed two fields away from the wreck, and ran over to see the kill I had made. I had hit the Hun about fifty times, and had nearly cut off both his legs at the hips.

There was nothing left in the line of souvenirs as the Tommies had gotten to the wreck before I did. I carried off a piece of his wing props, and had a stick made of it. That night we celebrated my first Hun brought down behind our own line since I had become a pilot.

Next day I went out to get another Hun to add to my collection. I was in the act of crossing the Hun lines when, bang! to the right of me came a thud, and my engine stopped. Revenge, I thought. I volplaned to the ground, made a good landing in a field, and then had another engine brought out to replace mine.

While with this squadron I witnessed one of the greatest air fights I was privileged to see. It took place above the cemetery of P—. Three Huns were aloft behind their own lines, and back of them was a patrol of their own. The Hun does not believe in coming over our lines whenever he can help it, and generally he will manoeuvre so that our boys who go up to fight him have to follow him over to his own territory.

One of our men, named Price, was just coming in from patrol. He suddenly found himself at the same height as three Huns,—which I judged to be about 12,000 feet. Price was well behind the Hun lines when the enemy saw him, and all three made for him at once. I was at an artillery observation post at the time, visiting a pal, and was able to get a good view of the combat.

The foremost of the Huns made straight for Price, and for a minute it looked as though he intended ramming him. They separated and began to fire upon one another, as the tut-tut-tut of the machine guns, which was faintly audible, told me. Of a sudden the Hun volplaned, while another Hun made straight for Price.

I wondered what Price would do under the circumstances, but saw the next moment that he zoomed over the second Hun machine, which just then swooped upon him for attack. While Price was doing this, I noticed that the first Hun was falling to the ground, having either been killed by Price's machine gun or disabled.

Within a few seconds the second Hun also crashed to the ground, and the third was now making for home as fast as his motor would carry him, but Price caught up with him very shortly. It was an exciting race. Price was working his machine gun for all the thing was worth, and before long the third Hun dashed to the ground.

The day following the fight I went out on another patrol. I rose up to about 15,000 feet and started across the lines. I had no trouble getting into Hunland. But the day was fairly clear and the Hun Archies were working overtime. I was about three miles behind the lines, when right ahead of me exploded a "woolly bear."

As soon as it had burst, my machine started to do a cake walk. I shut off power quickly and headed homeward, landing in an advance position of ours.

I will admit that I already had the greatest respect for the Hun Archie batteries. The woolly bear they had fired at me was something new, and since it had certainly done damage enough to my machine it increased that respect.

But duty is duty. After I had attached the propeller I went up again, but shrunk six inches when the next woolly bear exploded quite close to me. I ducked into the cockpit, although one is no safer in the cockpit than outside. When the machine crashes to the ground, the cockpit is still a part of it, of course, so far no means having been devised to anchor that cockpit to a cloud. Although the bus I was flying was a fast one, that Hun Archie battery did most creditable work. I must say that much for the Hun, although I hate him like poison.

The Huns were good shots, even at the elevation at which I was flying, which made my machine as seen from the ground no larger than a mosquito. I spent a very exciting day. The fire of the Hun Archies had never been as accurate as on that day, and those woolly bears seemed to have us all puzzled.

For all that, I had been lucky. When I returned to the aerodome it was merely to learn that old Pizzdoodle, a Scotch friend of mine, and as fine a boy as ever lived, had been brought down. Albert Ball, also of our squadron and the best pilot in the corps, perhaps, had likewise been shot down. The same fate had overtaken a number of others, many of whom I knew.

I spent a great deal of time that night wondering whether it would be my turn next. I remember looking over my medals and that peculiar mascot of mine, a Chinese doll. Life never seemed so uncertain or so short to me.

I had to wait next morning for quite some time before I received orders to go on patrol. Just before that I had learned that the King was coming to inspect our squadron, and I wondered whether I would have to hie myself into the blue just at the time when he would come. That was not to be the case, however.

Presently the King drove up in a car. We were lined and were looked over by the royal eye. The King shook hands with the commanding officer, chatted with him for awhile and then walked down our line. We were presented to him one by one, and the King had a kind word and a smile for every man.

After the King had addressed the man next to me, the wing commander told him that I was a Yankee, whereupon the King shook hands heartily with me and told me that he was proud of the Americans in the British service.

He asked me how I liked flying, and I told him that I had had no fair chance as yet, having been shot down only twice. The King laughed heartily, and told me that he had no fear for me, that I seemed quite able to take care of myself. He also remarked that it was his opinion that the United States of America would soon be doing good work and giving a good account of itself. Then he questioned me as to my length in the service and hoped that we would meet again.

When the King had left our camp, I started out on my patrol with a feeling that something would happen that day. I was rather blue and made up my mind that if I could prevent it old Archie, back of that Hun line, was not going to get me. I went up to 20,000 feet that morning, but had hardly done so when I noticed that there was a fight going on across the Hun lines. I wanted to see what was going on and made for the spot, but had not gone very far before old woolly bear picked us up. Soon the shells were bursting all around us.

Before long a gang of our men was making for the scene of the fight, and gave the Hun Archies every chance to send up their woolly bears. The seventh shell that exploded near me sent a steel fragment into my carburetor. Of a sudden my motor slowed down and, as usual, I had visions of having to make a forced landing in Hunland. The piece of the shell in coming down had done considerable damage to the sides of the cockpit, and for a moment I feared that it had smashed some of my control. But that fear was ungrounded, as I presently discovered. My controls were still intact, and for that reason I would be able to glide to the ground.

I swung my machine into position for a glide toward our line, and before very long was at 10,000 feet with the Hun shells keeping close to my back. Some of them exploded a little ahead of me, which is always a bad sign for a descending man. It shows that the Archie gunners have a good line on the course of the dive, and every next shell may be the last the man in the machine sees. It was so on this day. The woolly bears continued to stand in my way, and I sped through their fumes nearly all the way down. To this day I do not understand how I managed to land, as I finally did in a convenient field.

The forced landings keep a man's nerve on edge. With the motor dead the pilot has lost 85% of his power to control the machine, and generally he reaches the ground at too great a speed to make a landing that will keep his machine intact.

On this landing I hit the ground at a speed of about 55 miles per hour, and had the misfortune of being thrown to one side by a bump on the ground which was struck by one of the wheels. The next instant the machine was on its nose; it turned over on its back and collapsed.

During the somersault I had the misfortune to stun myself by being thrown against the instrument board. The result was that I was bruised all over, had my lip cut, eyes blackened and my chin bruised quite badly. I was unable to get out of the wreckage, and still had the fear that the gasoline, which was spilling from the tanks, would ignite,—in which case I would have met the fate of many another pilot.

THE GREAT AMERICAN ARMY

GERTRUDE STEIN

FROM JUNE 1918

*Written while volunteering as an ambulance driver in
France during World War I.*

I found an acorn to-day.
Green
In the center.
No, on the end.
And what is the name of the bridge?
This is what we say.
"The Great American Army,"—
This is what we say.

I write to loan.
We do work so well.
And what must *we* do?

In the world.
What do you call them?
Plates.
And where do you use them?
In guns.
The French pronounce it Guns.

So do the English.
What do the boys say?
"*Can* we?"

In the middle.
Or in the middle.
The Great American Army.
Nestles in the middle.
We have hope;
Certainly—
And Success!

THE GATEWAY TO AN ARTIFICIAL PARADISE: THE EFFECTS OF HASHISH AND OPIUM COMPARED

ARTHUR SYMONS

FROM OCTOBER 1918

Hashish (which is extracted from the flowering tops, and the tender parts of Indian hemp) is a drug which enslaves the imagination and changes the nature of the will. It is a magician who turns sounds into colors and colors into sounds. It annihilates space and time, and has the divinity of a sorceress, the charm of a dangerous and insidious mistress. It produces morbid effects on our senses and wakens fantastic visions in our half-closed eyes.

Like every form of drug intoxication the effects of hashish are malign, diabolical. When subjugated by it, a part of oneself becomes wholly dominated, so that it may truly be said of an addict: *Il a voulu devenir ange; il est devenu bête.*

After indulging in it, one sits, as in a theatre, seeing a drama acted on a stage. We see it all with eyes that—during these ecstatic hallucinations— behold an endless drama of dreams; that perceive the subtlest impressions, fairy pageants, ghostlike unrealities: eyes, in short, that envisage the borders of the infinite. Then—to show the fantastic nature of its miraculous powers—the grammar, the arid grammar itself, becomes, to the dreamer, something like an evoked sorcery. The words are alive—in flesh and in blood; the substantive, in its substantial majesty; the adjective, a transparent vestment that clothes it and colors it like a glacis: and the verb, an angel of movement, that gives a sort of rhythmic swing to the entire phrase.

With the coming of the hallucinations all exterior forms take on singular aspects; become deformed and transformed. Then come the transpositions of ideas, with unaccountable analogies that penetrate the spirit. Music, heard or unheard, seems immeasurable, more stirring and more sensual.

Sometimes, when one is under the spell of the drug, the idea of an evaporation—slow, successive, eternal—takes hold of your spirit and you soon apply this idea to your thoughts, to your mode of thinking. By a singular equivocation, by a kind of mental transportation, or intellectual *quid pro quo*, you find yourself evaporating. The instant becomes eternity; though the hallucination is sudden, perfect and fatal. One feels an excessive thirst, a physical restlessness, a nervous apprehension, which at last subsides into that strange state which the Orientals call *Kief.*

Hashish has a more troubling effect on one than opium. It is more vehement, more ecstatic, more malign, more evocative, more unseizable. It lifts one across more infinite horizons and carries us more passionately over the passionate waves of unknown storms on unseen seas. It takes us, not into eternities, not into chaos, not into Heaven, not into Hell (though these may whirl before one's endazzled vision) but into an incredible existence over which no magician rules, over which no God or witch presides.

The mental effects of hashish are, also, more *active* than those of opium. After smoking opium things grow somnolent, slow, wavering. Men and women become veiled—we never see their faces. There is light, but not the light of the sun, nor of the stars, nor of the moon. The houses have no windows; inside there are no mirrors. Everywhere, throughout the whole hallucination, one is aware of an odor, a stench—the stench superinduced by opium and by opium's moral degradations. The streets are thick with grass; such animals as one sees are, for some strange reason, stupefied. In fact, the sleeping world of opium has no foundations in action or life; the scenes in it exhale something worse than inaction— an inexplicable *stupefaction*.

The effects of hashish are more unexpected and more bizarre than those of opium. It is a drug which can separate ourselves from ourselves; change our very shapes into shapeless images; drown us in the deep depths of annihilation, out of which we emerge vaguely, slowly, pleasantly. It can bury us under the oldest roots of the earth; give us death in life and life in death; bestow upon us sleep that is not sleep, and waking dreams that are not any part of waking. There is nothing, in short, human or inhuman, moral or immoral, which this drug cannot give us.

Yet, all the time we are indulging in it, we know not what it is taking from us, nor what deadly exchange we are certain to be made to give for it; nor what intoxication will some day be produced *beyond* its intoxication; nor that it will soon become almost a habit of the Soul.

I magine a universe in disorder, peopled by strange beings who have no relation to each other; whose speech is jargon; where such houses as one sees are built in unbelievable ways—none with straight lines, many in triangles; where the animals are wholly unlike ours, some smaller than ants, some larger than beasts of the forest; where there are no churches, no apparent streets; where we see shadows, but not the shadows which the sun casts from our figures as we walk on the grass; not the moon's shadows that make mockery of us; but shadows from the veritable fire and fumes and flames of Hell; where, if one sees fire, the smoke goes downward; where flames leap out of the soil again only to turn into living serpents. Now one sees a python return into his proper flame. There seem to be no gods in this fantastic land, nor idols, nor priests, nor shrines; but only chaos, and smoke, and music, and the sound of dancing and carousing in innumerable brothels.

The seas storm the skies. See! They have swallowed up Heaven; and all that lives and all that dies has become indistinguishable.

Hashish, with all that is agreeable about it, is one of the most insinuating and terrible means employed by the Princess of Dreams to enslave humanity, to give to her victims a monstrous sense of the horror of life, of the wickedness, not only of living beings, but of Space and Time as well. Those who taste long of this supreme poison seem fated to be hurled—always, without ending—between violent and opposing whirlwinds of horror.

The pale and shadowy Princess of Dreams has a habit of appearing, in proper person, to her votaries in their drowsy visions. She guides them and hovers over them, all the time becoming more vicious and more formidable. And, pale though she is, and dead, and abnormal, and sinister, yet does she still continue the heroine of all their dreams.

And the Princess has a way of becoming—month by month—more cruel, more merciless. In her eyes there burns a more ardent and violent light; she becomes more insatiable than Death—more ravenous than Life.

It is, as a rule, the last sign of the drug's mastery over a man, when he begins to admire himself inordinately; when he glorifies himself; when he becomes the center of the whole universe; as certain of his virtues as of his genius and destiny. Then, with stupendous irony, he cries aloud: "I have become God." At last he wishes to tell the whole world of his divine attributes: to project himself out of himself—as if the will of a man liberated by intoxication had some magical and efficacious virtue—and to cry, again and again, with a cry that might strike down the scattered angels from the ways of the sky: "Look at me. Look at me well! I have become God."

OUR OFFICE: A HATE SONG

DOROTHY PARKER

FROM MAY 1919

An *Intimate Glimpse* of Vanity Fair—*En Famille*

I hate the office;
It cuts in on my social life.

There is the Art Department;
The Cover Hounds.
They are always explaining how the photographing machine works.
And they stand around in the green light
And look as if they had been found drowned.
They are forever discovering Great Geniuses;
They never fail to find exceptional talents
In any feminine artist under twenty-five.
Whenever the illustrations are late
The fault invariably lies with the editorial department.
They are always rushing around looking for sketches,
And writing mysterious numbers on the backs of photographs,
And cutting out pictures and pasting them into scrapbooks,
And then they say nobody can realize how hard they are worked—
They said something.

Then there is the Editorial Department;
The Literary Lights.

They are just a little holier than other people
Because they can write classics about
"'Brevity is the soul of lingerie', said this little chemise to itself";
And "Here are five reasons for the success of the Broadways plays".
They are all full of soul;
Someone is forever stepping on their temperaments.
They are constantly having nervous breakdowns
And going away for a few weeks.
And they only come in on Saturday mornings
To hold the franchise.
They tell you what good training editorial work is.
But they don't mean to stay in it—
Some day they will be Free Lances
And write the Great Thoughts that Surge within them.
They say they only wish they could get away from the office,—
That makes it unanimous.

Then there is the Fashion Department;
First Aids to Baron de Meyer.
If any garment costs less than $485
They think you ought to give it to the Belgians.
They look at everything you have on,
And then smile tolerantly
And say, "Sears, Roebuck certainly do a wonderful business, don't they?"
They are forever taking pictures of prominent Wild Women
Dressed as brides and kneeling at Property Altars.
And they write essays on Smart Fashions for Limited Incomes,—
The sky's the limit.

There is the Boss;
The Great White Chief.
He made us what we are to-day,—
I hope he's satisfied.

He has some bizarre ideas
About his employees' getting to work
At nine o'clock in the morning,—
As if they were a lot of milkmen.
He has never been known to see you
When you arrive at 8:45,
But try to come in at a quarter past ten
And he will always go up in the elevator with you.
He goes to Paris on the slightest provocation
And nobody knows why he has to stay there so long.
Oh, well—
You can't expect to keep him down on the farm.

I hate the office;
It cuts in on my social life.

1920s

WILLIAM SOMERSET MAUGHAM:
A PEN PORTRAIT BY A FRIENDLY HAND

HUGH WALPOLE

FROM JANUARY 1920

When I first saw William Somerset Maugham (it is a considerable number of years ago now) I was most acutely conscious of his grey top hat.

It must have been that same grey hat which figured so prominently in Gerald Festus Kelly's portrait—a grey hat set audaciously, cynically, with humor and with a quite definite pose of a dandyism in which the wearer obviously did not believe. That hat belonged to Maugham's earlier, more cynical days, the days of "Mrs. Dot" and "Smith," the days when he was out quite determinately to make money and had put behind him for the moment the unproductive austerities of "A Man of Honour" and "Liza of Lambeth."

I had the merest glimpse of him at that time wandering, under the grey hat, through the gardens of a Campden Hill retreat, where Violet Hunt was giving a literary garden party. How desperately those garden parties seem now to be things of the past! It was at the time when May Sinclair was showing her reverence for Henry James in her novel, "The Creators"; when untidy young men and women discussed, with bated breath, the audacities of the Vedrenne Barker management at the Cort Theatre. The days when Conrad was still despised and rejected, and Frank Harris was writing about Shakespeare, and Bernard Shaw was a freakish young thing who would write better one day.

Lord! What a long while ago and how scornfully Somerset Maugham moved amongst those shadows under the high trees and how he despised them for their high-brow sentiments and baggy-looking clothes!

That garden party at which I saw him must have been I think the very last of its series. I never went to one again. I never heard of one again. The London world moved on to a new phase.

The next time that I saw Maugham was in that gay discreet bandbox of a house in Mayfair that became, for many of us, one of the happiest, most hospitable, most amusing houses in London. I was, I remember, from the very first struck by the strange contrast of the lower social part of the house and the room on the top floor where he did his work. That top floor remains, after all these years, as the most ideal spot for a writing man that I have ever seen.

All rooms are, I suppose, symbolic of their owners. Maugham's had just that mingling of harsh reality with barbaric and preferably Eastern splendor that represents him. He had worn his grey top hat as the King of China might have worn it, and here was the King of China again among the squatting Eastern gods and the marvellous lacquer boxes and the heavy gold chests mysteriously engraven. And against this there was, in the very center of the wide bare room, a large rough deal table with good plain English legs and no nonsense about it. Here Maugham sat and cultivated his genius.

He was supposed, at the time of which I am speaking, to be giving himself up to the production of those merry superficial comedies that delighted the London world for so long. It was the characteristic thing to say at that time that Maugham had sold his soul for a "mess of pottage." He let the world say what it liked; admitted, if anyone asked him, that certainly "Mrs. Dot" was a more profitable lady than "Liza" and that one could live only once. Meanwhile, how characteristically he was producing through all those years what will remain. I am convinced, not only his masterpiece, but one of the great English novels of the period—"Of Human Bondage."

Only one or two of his friends knew of that book. He had for it that love which is beyond question the happiest thing in a writer's life, that love which is not pride nor conceit, but simply so deep an immersion in the thing that you are creating that you positively cannot pull yourself out of it. He lingered on and on over this "Pattern in the Carpet," as he called it, rewriting, adding, subtracting, knowing full well what every writer knows, that no book belongs to an author after its publication, that that intimacy of creation will never return once the world shares it with you.

He never tried during that time to persuade people of his other artistic self. That third book of his—"Mrs. Craddock"—still remains as one of the ablest, most poignant studies of woman in our generation. How many people here have read it?

Maugham never forced anyone to think about him at all, but the obtuseness of the world in general is one of his pleasantest private jokes. He prefers them obtuse.

The life of a popular and successful dramatist must be a very exciting and happy one. I should like immensely to be Mr. Hopwood, or Miss Zoë Akins or Mr. Knoblock. It has all the elements of horse-racing, Chemin-de-Fer, public oratory, the Episcopal Bench and proposals of marriage; it must make one simply conceited to death.

Maugham has never had that kind of conceit. He has, as have all artists who are any good at all, a justified sense of his own powers. He knows that he can write books that are worth the attention of serious people and plays that anyone, serious or not, is justified in going to see. He knows that he is better than Mr. Tom Noddy, who doesn't realize the first thing about stage technique, and Mr. Emery Paper, whose novel about Mormonism is being much read just now. But he also knows that Aristophanes and Aeschylus lived before him and understood quite a lot about the theatre and that Dostoiefsky and Flaubert wrote pretty good novels.

Into this happy and exciting existence then broke the war. Maugham was luckier in the war than many of us in that he found work that was exactly suited to him. The secret service job that fell to him was made for him, made for his knowledge of languages, his knowledge of human nature, his knowledge of when to speak and when to keep silent. I saw a little phase of his work in Russia. We were in Petrograd together during those months after the Revolution of March, 1917. Very depressing those months were, when the idealism of some of us got some hard knocks, and when all our preconceived notions of Russia and the Russian spirit fell to the ground one after another. I don't think that Maugham knew very much about Russia, but his refusal to be hurried into sentimental assumptions, his cynical pretence that "all was anyway for the worst" (he did not himself believe that for a single moment) gave him a poise and calm that some others of us badly needed. He watched Russia as we would watch a play, finding the theme, and then intent on observing how the master artist would develop it. He did not see the end of that play—the end indeed is not yet—but he sent home some pretty wise notions as to its probable last act.

It was in the last summer of the war that I caught quite a different glimpse of him. I stayed with him for a day or two in one of the loveliest houses in the whole of England, and it was at that time that he was writing "The Moon and Sixpence." I think that he had the idea of the book in his head long before he wrote it. He had always been passionately interested in modern painting, and I remember his saying to me a long while ago what a novel Gauguin's life would make. I don't think, however, that that artist gave him more than the starting-point for his story. Maugham's Strickland is his own creation; the technique of that fine book is his own technique, above all, the poetry of it is his own poetry. It does seem to me to rank among the very finest novels in English of the last ten or twenty years.

Maugham is still mid-way in his career. I for one do not believe that he has yet touched the heights that he will reach as a dramatist. His present visit to China should provide him with the motive that his strange talent, Eastern, Western, cynical, harsh and tender, demands.

MY AUTOBIOGRAPHY

A. A. MILNE

FROM JANUARY 1920

A few years ago I published a book. That is to say, I wrote the thing, and my agent induced a publisher to accept it, and the publisher tried to induce the public to buy it. We had quite a fair success; we sold a good seven copies. However, it is generally agreed among actuaries and others that we might have had a really big success, we might have sold nine, or even ten, copies, but for an unfortunate occurrence. I shall explain what happened.

At about the time that the book was accepted I wrote a story which appeared in an American magazine. I had never written in an American magazine before, and though my name is of course a household word in the uninhabited parts of China, it was felt that I needed a special introduction to the people of New York. My agent suggested, therefore, that I should write a short life of myself—two or three hundred words, say—explaining who the dickens I was, in order that the editor might print this alongside my story, as a sort of explanation why he did it. "This is the fellow," the editor was to be assumed as saying. "I thought we ought to give him a chance."

Naturally, when I sat down to write my life I began to wish that I had lived a better one. But it was then too late; the copy had to be in by Friday. I told them where and when I was born, where I was educated (when I say "educated," you know what I mean), and what made me first begin to write. I described my marriage, my permanent address and the regiment to which I had attached myself for the war. I mentioned my travel-book, "Half an Hour in the Malay Archipelago," and my detective-story, "The Crimson Cough." I wrote three hundred words all about myself—a fascinating subject—and sent them to my agent, and he wrote back to thank me, and said that he supposed it would have to do. But he seemed to be a little disappointed.

A week went by, and then I heard from my agent again. My book would be coming out soon, my first book in America. Widely quoted as I was on the desert islands of the Pacific, I was not (he opined) a very familiar personality to the library-subscribers of New York. The publisher suggested therefore that I should write a short life of myself—two or three hundred words, say—explaining who the devil I was, in order that he might circulate it in advance as a warning of what was coming.

So I sat down to write my life. It was rather a bore doing it again, and I wished that I had kept a copy of what I had written the week before. However, it was no good worrying about that now. Selecting a clean piece of paper, and dipping my pen in the ink, I told them where and when I was born, when I was educated and what made me first begin to write. I described my marriage, my home, my military experiences. I mentioned my detective-story, "The Crimson Cough," and my travel-book, "Half an Hour in the Malay Archipelago." I wrote three hundred words all about myself—a subject still fascinating, although some glamour had worn off—and I sent them to my agent.

The next morning he called me up on the telephone. He was very much upset.

"I say, really!" he expostulated. "This won't do at all."

"Why, what's the matter?"

"My dear fellow," he said, reproachfully, "this is the same life as the other one."

He thinks that, but for this, we might have sold nine, or even ten copies of the book.

THE HIGHER EDUCATION ON THE SCREEN

ROBERT E. SHERWOOD

FROM FEBRUARY 1920

The cinema is rapidly replacing the school as a medium of education for the young. School teachers and professors everywhere have been forced to admit that their youthful charges are learning a great deal more about life in the motion-picture palaces than they ever can in the class-rooms; and the resultant degree of precocity and sophistication in the young is cause for both amazement and alarm.

In fact, the day is actually at hand when the silver screen will supplant the blackboard. The present system of education has been weighed in the balance and found wanting—and not only the kindergartens and schools, but the universities as well, are doomed.

What will be the viewpoint, the attitude, of the average child of a few years hence—a child trained mentally by the cinema? How will this one differ from us, who had to content ourselves with the meager supply of information furnished in the old fashioned and soon-to-be-obsolete institutions of learning?

GEOGRAPHY

First, let us consider the study of geography. At an age corresponding to ours when we were just about capable of grasping the fact that Quito is the capital of Peru, the child of the future will have an adequate working knowledge of conditions in the Bad Lands of Montana, the Limehouse wharves in London, and the downtown districts of Shanghai. He will be perfectly acquainted with the habits and habitat of the Apaches—both Parisian and Arizonian—and will know things about the points east of Suez that Kipling never dreamed of. He will never have to open the pages of Rand-McNally, and will not be bothered with such details as the outline of continents or the tide tables in their relation to the lunar orbit; but every film trained child will be glad, upon examination, to disclose the following facts of geographic interest:

1. Africa is a vast expanse of passion bounded by Alla Nazimova and Theda Bara.
2. A forest is something which catches fire in Reel 4.
3. The Grand Canyon is that ditch which Douglas Fairbanks jumps across.
4. A desert island is a spot of land which yachts run into and which generally turns out to be inhabited by Norma Talmadge.
5. The Pacific Ocean is a body of water six paces due west of the Mack Sennett Bathing Girls.

And so forth.

SOCIOLOGY

Nor will the question of social values be neglected. The seething spirit of unrest—a spirit born of mutual distrust and jealousy—which breeds the

germ of revolution, will be killed in its infancy by the provisions of a mutual meeting ground for people in all stations of life. The man in the
street will condescend to fraternize with the man in the drawing room
because, having seen him in the pictures, he knows all there is to know
about him. For instance, every child who behaves himself and watches
the screen closely will know:

That a rich man is (9 times out of 10) a rascal bent upon the wooing of
Pearl White.

That he may be identified by his immaculate sartorial equipment,
which includes a belted waistcoat, a Glen-Urquhart plaid cap and cloth-
topped shoes.

That he lounges about in exclusive clubs which are heavily uphol-
stered in the neo-Selznick style, and drinks rows upon rows of whiskeys
straight.

That he shakes dice and the shimmy, and misleads parlor-maids when
not otherwise engaged.

Whereas:

A poor man is invariably noble.

That he, in his turn, may be identified by the fact that his shirt is always open, disclosing a corrugated neck and a liberal expanse of knotted
chest, which he thumps periodically.

That he likes nothing better than to murder his rivals "with his two
hands."

That, even if he "ain't long on book l'arnin'," he's "true blue."

History will, of course, receive a certain degree of attention. From now
on, contemporary events will be so effectively mirrored in motion pictures that future generations will have a living record of that which has
gone before, instead of the uninteresting and inaccurate volumes which
we, in our simple way, have had to muddle through with. The little schol-
ars of the future will be able to check up on the various shortcomings of
their predecessors in a manner hitherto undreamed of.

HISTORY OF THE WAR

The World War will be chiefly notable throughout the years to come because it is the first great historical event to be chronicled by means of the motion picture camera. The War has already received much valuable publicity on the screen, and there is no doubt but that it will furnish a well nigh inexhaustible source of entertainments and diversion for our descendants in the peaceful days of the future.

What a comfort for the man who has been Over There to know that his great-great-grandchildren will be privileged to see all the war photoplays which have descended upon us since "that mighty grey horde swept into Belgium" in August, 1914! Perhaps the man who has been Over There will wonder what impression this same great-great-grandchild will receive of his forefather's share in the famous victory; we hazard the opinion that the impressions (if the child has faithfully followed all the war films) will be something like this:

What did my great-great-grand-daddy do in the Great War?

He (1) captured a village, practically single-handed, just in time to save an exquisite French girl from an unspeakable fate.

(2) Lay wounded in the heart of No-Man's-Land until rescued by a Red Cross dog.

(3) Received the Légion d'Honneur and a kiss from Marshal Foch—a part posed by a corpulent old man with a walrus mustache and a Sam Browne belt over his left shoulder; and finally he

(4) returned home to find that he had been given up for lost by everyone except *her*—who had never wavered for so much as an instant.

There were many obstacles which blocked the path of the cameraman in Northern France, where many of the leading battles took place. The light was so poor (due to constant overdoses of high-explosive) as to preclude the possibility of any effective photography, the result being that the scenes had to be reproduced in California, some six thousand miles away. Motion picture promoters hope that the next war be staged in a more suitable location than the last one; and this hope is shared, to a certain extent, by the inhabitants of Northern France.

LITERATURE

Literature will not be quite submerged as a study, but it will receive the subordinate place which it deserves and will be offered only in supremely condensed form. The subtitles in photoplays will provide ample reading matter for the young and will serve to fulfill the mission in which such stalwart literateurs as Hans Anderson and Peter Grimm have utterly failed. The average romance could be told in a few sentences—punctuated, of course, with the real action on the screen—somewhat as follows:

"Pure and unsmirched as the driven lily, Myra Figgis was the only glint of sunshine which penetrated the dark shadows of Hell-bent Alley."

"Arnold Starchworthy, social vulture, cast doubtful eyes upon the little sunflower of the slums."

"And so—"

"Years sped past in their relentless flight."

"Jim Muldoon was a man who UNDERSTOOD."

"'You cur.'"

"'Jim! Oh, Jim! You've killed him.'"

"Down through the ages, pure as the sunset, comes the eternal message of LOVE—deathless, undying—without end."

"Next week—The screen version of Ibsen's 'Ghosts' with Roscoe (Fatty) Arbuckle."

THE MILLENNIUM

The result of this is obvious—the mind will mature far earlier than the body and the physical will become subservient to the intellectual. This approximates the ideal state.

Could we but see and talk with some of these prodigies of the future, we would gain a faint conception of the narrowness of our own minds in this primitive age. Think of it!—a nine-year-old child of today is incapable of writing anything less puerile than "The Young Visiters," for instance. Tomorrow after the cinema has replaced the school, our kiddies will be composing unexpurgated versions of "The Thousand and One Nights."

Then, indeed, will we be able to open up the flood gates and let the millennium rush in.

MR. WILSON'S INELASTIC INTELLIGENCE

JOHN JAY CHAPMAN

FROM FEBRUARY 1920

No wonder that Europe has found it hard to understand the American mind. The American can see things in the clouds: he has magnificent visions and enthusiasms. He can also see a thing which he holds in his hands, or the branch of a tree when it is very near him, and is perhaps about to put out one of his eyes. But the mind of the American has no middle distance. He is either star-eyed and idealistic about a dim future, or else he is deadly practical and very efficient about some necessary job.

It was this blindness to things in the middle distance that prevented America from seeing the war as it came on. The war was not in the skies but on earth; it contradicted our theories and our beliefs, and we couldn't really believe in it till it was close upon us. Then, in a flash, we saw it plainly, sized it up accurately, treated it as a practical job and finished it off magnificently.

Much the same thing happened with regard to the League of Nations. So long as the League was a splendid dream we loved it. [President Woodrow] Wilson, who for all his eccentricities is a stamped and patented American mind, espoused the League idea platonically. He swallowed it whole: the world must have a League that should govern Humanity. The war itself and the Treaty of Peace sank in his mind to insignificance before the thought of the League. He was at home in the Empyrean, and was going to set the stars in order. He didn't in the least see the middle distance of practical difficulties which lay between him and his League. He cared nothing about difficulties; they would, he thought, settle themselves. Of course, if he had been a European he would first have put through a Treaty of Peace, and then later formed some sort of a League, devoted to certain practical ends, a utilitarian and not very noble affair.

Such a plan would, however, have excited little interest in America. It would not have been big enough, new enough, ideal enough for us. It would have seemed like the Hague over again. But Mr. Wilson's scheme was large enough to suit us. It was all theory, and in theory we are at home. Now when the great League constitution was perfected (at least printed) and presented to the American people, a strange and quite unexpected thing happened. The theory of the plan conflicted with the American Constitution. We now saw for the first time, what any thoughtful person should have seen from the start, that there were practical and peculiar difficulties in hitching the United States to the League. Our people gave no thought to such problems till the crisis was upon them. It wasn't until the World Ship which we had launched ourselves was about to run down the U.S.S. Constitution that we woke up.

The Americans now began to follow the discussions of the United States Senate, first, with a sort of surly half approval of the Senate's reservations, and later with the dismayed, undisguised conviction that the League must be amended. We became confused and uncomfortable, did nothing, and hoped for the best.

All this time the thing which Europe really wanted and would have worked out for herself if the Americans hadn't been there, was a *makeshift*. The European is (compared to the American), a cynical person, and is anxious for a quiet life and enough to eat. He fell in with the Platonic and universal theories of Mr. Wilson only because there seemed no other way of getting America to co-operate and lend a helping hand toward setting Europe's house in order. He wanted the aid of American idealism in making and guarding his new home. In order to get this aid the European consented to Wilson's new Cosmic Machine which was larger than he had really wished for. When Europe found that the American people were growing cold toward the League she was grieved and surprised, and no wonder. How should Europe know that before the distant, rosy, academic League, so clearly seen and deeply loved by the American could approach the American eye and get into a range where the American could see it as a fact, realize it as a claim, and act upon it in a commonplace, efficient way,—how could the European know that that rosy vision must pass through the middle distance, lose its shine, grow vague, grow almost invisible, and finally reveal itself to the Americans as very near at hand, very insistent, very imperfect,—straggling into sight as the thing it really was all the while, the thing which Europe wanted all along,—a *makeshift?*

As soon as the American saw that the League was a makeshift he began to be sensible about the matter.

I n looking back over the whole historic episode we must try to divest it of its personalities, however startling they may have been, and see only national traits and great public currents of thought in the story. You and I are Wilson. We may not like him, but we are like him. You and I are the Senate. We may not like them, but we *are* like them. The American mind in its first contact with Europe,—*i.e.,* in the War, began by seeing the issue in a fog of false idealism and fumbling at it, but ended by seeing that the matter in hand was a job, and doing it.

In this second episode—the League of Nations—the American mind followed the same course. First it bit off more than it could chew and then with great deliberation spat it all out, in the face of all men.

If Mr. Wilson had had a more elastic intelligence, that is to say, had our people possessed more common sense, he would have drafted a common-sense League, in Paris, and we should have adopted it. If Mr.

Wilson could only have seen that part of the world which lies between the horizon line and the veranda railing, he would have done this, or rather *we* should have done it. But our favorite proverb is "Never cross a bridge till you come to it." And, accordingly, we shouted at the outset, "League, League and nothing but the League!" Then later we shouted, "Down with the League, damn the League!" and, finally, we shouted, "Up with the League, after all!"

This is our way of doing things.

But note this: On all these occasions we acted with substantial unanimity: we were governed by a great wave of public thought. Another fact must be noted, for it is very extraordinary. Our final shout of "Up with the League, after all!" was a *silent* shout: no procesions, denunciatory monster meetings, but just an invisible mandate which issued from everyone and informed the Senators that the United States must enter the League.

One cannot blame Europe for being puzzled by all these gyrations of ours. This vast and complex American people is a thinking-machine, and it all thinks together. It arrives at results through an infinite clatter, an infinite bable and confusion, interrupted by periods of subsidence and of creakings that seem to be premonitory of a breakdown. And then, suddenly, some conclusion is registered on the dial. The machine hands you out a printed slip. On the last occasion the lettering of the slip read: "Take the Makeshift."

This short edict represents a great advance in wisdom over our clamorous rejoicing when the League was born in Paris, and when Mr. Wilson was promising peace and happiness to mankind. We are less callow now, less *idée fixe*, more worldly wise.

We are cutting our eye teeth.

THE LAMPS OF LIMEHOUSE

THOMAS BURKE

FROM MARCH 1920

In the featureless twilight of the Causeway, Sing-a-song Joe, the loony of Poplar, the half-witted drunkard, the sport of idle crowds, took his tin whistle from under his coat, put it to his lips, and blew a piercing cry. Drawn by the note, a group of street boys . . . soon surrounded him, crying to others: "Come on, boys! We got Sing-a-song! Now we'll 'ave some sport!"

They gathered about him and hustled him to the wall, jeering and baiting him; while he, with wide grins and aimless gestures, made mild protest, and palpably took pride in the attention he commanded. Yet something in his face and demeanor was markedly incongruous to his situation. His wayward hair, pinched face, and starveling eye belonged rather to the dreamer than to the self-sufficient street-waif. And a dreamer he was; he was Sing-a-song Joe: a name that was fixed upon him by his ready offers to sing a song in return for cigarette, drink, or bread. All Poplar knew that witless voice that cried so shockingly the obscenities of sea-chanties or inane jingles of his own impromptu invention; but of the strange heart of the singer that hung tangled in a net of stars and flowers, Poplar knew nothing.

At a point when jeering ceased, and sharp physical violence began, he broke away from his persecutors, fled down the Causeway, and, whistle in hand, darted through an open door. The sanctuary to which he fled was the little store of John Sway Too, who alone showed him kindness unmixed with taunts or blows; for to John Sway Too he was useful as a casual enter-tainment to his evening customers. [The proprietor] received him with an inexpressive smile, and waved him to a seat. He went to a seat in the back room, deliberately, as one who took his rights, and, placing the whistle again between his teeth, made shrill music, his lean fingers fluttering merrily over its stops. John Sway Too, still smiling, poured out a tumbler of rice-spirit, and handed it to him. He drank it in two gulps.

A few casuals of the docks, who were eating at adjoining tables, cocked eyes at him. One spoke:

"Sing us a song, Joe. 'Ere's a fag for yeh. Catch!"

The boy caught deftly the thrown cigarette, and, laying aside his whistle, threw back his head, and screamed in thin tones traditional lewd verses of waterside life. The guests gave ironical applause, and threw pieces of bread at him. Somebody charged his glass, and under its influ-ence he expanded. He lolled in his chair. He threw a wide arm, and babbled.

"I'm a poet!" he cried. "I make poems out of my own head. I'd show them to you if you could understand them. But you couldn't; so I keep 'em to myself. But I'm a great poet all the same. Ha!"

The company sniggered drily. They had heard this many times before. It was time, they said, that he thought of some new gag. At this moment the latch of the shop-door clicked, and two girls entered; one self-consciously, the other swinging in self-possession. John Sway Too ambled forward, and bowed them to the back room and seats. They ordered chow-chow and tea: and at the sound of their voices, Sing-a-song, whose head had fallen to his breast, sharply looked up. The drink was working within him, and he could see but one object at a time. That on which his heavy-lidded gaze rested was the shy girl: a slim, slight figure, with white face and dense black hair encircling it; all grace and unappeased expectancy. So keen was his look that her eyes were withdrawn from the multitude of novel and distracting points of interest in this grotesque establishment, towards him. The stare was noted by the loungers, who muttered ribald epithets, spattered with chill giggles from the girl's companion.

"Say, Mag," said this one, "you've got orf this time. You've clicked all right!"

The dark girl made no comment. What was passing in her mind was beyond conjecture; but she glanced back and forth at the boy, and caught his hot, hungry eyes with hers, and seemed in nowise affronted. While they were eating, the minstrel turned from them, and called to John Sway Too.

"Sti-sti-stick us a pipe, Johnny!"

Johnny regarded him with grave reproof. "Ho no. Li-un veh de-ar. Hi give you whole bottle hof rice-spillit. You be qui-et."

"Give us a tune, Sing-a-song!" shouted one. "Give us another song—something new."

Glass in hand, the boy rose from his seat and threw his arm in a grandiose gesture. The empty glass shot to the wall with a light crash, which was echoed by thick laughter.

"I am a poet!" he asserted. "I do not sing for people like you. I sing to ladies and princesses. I will sing for *her!*" He darted a lean arm towards the dark girl; then moved to her table. The company at the tables directed at her a volley of large winks and grimaces, intended to encourage her to keep up the jest.

"Lady, buy me a pipe, and I'll make a beautiful poem. A lovely poem—all about you."

The girl looked up, uncertain of her cue; embarrassed, half-amused, and just a little apprehensive; wondering how she was expected to treat this encounter. She had been brought into this strange atmosphere by her friend, as an escapade. It was to her a glimpse of Bohemian life. She had heard of ungainly, vociferous poets in the cafes of Montmartre, and assumed that this was a London reconstruction of Montmartre. It fed her with hints of rare adventure; and, at a kick on the ankle from her friend, she called decisively to John Sway Too. "Give him what he wants. I'll pay."

John moved to a blue curtain, which shielded a deep, dark recess, and beckoned to Sing-a-song, who, after a prodigious inclination to the girl, followed him. Those in the shop heard the splutter of a match and the sizzling of chandu. Then John returned alone, and Sing-a-song was forgotten. Fresh customers came in, with fresh topics for talk; those who had finished their meal went out; and the two girls talked in self-conscious murmurs.

Suddenly, through a lull in the conversation, came the piercing note of a whistle from the recess. The company started. The note was followed by a tuneless trill. Next moment, the curtain was violently torn apart, and Sing-a-song Joe, with whistle at lips, reeled shapelessly down the two steps into the shop. He sagged from side to side, still blowing. His eyes were starry; his face was livid. Then, while the customers gaped in wonder, he swerved round toward the dark girl. The whistle fell from his mouth to the floor, and he stretched arms to her and spoke.

"My princess! At last I have found you." He swayed from side to side: then braced himself sharply, and a torrent of hot language gushed from him. "Beautiful lady!" he tried in shrill tones, "your poet has found you. For many years I have been making songs. Songs to hurt men's hearts and fill young girls with beauty. Songs that none have heard, because they have remained locked in my heart, waiting for the maid who alone shall release them and hear them. Beautiful girl, I have waited so long for you, and now you have come to me. Now I will take you from these bleak, rough places to a dim forest that I know; and there I will take from you your garments, and will gather all your beauty to myself, and my arms shall bind you to me; and your white limbs shall light the recesses of the woodland like bright torches. It is far from here, this secret forest of mine. No woman has yet walked therein; and one woman only ever shall walk therein—the princess for whom I have kept it.

"O lovely girl, answer me. Give me your bright mouth, and I will make songs of you that shall be sung in high places throughout the world, and wherever men shall meet they shall talk of your beauty. Give me your loveliness, and come with me, O lady, and I will teach you wonderful things, and will cherish you and keep you harmless from all unkindness. Look up at me, my beautiful!"

The girl sat motionless at the table, all throughout this harangue, until the sharp command. So sudden and impetuous was his flood of language that it had washed from her all consciousness of onlookers. She was aware only of him, in this anomalous world where the amazing seemed to be the normal. A long-imprisoned self stirred within her; and she looked up, and saw, not a figure of ridicule, but a symbol of high adventure. As he met her glance, he took a step forward, knelt to her, very gently took her hand, and kissed it many times.

Then a well-aimed tomato caught him in the face. A cup of tea shot down his neck. A tea canister struck the back of his head. And a big hand gripped his collar, twisted him round on his knees, and flung him full length. A chorus of voices sang about him.

"Look 'ere," said the man who had thrown him, "you just behave yesself, me boy. Don't you go interferin' wiv respectable girls. Else you'll get into trouble—pretty quick, too. See?"

"No—no—lemme get up!" he protested with his wide grin. "Lemme get up, boys!"

They crowded him.

And suddenly a shock passed across his face. His eyes clouded. He lifted a hand to his head. The girls, who had nervously left their chairs, looked on in some concern. "Don't hurt him—you!" cried the dark girl. "He wasn't interfering with you—he was only talking to me."

"P'raps 'e was. And p'raps 'e might 'a done more than talk. You never know wiv 'im. D'you know who 'e is?"

"No, I don't."

"Well, you want to be careful who you talk to, when you come to these places. 'E's Sing-a-song Joe. 'E's a loony. 'E's barmy!" He pointed a thick arm at the lad, who stood, scarecrow fashion, his disarranged rags flapping about him. He grinned vacuously, and bleated, "Stop it, now, boys. Lemme go!"

The girl turned to look at him, and a light shriek shot from her, as she cowered to the wall. "Oh, take him away, take him away. Don't let him come near me. Ugh!"

They took him away. They turned him round and round, and hustled him from shoulder to shoulder until he was pitched into the greasy street, and his whistle tossed after him.

Grinning and giggling, he picked himself up and shuffled to his customary bed among the dark arches of the Isle of Dogs. There, as he lay in a corner sheltered from the night wind, and waited for sleep, came to him, from the chaos of his mind, a vague memory of a princess who had received him as her prince and had given him her hand. When it had happened he did not know. But he knew that he had made a wondrous poem to a princess, and had delivered it to her in the guest-chamber of her palace; and he remembered being thrown by rough men from her presence into exile. And suddenly he became haughty towards those among whom he lived. He was far above such louts and knaves. Though impotent to disclose to their base minds his glory, or to resent their torments, he yet despised them. These poor, half-witted fellows could never know what he had known.

And in the shadow of the Limehouse arches, he arose, held himself erect, put his whistle to his lips, and strutted.

"HIPPOCKETIQUETTE"

RICHARD CONNELL

FROM APRIL 1920

A terrible discovery has lately been made with regard to New York society. We who inhabited it had a way of thinking that it was the ladies, the wits, the spirit of *badinage* that made our dinners and evening parties so agreeable, so desirable, so much worth while struggling to attend. But along comes January 16th [1920—the start of Prohibition] and opens our eyes to the true facts of the case. It was Alcohol that was really king; it was champagne that we mistook for wit, and cocktails that put in our minds the idea that men were brave and women beautiful. Words cannot give any idea of the desolation, the boredom of a dinner given to-day in the smartest set in New York.

Yes, high society is now not only high but dry. No longer are mint juleps minted; no longer do the Haig boys lead the cotillions; no longer does the Martini rear its noble head along the golden shores of Central Park. That is—ostensibly. In reality, of course, there is still some very serious and effective drinking being done, but it is not being done with the abandon which characterized the pre-Wilsonic dynasties.

While the theatres are hanging out the "S. R. O." sign, the hostesses are hanging out the "B. Y. O." sign. "BRING YOUR OWN."

Formerly, a man went to a dinner with the cheerful certainty that if he didn't like the company, he'd probably like the wine. But now, as the taxi purrs toward your hostesses' house, it seems to hum a plaintive little tune, "Will they have some? Will they have some?"

That is the question of the day. To know or not to know in advance whether your host is a jolly good fellow, which nobody can deny, or simply a director of the Croton Water Works. It is true that while there is lucre there will be liquor. But who has it? This is the problem that is causing furrows of perplexity to line the foreheads of the most seasoned dinner-beagles in New York society.

Mr. Martyn S. C. Symington, the well-known authority on etiquette, the etiquette editor of this magazine, and author of the always popular book, "Which Fork?" has studied this important problem and has, at last, formulated a set of rules for the dry season. These rules will shortly be published in book form under the title "Hippocketiquette," which word the author learnedly explains, is derived from the Greek compound "hippocket",—and the French root, "etiquette". The subjoined quotations will suggest the volume's timely interest.

Form of invitation for a dinner, given by a man with an opulent cellar:

Mr. and Mrs. Merrick Huntington
request the pleasure of
Mr. Loring's
company at dinner on
Thursday evening, at eight o'clock
DRINKING

If "R. S. V. P." is in the left hand corner of an invitation, it has the customary meaning, but if it is in the RIGHT corner, it means "Real Scotch Voluminously Provided".

The committee of a charity ball for the starving something of somewhere, will induce lavish generosity on the part of the guests if the invitations are in the following form:

The Society of Colonial Janes
requests the pleasure of
Mr. Loring's company

at a Charity Ball in the
Bryan Room of the Hotel Loganberry,
on Friday evening at 11 o'clock
Subscriptions, consisting of $10 and One Pint,
may be sent to the Secretary

A delicate way of inviting a man known to have a private stock to your country place for a week-end is suggested by the following letter which Mr. Symington received from a lady of the highest standing in society and with the wholesale liquor houses:

"My Dear Mr. Symington:

"I should like it so much if you could run down to Glen Cove for the week-end. I have heard that you always take two hat boxes with you when you visit, but only one hat. Naughty man! May I not expect you and your hat boxes this week?

"Glen Cove is quite pleasant, although the weather has been so dry. Perhaps your coming will bring us better weather. Do come down.

"Cordially yours,
"Eugenia Rutherford."

It is hoped that the Social Register, and the various Blue Hooks, will adopt a System of marking the elect whose names appear in them, with some symbol indicating, not only their clubs but their cellars. For example, you receive an invitation to dine with Percy Wimples, and you wonder what the convivial prospects are. A glance at the revised Register gives you the following information—Wimple. Mr. Percy W.—Mt. Un. PS. Gw. H. 94. 19 E. 78.

At once, you may know, not only the unimportant fact that Wimple is a '94 Harvard man who is a member of the Metropolitan and Union

Clubs, but the much more vital information that he has a "Private Stock", and that his dinners are "Generally Wet".

You accept.

If, on the other hand, the damning symbols should be, Wo—or Pst., which, according to Prof. Symington, would indicate "Water only", or "Private stock, but tight with it," you are warned beforehand.

In informal notes it is always well, indeed it is quite necessary, to include some graceful hint as to the probable humidity of the occasion. Just a neat postscript will do, such as "To meet Messrs. Moet and Chandon," or "Presents her niece, Miss Gordon Ginevra Bottle."

Mr. Symington's book fills a long-felt want and should be in every home.

POEMS

EDNA ST. VINCENT MILLAY

FROM NOVEMBER 1920

WILD SWANS

I looked in my heart while the wild swans
      went over;—
And what did I see I had not seen before?
Only a question less or a question more;
Nothing to match the flight of wild birds flying.
Tiresome heart, forever living and dying!
House without air! I leave you and lock your
      door!
Wild swans, come over the town, come over
The town again, trailing your legs and crying!

THE SINGIN' WOMAN FROM THE WOOD'S EDGE

What should I be but a prophet and a liar
Whose mother was a leprechaun, whose
      father was a friar?
Teethed on a crucifix and cradled under water,
What should I be but the fiend's god-daughter?

And who should be my playmates but the adder
      and the frog,
That was got beneath a furze-brush and born in a bog?
And what should be my singin', that was christened
      at an altar,
But Aves and *Credos* and psalms out of the psalter?

You will see such webs on the wet grass, maybe,
As a pixie-mother weaves for her baby;
You will find such flames at the wave's weedy ebb
As flashes in the meshes of a mermother's web.

But there comes to birth no common spawn
From the love of a priest for a leprechaun,
And you never have seen and you never will see
Such things as the things that swaddled me!

After all's said and after all's done,
What should I be but a harlot and a nun?

In through the bushes on any foggy day
My da would come a-swishin' of the drops away,
With a prayer for my death and a groan for my
      birth,
A-mumblin' of his beads for all that he was worth;

And there'd sit my ma with her knees
      beneath her chin,
A-lookin' in his face and a-drinkin' of it in,
And a-markin' in the moss some funny little sayin'
That would mean just the opposite of all that he
      was prayin'.

Oh, the things I haven't seen and the things I
      haven't known,
What with hedges and ditches till after I was grown,
And yanked both ways by my mother and my father,
With a *Which-would-you-better?* and a *Which-*
      would-you-rather?

He taught me the holy talk of vesper and of matin,
He heard me my Greek and he heard me my
      Latin;
He blessed me and crossed me to keep my soul
      from evil,
And we watched him out of sight and we conjured up the devil!

With him for a sire and her for a dam,
What should I be but just what I am?

FOUR SONNETS

I

When you, that at this moment are to me
Dearer than words on paper, shall depart,
And be no more the warder of my heart,
Whereof again myself shall hold the key;
And be no more—what now you seem to be—
The sun, from which all excellencies start
In a round nimbus, nor a broken dart
Of moonlight, even, splintered on the sea;

I shall remember only of this hour—
And weep somewhat, as now you see me weep—

The pathos of your love, that, like a flower,
Fearful of death yet amorous of sleep,
Droops for a moment and beholds, dismayed,
The wind whereon its petals shall be laid.

II
Here is a wound that never will heal, I know,
Being wrought not of a dearness and a death,
But of a love turned ashes and the breath
Gone out of beauty; never again will grow
The grass on that scarred acre; though I sow
Young seed there yearly and the sky bequeath
Its friendly weathers down, far underneath
Shall be such bitterness of an old woe.

That April should be shattered by a gust,
That August should be levelled by a rain,
I can endure, and that the lifted dust
Of man should settle to the earth again;
But that a dream can die, will be a thrust
Between my ribs forever of hot pain.

III
Pity me not because the light of day
At close of day no longer walks the sky;
Pity me not for beauties passed away
From field and thicket as the year goes by;
Pity me not the waning of the moon,
Nor that the ebbing tide goes out to sea,
Nor that a man's desire is hushed so soon,
And you no longer look with love on me.

This have I known always: love is no more
Than the wide blossom which the wind assails,
Than the great tide that treads the shifting shore,
Strewing fresh wreckage gathered in the gales;
Pity me that the heart is slow to learn
What the swift mind beholds at every turn.

IV

What lips my lips have kissed, and where,
       and why,
I have forgotten, and what arms have lain
Under my head till morning; but the rain
Is full of ghosts tonight, that tap and sigh
Upon the glass and listen for reply,
And in my heart there stirs a quiet pain
For unremembered lads that not again
Will turn to me at midnight with a cry.

Thus in the winter stands the lonely tree,
Nor knows what birds have vanished one by one,
Yet knows its boughs more silent than before:
I cannot say what loves have come and gone,
I only know that summer sang in me
A little while, that in me sings no more.

SPRING

To what purpose, April, do you return again?
Beauty is not enough.
You can no longer quiet me with the redness
Of little leaves opening stickily.

I know what I know.
The sun is hot on my neck as I observe
The spikes of the crocus.
The smell of the earth is good.
It is apparent that there is no death.
But what does that signify?
Not only under ground are the brains
              of men
Eaten by maggots.
Life in itself
Is nothing,—
An empty cup, a flight of uncarpeted stairs.
It is not enough that yearly down this hill
April
Comes like an idiot, babbling and
              strewing flowers!

WEEDS

White with daisies and red with sorrel
And empty, empty under the sky!
Life is a quest and love a quarrel;
Here is a place for me to lie.

Daisies spring from damnéd seeds,
And this red fire that here I see
Is a worthless crop of crimson weeds,
Cursed by farmers thriftily.

But here, unhated for an hour,
The sorrel runs in ragged flame;

The daisy stands, a bastard flower,
Like flowers that bear an honest name.

And here awhile, where no wind brings
The baying of a pack athirst,
May sleep the sleep of blessed things
The blood too bright, the brow accurst.

THIS IS A MAGAZINE

F. SCOTT FITZGERALD

FROM DECEMBER 1920

The scene is the vast and soggy interior of a magazine—not ponder or pistol, but paper and popular. Over the outer curtain careens a lady on horseback in live colours. With one hand she raises a cup of tea to her glossy lips while with the other she follows through on a recent mashie shot, meanwhile keeping one rich-tinted, astounding eye upon the twist of her service and its mate on the volume of pleasant poetry in her other hand. The rising of the curtain reveals the back-drop as a patch-work of magazine covers. The furniture includes a table on which lies a single periodical, to convey the abstraction 'Magazine', and around it your players sit on chairs plastered with advertisements. Each actor holds a placard bearing the name of the character represented. For example, the Edith Wharton Story holds a placard which reads "By Edith Wharton, in three parts."

Near (but not in!) the left hand stage box is stationed a gentleman in underwear holding a gigantic placard which announces that "THIS IS A MAGAZINE".

As the Curtain rises the audience discovers the Edith Wharton Story attempting a tête à tête with a somewhat arrogant British Serial.

THE EDITH WHARTON STORY (*a bit bitterly*): And before I could so much as shoot a saucy subtlety, there I was plumped down between an odious fable in broken Yiddish and this—this affair next to me.

'This affair' is a very vulgar and proletarian Baseball Yarn who sprawls colloquially in his chair.

THE BASEBALL YARN: Was you speakin' to me, lady?

(*On the lady's part a frigid and Jamesian silence. She looks, by the way, like a lady who has lived all her life in three-room apartments and had her nerves ruined by impulsive elevator boys.*)

THE BASEBALL YARN (*in brutal soliloquy*): If they could jes' stick a guy in a magazine where he could borrer one good chewterbacker!

A DETECTIVE STORY (*in a tense whisper*): There's one in my third paragraph. But be quiet and be careful not to break any retorts.

THE BASEBALL STORY (*facetiously*): Or make any, eh? Ha! Ha! Ha!

THE BRITISH SERIAL (*to The Edith Wharton Story*): I say, who's that little story over near the Editorial? Don't fancy I've seen her before since I've been running.

THE EDITH WHARTON STORY (*lowering her voice*): My Dear Man, she's a nobody. Seems to have no family—nothing but a past.

THE BRITISH SERIAL: She has a certain charm, but a deuced vulgar plot. (*He yawns.*)

THE BASEBALL YARN (*in a rude aside to the Detective Story*): The noble Duke looks a bit padded his own self. Say! Pipe the old grampa asleep on his advertisements.

THE DETECTIVE STORY: That's the Robert Chambers Serial. He's through this issue.

THE BASEBALL YARN: Kinda like that little thing next to him. New in here ain't she?

THE DETECTIVE STORY: New and scared.

THE BASEBALL YARN: Looks as if she was wrote with a soft pencil.

THE DETECTIVE STORY: Overdressed! Her illustrations cost more than she did.

(*Several chairs down, a little Love Poem leans tenderly across a story to another Love Poem.*)

THE FIRST LOVE POEM: I adore your form.

THE SECOND LOVE POEM: You've got a good figure yourself—in your second line. But your meter looks a little strained.

THE FIRST LOVE POEM: You are the caesura in the middle of all my lines. Alas! someone will cut you out and paste you on a mirror—or send you to his sweetheart with "Isn't this lovely!" scrawled across you—or passepartout you.

THE SECOND LOVE POEM (*coyly*): Now you just get right back to your own page.

(*At this point, the Robert Chambers Story awakens with a start, and walks rheumatically over to the Edith Wharton Story.*)

THE ROBERT CHAMBERS STORY (*asthmatically*): May I join you?

THE EDITH WHARTON STORY (*acidly*): You seemed well content to flirt with that sentimental little piece, behind the advertisements.

THE ROBERT CHAMBERS STORY: On the contrary, she bores me. Every character in her is born in wedlock. Still she's a relief from the Commercial yarns.

THE BRITISH SERIAL: You can be thankful you haven't got your feet between two smelly soap advertisements. (*He points to what appears to be a paralytic dwarf at his feet.*) Look! There's my Synopsis of Preceding Chapters all tangled up again.

THE ROBERT CHAMBERS STORY: Thank heavens, I'm published! I've had some annoying experiences in the last eight months. In one issue there was a Penrod Story next to me making so much noise that I couldn't hear my own love scenes.

THE EDITH WHARTON STORY (*cruelly*): Never mind. The shop-girls could fill them in with their eyes closed.

THE ROBERT CHAMBERS STORY (*sourly*): My dear lady, your climax is on crooked.

THE EDITH WHARTON STORY: At least I have one. They tell me you drag horribly.

THE BASEBALL YARN: Well, if the swells ain't scrappin' with each other!

THE EDITH WHARTON STORY: No one invited your comments.

THE BASEBALL YARN: Go on! You're full of dots!

THE EDITH WHARTON STORY: At least, I'm not full of mixed metaphors!

THE ROBERT CHAMBERS STORY: Weak repartee! Columnist's humor.

(A *new voice, very oratorical and sonorous, breaks in. It is—*)

THE POLITICAL ARTICLE: Come! There's nothing irreconcilable there. There's no knot so tight that there isn't a way out of the labyrinth.

THE LITTLE STORY WITHOUT A FAMILY (*timidly*): Dear folks, it's a sweet cosy world. So don't poison your little lungs with naughty unkind words.

THE BRITISH SERIAL: Shades of those Porter women!

THE LITTLE STORY WITHOUT A FAMILY: You don't know what abuse is until you've been returned with "Join the Navy" stamped on your envelope.

THE BRITISH SERIAL: If I had been fished out of the waste-basket, I shouldn't boast about it!

THE BASEBALL YARN: Let her alone! She's a honest Gurl. I'll kick you one in the conclusion!

(*They rise and square off, eying each other menacingly. A contagious excitement springs up; the Basil King Revelation forgets its credulous queens and tears over; an Efficiency Article loses its head and runs wildly through the issue, and even the illustrations leap out of their borders, the half-tones vying democratically with the Ben Days, in reaching the scene. The excitement spreads to the advertisements. Mr. Madison Whims of Seattle falls into a jar of No-Hairo Cold Cream. A Health and Strength Giant arrives clinging to an earphone; a Short Story Course becomes covered with Rat Poison. The Circulation increases.*

In fact, for a minute everything is something awful! Just as the number's minutes seem as numbered as its pages, a stentorian voice proceeds from the Table of Contents, an efficient looking gentleman with a megaphone who has been sitting unnoticed in the orchestra: "Places! A Reader!" A hush falls; everyone scurries back into position, just as a thick and impenetrable dark descends upon the stage through which emerge, as an emanation from limbo, the large glossy eyes of the cover girl, on horseback in five colours.

A voice comes out of the dark and, in the great quiet, it is like the voice of God.)

THE VOICE: Wonder if there's anything in this worth readin'. Sure is some queen on the cover!

AN INSERT JOKE (*laughing feebly*): Hee! Hee! Hee! (*It is the grotesque and horrible cackle of an old man.*)

The lights go on to show that the curtain is now down, in front of it sits a reader, a lone stage hand. He wears an expression of tremendous and triumphant boredom. He is reading the magazine.

SPORT FOR ART'S SAKE

HEYWOOD BROUN

FROM SEPTEMBER 1921

For years we had been hearing about moral victories and at last we saw one. This is not intended as an excuse for the fact that we said before the fight that Carpentier would beat Dempsey. We erred with Bernard Shaw, who declared that the odds ought to be fifty to one on the Frenchman. Swayed by the master we bet, and our half dollar is gone, but we are not minded to moan about it. The surprising revelation which came to us on this July afternoon was that a thing may be done well enough to make victory entirely secondary. We have all heard, of course, of sport for sport's sake, but Georges Carpentier established a still more glamorous ideal. Sport for art's sake was what he showed us in the big wooden saucer over on Boyle's dirty acres.

It was the finest tragic performance in the lives of ninety thousand persons. We hope that Professor George Pierce Baker sent his class in dramatic composition. We will be disappointed if Eugene O'Neill, the white hope of the American drama, was not there. Here for once was a laboratory demonstration of life. None of the crowds in Greece who went to somewhat more beautiful stadiums in search of Euripides ever saw the spirit of tragedy more truly presented. And we will wager that Euripides was not able to set his crowd up upon its hind legs into a concerted shout of "Medea! Medea! Medea!" as Carpentier moved the fight fans over in Jersey City in the second round. In fact it is our contention that the fight between [Jack] Dempsey and [Georges] Carpentier was the most inspiring spectacle which America has seen in a generation.

Personally we would go further back than that. We would not accept a ticket for David and Goliath as a substitute. We remember that in that instance the little man won, but it was a spectacle less fine in artistry from the fact that it was less true to life. The tradition that Jack goes up the beanstalk and kills his giant, and that Little Red Ridinghood has the better of the wolf, and many other stories are limited in their inspirational quality by the fact that they are not true. They are stories that man has invented to console himself on winter's evenings for the fact that he is small and the universe is large. Carpentier showed us something far more thrilling. All of us who watched him know now that man cannot beat down fate, no matter how much his will may flame, but he can rock it back upon its heels when he puts all his heart and his shoulders into a blow.

That is what happened in the second round. Carpentier landed his straight right upon Dempsey's jaw and the champion, who was edging in toward him, shot back and then swayed forward. Dempsey's hands dropped to his side. He was an open target. Carpentier swung a terrific right hand uppercut and missed. Dempsey fell into a clinch and held on until his head cleared. He kept close to Carpentier during the rest of the fight and wore him down with body blows during the infighting. We know of course that when the first prehistoric creature crawled out of the ooze up to the beaches (see *The Outline of History* by H. G. Wells, some place in the first volume, just a couple of pages after that picture of the big lizard) it was already settled that Carpentier was going to miss that uppercut. And naturally it was inevitable that he should have the worst of it at infighting. Fate gets us all in the clinches, but Eugene O'Neill and all our young writers of tragedy make a great mistake if they think that the poignancy of the fate of man lies in the fact that he is weak, pitiful and helpless. The tragedy of life is not that man loses but that he almost wins. Or, if you are intent on pointing out that his downfall is inevitable, that at least he completes the gesture of being on the eve of victory.

For just eleven seconds on the afternoon of July 2 we felt that we were at the threshold of a miracle. There was such flash and power in the right hand thrust of Carpentier's that we believed Dempsey would go down, and that fate would go with him and all the plans laid out in the days of the oozy friends of Mr. Wells. No sooner were the men in the ring together than it seemed just as certain that Dempsey would win as that the sun would come up on the morning of July 3. By and by we were not so sure about the sun. It might be down, we thought, and also out. It was included in the scope of Carpentier's punch, we feared. No, we did not exactly fear it. We respect the regularity of the universe by which we live, but we do not love it. If the blow had been as devastating as we first believed, we should have counted the world well lost.

Great circumstances produce great actors. History is largely concerned with arranging good entrances for people; and later exits not always quite so good. Carpentier played his part perfectly down to the last side. People who saw him just as he came before the crowd reported that he was pitifully nervous, drawn, haggard. It was the traditional and becoming nervousness of the actor just before a great performance. It was gone the instant Carpentier came in sight of his ninety thousand. His head was back and his eyes and his smile flamed as he crawled through the ropes. And he gave some curious flick to his bathrobe as he turned to meet the applause. Until that very moment we had been for Dempsey, but suddenly we found ourself up on our feet making silly noises. We shouted "Carpentier! Carpentier! Carpentier!" and forgot even to be ashamed of our pronunciation. He held his hands up over his head and turned until the whole arena, including the five-dollar seats, had come within the scope of his smile.

Dempsey came in a minute later and we could not cheer, although we liked him. It would have been like cheering for Niagara Falls at the moment somebody was about to go over in a barrel. Actually there is a difference of sixteen pounds between the two men which is large enough, but it seemed that afternoon as if it might have been a hundred. And we knew for the first time that a man may smile and smile and be an underdog.

We resented at once the law of gravity, the Malthusian theory and the fact that a straight line is the shortest distance between two points. Everything scientific, exact, and inevitable was distasteful. We wanted the man with the curves to win. It seemed impossible throughout the first round. Carpentier was first out of his corner and landed the first blow, a light but stinging left to the face. Then Dempsey closed in and even the people who paid only thirty dollars for their seats could hear the thump, thump of his short hooks as they beat upon the narrow stomach of Carpentier. The challenger was only too evidently tired when the round ended.

Then came the second and, after a moment of fiddling about, he shot his right hand to the jaw. Carpentier did it again, a second time, and this was the blow perfected by a life time of training. The time was perfect, the aim was perfect, every ounce of strength was in it. It was the blow which had downed Bombardier Wells, and Joe Beckett. It rocked Dempsey to his heels, but it broke Carpentier's hand. His best was not enough. There was an earthquake in Philistia but then out came the signs "Business as usual" and Dempsey began to pound Carpentier in the stomach.

The challenger faded quickly in the third round, and in the fourth the end came. We all suffered when he went down the first time, but he was up again, and the second time was much worse. It was in this knockdown that his head sagged suddenly, after he struck the floor, and fell back upon the canvas. He was conscious and his legs moved a little, but they would not obey him. A gorgeous human will had been beaten down to a point where it would no longer function.

If you choose that can stand as the last moment in a completed piece of art. We are sentimental enough to wish to add the tag that after a few minutes Carpentier came out to the center of the ring and shook hands with Dempsey and at that moment he smiled again the same smile which we had seen at the beginning of the fight when he stood with his hands above his head. Nor is it altogether sentimental. We feel that one of the elements of tragedy lies in the fact that Fate gets nothing but the victories and the championships. Gesture and glamour remain with Man. No in-fighting can take that away from him. Jack Dempsey won fairly and squarely. He is a great fighter, perhaps the most efficient the world has ever known, but everybody came away from the arena talking about Carpentier. He wasn't very efficient. The experts say he fought an ill considered fight and should not have forced it. In using such a plan, they say, he might have lasted the whole twelve rounds. That was not the idea. As somebody has said "Better four rounds of—" but we can't remember the rest of the quotation.

Dempsey won and Carpentier got all the glory. Perhaps we will have to enlarge our conception of tragedy, for that too is tragic. Surely here, if anywhere, was a protagonist striving bravely against a fate "too strong, too clever, too relentless for the sons of men!"

MEMOIRS OF COURT FAVOURITES

NOËL COWARD

FROM NOVEMBER 1921

MADCAP MOLL
(THE ENGLISH SCHOOL OF BIOGRAPHY)

Nobody who knew George I could help loving him—he possessed that peculiar charm of manner which had the effect of subjugating all who came near him into immediate slavery. Madcap Moll, his true love, his one love, adored him with such devotion as falls to the lot of few men, be they kings or beggars.

They met first in the New Forest, where Moll spent her wild, unfettered childhood. She was ever an undisciplined creature, snapping her shapely fingers at bad weather, and riding for preference without a saddle—as hoydenish a girl as one could encounter on a day's march. Her auburn ringlets, ablow in the autumn wind, her cheeks whipped to a flush by the breeze's caress, and her eyes sparkling and brimful of mischief and roguery! This, then, was the picture that must have met the King's gaze as he rode with a few trusty friends through the forest for his annual week of otter shooting. Upon seeing him, Moll gave a merry laugh and crying, "Chase me, Laddie", in provocative tones, she rode swiftly away on her pony. Many of the courtiers trembled at such a daring exhibition of *lèse majesté*, but the King, provoked only by her winning smile, set off in hot pursuit. Eventually he caught his roguish quarry seated by the banks of a sunlit pool. The King cast an appraising glance at her shapely figure and tethered his horse.

"Are you a creature of the woods?" he said.

Madcap Moll tossed her curls. "Ask me!" she cried derisively.

"I *am* asking you", replied the King.

"'Odd's fudge—you have spindleshanks!" cried Madcap Moll irrelevantly. The King was charmed. He leaned toward her.

"One kiss, mistress!" he implored. At that she slapped his cheek good naturedly. He was captivated.

"I faith, my daring girl!" he cried delightedly. "Knowst that I am George the First?" said the King, rising.

Madcap Moll blanched.

"Sire", she murmured, "I did not know—a poor unwitting country lass—have mercy!"

The King touched her lightly on the nape.

"Arise", he said gently, "you are as loyal and spirited a girl as one could meet. Hast a liking for Court?"

"Oh, sire!" answered the girl.

Thus did the King meet her who was soon to mean everything in his life—and more.

MAGGIE McWHISTLE
(THE SCOTCH SCHOOL OF BIOGRAPHY)

Born in an obscure Scotch manse of Jacobite parents, Maggie McWhistle will go down to immortality as perhaps the greatest heroine of Scottish history.

And perhaps not.

What did Maggie know of the part she was to play in the history of her country? Nothing. She lived through her girlhood, unheeding; she helped her mother with the baps and her father with the haggis; and occasionally she would be given a new plaidie.

A word must be said of her parents. Her father was known all along Deeside as Handsome Jaimie—and oh, how the light-hearted village girls mourned when he turned minister; he was high, high above them. Of his meeting with Janey McToddle, the Pride of Bonny Deeside, and the mother of Maggie, very little is written. Some say that they met in a snow-storm on Ben Lomond, where she was tending her kine; others say that they met on the high road to Aberdeen, and that his collie Jeannie bit her collie Jock—thus cementing a friendship that was later on to ripen into more and more.

History tells us that Maggie's griddle cakes were famous adown the length and breadth of Aberdeen, and that gradually a little path came to be worn between the manse and the kirk, seven miles away, where Maggie's feet so often trod on their way to their devotions. She was an intensely religious child.

One dark night, so the story runs, there came a hammering on her door. Maggie leapt out of her truckle, and, wrapping her plaidie round her—for she was a modest girl, she ran to the window.

"Wha is there?" she cried in Scotch.

The answer came back through the darkness, thrilling her to the marrow.

"Bonnie Prince Charlie!"

Maggie gave a cry and, running downstairs, opened the door and let him in. She looked at him by the light of her homely candle. His brow was amuck with sweat; he was trembling in every limb.

"I am pursued", he said, hoarse with exertion and weariness. "Hide me, bonnie lassie, hide me".

Quick as thought, Maggie hid him behind a pile of cold griddle cakes, and not a moment too soon, for there came a fresh hammering at the door. Maggie opened it defiantly and never flinched at the sight of so many men.

"We want Bonnie Prince Charlie", said the leader of the crew in Scotch.

Then came Maggie's well known answer, also in Scotch.

"Know you not that this is a manse?"

History has it that the men fell back as though struck dumb, and one by one awed by the still purity of the white-faced girl, the legions departed into the night. Thus Maggie McWhistle proved herself the saviour of Bonnie Prince Charlie for the first time.

There were many occasions after that in which she was able to save and hide him. She would conceal him up a tree or in an oven at the slightest provocation. Soon there were no trees for miles around in which she had not hidden him at some period or other.

Poor Maggie—perchance she is finding in Heaven the peaceful rest which was so lacking in her life on earth. For legend hath it that she never had two consecutive nights' sleep for fifteen years, so busy was she in saving and hiding her Bonnie Prince Charlie.

LA BIBI

(THE FRENCH SCHOOL OF BIOGRAPHY)

Hortense Poissons—"La Bibi" the dancer. What memories that name conjures up! The incomparable—the lightsome—the effervescent! Her life, a rose-coloured smear across the history of France; her smile—tier upon tier of sparkling teeth; her heart, that delicate organ for which kings fought in the streets—but enough. Let us trace her to her obscure parentage. You all know the Place de la Concorde—she was not born there. You have all visited the Champs Elysées—she was not born there. And there's probably no one who doesn't know of the Faubourg St. Honoré—but she was not born there. Sufficient to say that she was born. Her mother, poor, honest, *gauche*, was an unpretentious seamstress; she seamed and seamed until her death in 1682 or 1683. Bibi at the age of ten, flung upon the world homeless, motherless, with nothing but her amazing beauty to save her from starvation—or worse. Who can blame her for what she did—who can question or condemn her motives? She was alone. Then Armand Brochet (who shall be nameless) came into her life. What should she do? Refuse the roof he offered her? This waif (later on to be the glory of France) was a leaf blown hither and thither by the winds of Destiny. What was she to do?

Enough that she did it.

Paris, a city of seething vice and corruption—her home, the place wherein she danced her first catoucha, that catoucha which was so soon to be followed by her famous Peruvian minuet. Voltaire wrote many books, but he didn't mention her; Jean Jacques Rousseau never so much as referred to her; even Molière was so reticent about her charms that no single word about her can be found in any of his works.

Her life with Armand Brochet—three years before she stepped on the boards—how well we all know it. Her first appearance on the stage was in Paris, 1690, at the Opera when this airy, fairy thing danced her way into the hearts of the multitudes. Oh, Bibi—"Bibi, Coeur d'Or", as she was called so frequently by her adorers—would that in these mundane days you could revisit us with your girlish laugh and supple dancing form! Look at the portrait of her, painted by Coddlé, at the height of her amazing beauty; note the sensitive nostrils, the delicate little mouth, the graceful neck and shoulders, and those eyes—the gayest, merriest eyes that ever charmed a king's heart.

In November, 1701, she introduced her world-famed Bavarian fandango, which literally took Paris by storm—it was in her dressing room afterward that she made her celebrated *bon mot* to Maria Pipello, her only rival. Maria came ostensibly to congratulate her on her success but really to insult her. *"Ma petite"*, she said, *"l'hibou, est-il sur le haie?"* Quick as thought Bibi turned round and replied with a gay toss of her curls, *"Non, mais j'ai la plume de ma tante."*

Oh, witty, sharp-tongued Bibi!

A word must be said of the glorious ballets she originated which charmed France for nearly thirty years. They were, "The Life of a Raindrop" and "Angels Visiting a Ruined Monastery at Night". People flocked to the Opera again and again in order to see them and applaud their ravishing originator. Then came her meeting with the King in his private box. We are told she curtsied low and glancing up at him coyly from between her bent knees, gave forth her world-renowned epigram, *"Comment ça va, papa?"* Louis was charmed by this exquisite exhibition of drollery, and three weeks later she was brought to Versailles.

La Belle Bibi was certainly not one to miss opportunities, and only one month later she found herself installed at Court—the King's right hand. Then began that amazing reign of hers—short lived, but oh, how triumphant. Dukes, duchesses, countesses, even princes paying homage at the feet of La Bibi, the dancer, now Hortense, Duchesse de Mal-Moulle. Did she abuse her power? Some say she did, some say she didn't. Every afternoon, Louis was wont to visit her apartments; together they would pore over the plans and campaigns of war drawn up and submitted by his generals. Then, when Louis was weary, Bibi would put the maps in the drawer, draw his head on to her breast and sing to him songs of her youth. Meanwhile, intrigue was placing its evil fingers upon the strings of her fate. Lampoons were launched against her, pasquinades were written of her. When she went driving, fruits and vegetables were hurled at her.

Absinthe was her one consolation. Her gay humour remained with her to the end. As she lay on her death-bed she uttered the supreme *bon mot* of her brilliant life. Stretching out her wasted arm to the nearly empty absinthe bottle by her bed, she made a slightly resentful mouth at the physician and murmured, "Encore!"

Oh brave, witty Bibi!

Note: These biographical sketches of famous court beauties are abbreviated versions of a series of essays shortly to be published for Mr. Coward by Christopher's in London under the title of A Withered Nosegay. *Those familiar with the large and beautifully bound—oh, always beautifully bound, and emblazoned in gold with coronets and what-nots—memoirs, inevitably to be found in the libraries of our best non-reading families, will appreciate the justice of Mr. Coward's little parodies.*

JAMES JOYCE

DJUNA BARNES

FROM APRIL 1922

There are men in Dublin who will tell you that out of Ireland a great voice has gone; and there are a few women, lost to youth, who will add: "One night he was singing and the next he wasn't, and there's been no silence the like of it!" For the singing voice of James Joyce, author of *The Portrait of the Artist as a Young Man* and of *Ulysses* is said to have been second to none.

The thought that Joyce was once a singer may not come as a revelation to the casual reader of his books; one must perhaps have spent one of those strangely aloof evenings with him, or have read passages of his *Ulysses*, as it appeared in *The Little Review* to have realized the singing quality of his words. For tradition has it that a singer must have a touch of bravado, a joyous putting forth of first the right leg and then the left, and a sigh or two this side of the cloister, and Joyce has none of these.

I had read *Dubliners* over my coffee during the war, I had been on one or two theatrical committees just long enough to suggest the production of *Exiles*, his one play. The *Portrait* had been consumed, turning from one elbow to the other, but it was not until I came upon his last work that I sensed the singer. Lines like: "So stood they both awhile in wan hope sorrowing one with other" or "Thither the extremely large wains bring foison of the fields, spherical potatoes and iridescent kale and onions, pearls of the earth, and red, green, yellow, brown, russet, sweet, big bitter ripe pomillated apples and strawberries fit for princes and raspberries from their canes," or still better the singing humour in that delicious execution scene in which the "learned prelate knelt in a most Christian spirit in a pool of rainwater."

Yes, then I realized Joyce must indeed have begun life as a singer, and a very tender singer, and—because no voice can hold out over the brutalities of life without breaking—he turned to quill and paper, for so he could arrange, in the necessary silence, the abundant inadequacies of life, as a laying out of jewels—jewels with a will to decay.

Yet of Joyce, the man, one has heard very little. I had seen a photograph of him, the collar up about the narrow throat, the beard, heavier in those days, descending into the abyss of the hidden bosom. I had been told that he was going blind, and we in America learned from Ezra Pound that "Joyce is the only man on the continent who continues to produce, in spite of poverty and sickness, working from eight to sixteen hours a day."

I had heard that for a number of years Joyce taught English in a school in Trieste, and this is almost all of his habits, of his likes and his dislikes, nothing, unless one dared come to some conclusion about them from the number of facts hidden under an equal number of improbabilities in his teeming *Ulysses*.

And then, one day, I came to Paris. Sitting in the café of the Deux Magots, that faces the little church of St. Germain des Près, I saw approaching, out of the fog and damp, a tall man, with head slightly lifted and slightly turned, giving to the wind an orderly distemper of red and black hair, which descended sharply into a scant wedge on an out-thrust chin.

He wore a blue grey coat, too young it seemed, partly because he had thrust its gathers behind him, partly because the belt which circled it, lay two full inches above the hips.

At the moment of seeing him, a remark made to me by a mystic flashed through my mind "A man who has been more crucified on his sensibilities than any writer of our age," and I said to myself—"this is a strange way to recognize a man I never laid my eyes on."

Because he had heard of the suppression of *The Little Review* on account of *Ulysses* and of the subsequent trial, he sat down opposite me, who was familiar with the whole story, ordering a white wine. He began to talk at once. "The pity is," he said, seeming to choose his words for their age rather than their aptness, "the public will demand and find a moral in my book—or worse they may take it in some more serious way, and on the honour of a gentleman, there is not one single serious line in it."

For a moment there was silence. His hands, peculiarly limp in the introductory shake and peculiarly pulpy, running into a thickness that the base gave no hint of, lay, one on the stem of the glass, the other, forgotten, palm out, on the most delightful waistcoat it has ever been my happiness to see. Purple with alternate doe and dog heads. The does, tiny starlet tongues hanging out over blond lower lips, downed in a light wool, and the dogs no more ferocious or on the scent than any good animal who adheres to his master through the seven cycles of change.

He saw my admiration and he smiled. "Made by the hand of my grandmother for the first hunt of the season" and there was another silence in which he arranged and lit a cigar.

"All great talkers," he said softly, "have spoken in the language of Sterne, Swift or the Restoration. Even Oscar Wilde. He studied the Restoration through a microscope in the morning and repeated it through a telescope in the evening."

"And in *Ulysses?*" I asked.

"They are all there, the great talkers" he answered, "them and the things they forgot. In *Ulysses* I have recorded, simultaneously, what a man says, sees, thinks, and what such seeing, thinking, saying does, to what you Freudians call the subconscious,—but as for psychoanalysis" he broke off, "it's neither more nor less than blackmail."

He raised his eyes. There is something unfocused in them,—the same paleness seen in plants long hidden from the sun,—and sometimes a little jeer that goes with a lift and rounding of the upper lip.

People say of him that he looks both sad and tired. He does look sad and he does look tired, but it is the sadness of a man who has procured some medieval permission to sorrow out of time and in no place; the weariness of one self-subjected to the creation of an over abundance in the limited.

If I were asked what seemed to be the most characteristic pose of James Joyce I should say that of the head; turned farther away than disgust and not so far as death, for the turn of displeasure is not so complete, yet the only thing at all like it, is the look in the throat of a stricken animal. After this I should add—think of him as a heavy man yet thin, drinking a thin cool wine with lips almost hidden in his high narrow head, or smoking the eternal cigar, held slightly above shoulder level, and never moved until consumed, the mouth brought to and taken away from it to eject the sharp jets of yellow smoke.

Because one may not ask him questions one must know him. It has been my pleasure to talk to him many times during my four months in Paris. We have talked of rivers and of religion, of the instinctive genius of the church which chose, for the singing of its hymns, the voice without "overtones"—the voice of the eunuch. We have talked of women, about women he seems a bit disinterested. Were I vain I should say he is afraid of them, but I am certain he is only a little skeptical of their existence. We have talked of Ibsen, of Strindberg, Shakespeare. "Hamlet is a great play, written from the standpoint of the ghost," and of Strindberg, "No drama behind the hysterical raving."

We have talked of death, of rats, of horses, the sea; languages, climates and offerings. Of artists and of Ireland.

"The Irish are people who will never have leaders, for at the great moment they always desert them. They have produced one skeleton— Parnell—never a man."

Sometimes his wife, Nora, and his two children have been with him. Large children, almost as tall as he is himself, and Nora walks under fine red hair, speaking with a brogue that carries the dread of Ireland in it; Ireland as a place where poverty has become the art of scarcity. A brogue a little more defiant than Joyce's which is tamed by preoccupation.

Joyce has few friends, yet he is always willing to leave his writing table and his white coat of an evening, to go to some quiet near-by café, there to discuss anything that is not "artistic" or "flashy" or "new." Callers have often found him writing into the night, or drinking tea with Nora. I myself once came upon him as he lay full length on his stomach poring over a valise full of notes taken in his youth for *Ulysses*,—for as Nora says, "It's the great fanaticism is on him, and it is coming to no end." Once he was reading out of the book of saints (he is never without it) and muttering to himself that this particular day's saint was "A devil of a fellow for bringing on the rain, and we wanting to go for a stroll."

However it is with him, he will come away for the evening, for he is simple, a scholar, and sees nothing objectionable in human beings if they will only remain in place.

Yet he has been called eccentric, mad, incoherent, unintelligible, yes and futuristic. One wonders why, thinking what a fine lyric beginning that great Rabelaisian flower *Ulysses* had, with impartial addenda for foliage,—the thin sweet lyricism of *Chamber Music*, the casual inevitability of *Dubliners*, the passion and prayer of Stephen Dedalus, who said that he would go alone through the world.

"Alone, not only separate from all others, but to have not even one friend," and he has, if we admit Joyce to be Stephen, done as he said he would do. "I will not serve that which I no longer believe, whether it call itself my home, my fatherland, or my church: and I will try to express myself in my art as freely as I can and as wholly as I can, using for my defense the only arms I allow myself to use, silence, exile and cunning."

This is somehow Joyce, and one wonders if, at last Ireland has created her man.

WITHOUT THE CANE AND THE DERBY

Charlie Chaplin Playing for
His Friends After Dinner

CARL SANDBURG

FROM MAY 1922

The woman had done him wrong.

Either that.. or the woman was clean as a white rose in the morning gauze of dew.

It was either one or the other or it was the two things, right and wrong, woven together like two braids of a woman's head of hair hanging down woven together.

The room is dark. The door opens. It is Charlie playing for his friends after dinner, "the marvelous urchin, the little genius of the screen," (chatter it like a monkey's running laughter cry).

No.. it is not Charlie.. it is somebody else. It is a man, gray shirt, bandanna, dark face. A candle in his left hand throws a slant of light on the dark face. The door closes slow. The right hand leaves the door knob slow.

He looks at something. What is it? A white sheet on a table. He takes two long soft steps. He runs the candle light around a hump in the sheet. He lifts the sheet slow, sad like.

A woman's head of hair shows, a woman's white face. He takes the head between his hands and looks long at it. His fingers trickle under the sheet, snap loose something, bring out fingers full of a pearl necklace.

He covers the face and the head of hair with the white sheet. He takes a step toward the door. The necklace slips into his pocket off the fingers of his right hand. His left hand lifts the candle for a good-by look.

Knock knock, knock. A knocking the same as the time of the human heartbeat.

Knock, knock, knock, first louder, then lower. Knock, knock, knock, the same as the time of the human heartbeat.

He sets the candle on the floor.. leaps to the white sheet.. rips it back.. has his fingers at the neck, his thumbs at the throat, and does three slow fierce motions of strangling.

The knocking stops. All is quiet. He covers the face and the head of hair with the white sheet, steps back, picks up the candle and listens.

Knock, knock, knock, a knocking the same as the time of the human heartbeat.

Knock, knock, knock, first louder, then lower. Knock, knock, knock, the same as the time of the human heartbeat.

Again the candle to the door, the leap, the slow fierce motions of strangling, the cover-up of the face and the head of hair, the step back, the listening.

And again the knock, knock, knock.. louder.. lower.. to the time of the human heartbeat.

Once more the motions of strangling.. then.. nothing at all.. nothing at all.. no more knocking.. no knocking at all.. no knocking at all.. in the time of the human heartbeat.

He stands at the door.. peace, peace, peace everywhere only in the man's face so dark and his eyes so lighted up with many lights, no peace at all, no peace at all.

So he stands at the door, his right hand on the door knob, the candle slants of light fall and flicker from his face to the straight white sheet changing gray against shadows.

So there is peace everywhere.. no more knocking.. no knocking at all to the time of the human heartbeat.. so he stands at the door and his right hand on the door knob.

And there is peace everywhere.. only the man's face is a red gray plaster of storm in the center of peace.. so he stands with a candle at the door.. so he stands with a red gray face.

After he steps out the door closes: the door, the door knob, the table, the white sheet; there is nothing at all; the owners are shadows; the owners are gone; not even a knocking; not even a knock, knock, knock.. louder, lower, in the time of the human heartbeat.

The lights are snapped on. Charlie, "the marvelous urchin, the little genius of the screen" (chatter it with a running monkey's laughter cry). Charlie is laughing a laugh the whole world knows.

The room is full of cream yellow lights. Charlie is laughing.. louder.. lower..

And again the heartbeats laugh.. the human heartbeats laugh..

I LIKE AMERICANS—
THEY ARE SO RIDICULOUS

EDNA ST. VINCENT MILLAY (PSEUDONYM NANCY BOYD)

FROM AUGUST 1922

I like Americans.

You may say what you will, they are the nicest people in the world.

They sleep with their windows open.

Their bath-tubs are never dry.

They are not grown-up yet. They still believe in Santa Claus.

They are terribly in earnest.

But they laugh at everything.

They know that one roll does not make a breakfast.

Nor one vermouth a cocktail.

I like Americans.

They smoke with their meals.

The Italians are nice.

But they are not so nice as the Americans.

They have been told that they live in a warm climate.

And they refuse to heat their houses.

They are forever sobbing Puccini.

They no longer have lions about, to prey on Christian flesh.

But they have more than a sufficient supply of certain smaller
carnivora.

And if you walk in the street alone, somebody pinches you.

I like Americans.

They give you the matches free.

The Austrians are nice.

But they are not so nice as the Americans.

They eat sausages between the acts at the opera.

But they make you go out into the snow to smoke.

They are gentle and friendly. They will walk ten blocks out of their way
    to show you your way.

But they serve you paper napkins at the table.

And the sleeves of their tailored blouses are gathered at the shoulder.

And they don't know how to do their hair.

I like Americans.

They dance so well.

The Hungarians are nice.

But they are not so nice as the Americans.

They make beautiful shoes.

Which are guaranteed to squeak for a year.

Their native tongue is like a typewriter in the next room, and every word
    beginning with the shift-key.

Their wines are too sweet.

I like Americans.

They are the only men in the world, the sight of whom in their shirt-
    sleeves is not rumpled, embryonic, and agonizing.

They wear belts instead of suspenders.

The French are nice.

But they are not so nice as the Americans.

They wear the most charming frocks in the world.

And the most awkward underclothes.

Their shoes are too short.

Their ankles are too thick.

They are always forgetting where they put their razors.

They have no street-corner shoe-shining palaces, where a man can be a
    king for five minutes every day.
Nor any Sunday supplement.
Their mail-boxes are cleverly hidden slits in the wall of a cigar store.
They put all their cream into cheese.
Your morning cup of chicory is full of boiled strings.
If you want butter with your luncheon, they expect you to order radishes.
And they insist on serving the vegetables as if they were food.
I like Americans.
They make a lot of foolish laws.
But at least their cigarettes are not rolled by the government.
The material of which the French make their cigarettes would be used
    in America to enrich the fields.

In the city the French are delightful.
They kiss in the cafés and dine on the sidewalks.
Their dance halls are gay with paper ribbons and caps and colored
    balloons.
Their rudeness is more gracious than other people's courtesy.
But they are afraid of the water.
They drink it mixed with wine.
They swim with wings.
And they bathe with an atomizer.
Their conception of a sport suit is a black taffeta gown, long gloves with
    fringe on, a patent leather hand-bag, and a dish-mop dog.
In the country they are too darned funny for words.
I like Americans.
They carry such pretty umbrellas.
The *Avenue de l'Opera* on a rainy day is just an avenue, on a rainy day.
But Fifth Avenue on a rainy day is an old-fashioned garden under a
    shower.
The French are a jolly lot.
Their cities have no traffic regulations.

And no speed limit.

And if you get run over, you have to pay a fine for getting in the way.

They have no ear drums.

Paris is the loveliest city in the world.

Until she opens her mouth.

Should the French go forth to battle armed only with their taxi horns,
    they would drive all before them.

I would liefer live in a hammock slung under the "L" at Herald Square,
    than in a palace within ear-shot of the *Place de la* Harmony.

I like Americans.

They are so ridiculous.

They are always risking their lives to save a minute.

The pavement under their feet is red-hot.

They are the only people in the world who can eat their soup without a
    sound as of the tide coming in.

They sell their bread hygienically wrapped.

The Europeans sell it naked.

They carry it under the arm.

Drop it and pick it up.

Beat the horses with it.

And spank the children.

They deliver it at your apartment. You find it lying outside your door on
    the door-mat.

And European hotels are so hateful and irritating.

There is never an ash-tray in your bedroom.

Nor a waste-basket.

Nor a cake of soap.

No sweet little cake of new soap all sealed in paper!

Not even a sliver left behind by a former guest.

No soap.

No soap at all.

And there's always a dead man in a blanket across the head of the bed.

And you can't get him out. He's tied there.
And the pillow-slips are trimmed with broken buttons.
That scratch your ear.

Then there are their theatres.
They make you tip the usher.
And pay for your program.
The signal for the curtain to rise is the chopping of wood, off stage.
Then the railroad system.
Especially in France.
Have to get there forty-five minutes ahead of train time, or stand in the
    aisle all day.
Pay for every pound of trunk.
Never a soul in sight who knows anything about anything.
No place to sit.
No place to powder up.
And before they will let you into the station at all, they insist on your
    pushing two sous into a slot-machine.
When you have just had your pocket picked of the last sou you had in
    the world.
And are expecting your only husband on the express from Havre.
I like Americans.
They let you play around in the Grand Central all you please.
Their parks are not locked at sunset.
And they always have plenty of paper bags.
Which are not made of back numbers of *Le Rire*.

The English are nice.
But they are not so nice as the Americans.
They wear much too much flannel.
No matter with whom they are dancing, they dance a solo.
And no matter where they go, they remain at home.
They are nice. They keep the tea-set at the office.

But the Americans keep the dish-pan in the music-room.

The English are an amusing people.

They are a tribe of shepherds, inhabiting a small island off the coast of France.

They are a simple and genial folk.

But they have one idiosyncrasy.

They persist in referring to their island as if it were the mainland.

The Irish are nice.

But they are not so nice as the Americans.

They are always rocking the boat.

I like Americans.

They either shoot the whole nickel, or give up the bones.

You may say what you will, they are the nicest people in the world.

THE PUBLIC AND THE ARTIST

JEAN COCTEAU

FROM OCTOBER 1922

I am working at my wooden table, seated on my wooden chair with my wooden penholder in my hand, but this does not prevent me from being, in some degree, responsible for the course of the stars.

A dreamer is always a bad poet.

Nietzsche was afraid of certain "ands"; Goethe *and* Schiller, for example, or, worse still, Schiller *and* Goethe. What would he say at seeing the spread of the cult of Nietzsche and Wagner or, rather, Wagner *and* Nietzsche!

The opposition of the masses to the elite has always stimulated individual genius. This is the case in France. Modern Germany is dying of approbation, carefulness, faithful application and a scholastic vulgarization of aristocratic culture.

Let us keep clear of the theatre. I regret to have felt its temptation and to have introduced to it two great artists. "Well, then, why do you write for the theatre?" That is precisely the weak point about the theatre; it is forced to depend, for its very existence, upon *immediate* successes.

When I say that I prefer certain circus or music-hall turns to anything given in the theatre, I do not mean that I prefer them to anything that *might* be given in the theatre.

One day I was looking at a children's puppet show in the Champs Elysées when a dog came on the stage, or rather a dog's head, as big in itself as the two other actors put together. "Look at that monster," said a mother to her child. "That is not a monster, it is a dog," said her little boy. Men, as they grow older, lose—when in a theatre—the clairvoyance they had as children.

Tradition appears at every epoch under a different disguise, but the public does not recognize it under its masks.

That which makes the public laugh is not inevitably beautiful or new, but that which is beautiful and new inevitably makes the public laugh.

"Cultivate those qualities in thee for which the public blames thee: they are Thyself." Get this idea well into your head. This advice ought to be written up everywhere like an advertisement of "Pear's Soap." As a matter of fact, the public likes to "recognize" what is familiar. It hates to be disturbed. It is shocked by surprises. The worst that can happen to a work of art is to have no fault found with it, so that its author is not obliged to take up an attitude of opposition.

The public only takes up yesterday as a weapon with which to castigate today.

There are people who are considered quite intelligent, but who do nothing but *lean* toward good things in art. Their heads get near them, but the rest of their bodies remain rooted.

A favorite phrase of the public is: "I don't see what that's meant to be." The public wants to understand first and to feel afterwards.

A fall makes people laugh. The mechanism of falling plays an important part in causing the laughter which greets a new work. The public, not having followed the curve which leads up to this work, stumbles suddenly from where it was standing, down on to the work which it is now seeing or hearing. Consequently a fall takes place—and laughter.

A short phrase quickly spoken and full of meaning traverses the brain like a surgeon's lancet. Ten minutes later it is no longer there.

We have in our keeping an angel whom we are continually shocking. We must be that angel's guardian.

One does not blame an epoch; one congratulates oneself on not having belonged to it.

INSTINCT AND THE ARTIST

Art is science—in the flesh.

Genius, in art, consists in knowing how far we may go too far.

There is a house, a lamp, a plate of soup, a fire, wine and pipes at the back of every important work of art.

Instinct, in art, needs to be trained by method; but instinct alone helps us to discover a method which will suit us, and thanks to which our instinct may be trained.

In feeling his way, an artist may open a secret door and never discover that, behind that door, a whole world lies concealed.

When a work of art appears to be in advance of its period, it is really the period that has lagged behind the work of art.

There is a moment when every work, in the process of being created, benefits from the glamour attaching to uncompleted work. "Don't touch it any more!" cries the amateur. It is then that the true artist takes his chance.

Sculpture, so neglected on account of the current contempt for form and mass, is one of the noblest arts. To begin with, it is the only one which obliges us to move round it.

"Look," said a lady to her husband in front of one of Claude Monet's paintings of a cathedral. "It looks likes melting ice-cream." In this particular case the lady spoke the truth, but she had not acquired the *right* to do so.

The artist must always be partly man and partly woman. Unfortunately the woman part is almost always unbearable.

Every masterpiece having once been in the fashion goes out of fashion, and, long afterwards, finds an everlasting equilibrium. Generally it is when it is out of fashion that a masterpiece appeals to the public.

MUSIC—GOOD AND BAD

The musician opens the cage-door to arithmetic; the draughtsman gives geometry its freedom.

Beethoven is irksome in his developments, but not Bach, because Beethoven develops the *form* and Bach the *idea*.

The bad music, which superior folk despise, is agreeable enough. What is really intolerable is what they think *good* music.

Wagner's works are long works which are not only long, but *long-drawn-out*, because this old sorcerer looked upon boredom as a useful drug for the stupefaction of the faithful. It is the same with mesmerists who hypnotise in public. The genuine "pass" which puts the subject to sleep is usually very short and simple, but they accompany it with a score of sham passes which impress the crowd. The crowd is won by lies; it is deceived by the truth, which is too simple, and not sufficiently shocking.

The public is shocked at the charming absurdity of Erik Satie's titles and system of notation, but respects the ponderous absurdity of the libretto of "Parsifal."

Satie does not pay much attention to painters, and does not read the poets, but he likes to live where life ferments; he has a flair for good inns. Debussy established, once for all, the Debussy atmosphere. Satie evolves. Each of his works, intimately connected with its predecessor, is, nevertheless, distinct and lives a life of its own. They are like a new kind of pudding, a surprise and a deception for those who expect one always to keep on treading the same piece of ground. Satie teaches what, in our age, is the greatest audacity—simplicity.

Nothing is so enervating as to lie and soak for a long time in a warm bath. Enough of music in which one lies and soaks. Enough of clouds, waves, aquariums, water-sprites, and nocturnal scents; what we need is a music of the earth, every-day music. Enough of hammocks, garlands, and gondolas; I want someone to build me music I can live in, like a house.

Music is not all the time a gondola, or a race-horse, or a tight-rope. It is sometimes a chair as well.

We may soon hope for an orchestra where there will be no caressing strings. Only a rich choir of wood, brass and percussion.

All good music *resembles* something. Good music arouses emotion owing to its mysterious resemblance to the objects and feelings which have motivated it.

Pelléas is an example of music to be listened to with one's face in one's hands. All music which has to be listened to through the hands is suspect. Wagner is typically music which is listened to through the hands.

Too many miracles are expected of us; I consider myself very fortunate if I have been able to make a blind man hear.

THE HIGH-LOW CONTROVERSY

RANDOLPH DINWIDDIE

FROM JANUARY 1923

The important question of the proper length of dress skirts is again racking the public press and putting a large part of our female population completely off their feed. This particular phase of fashion is the most vital of the many whimsies which are yearly dallied with by the smart modistes and couturières. Pre-eminent in importance among dress questions is the height above see level of the human hem. It affects the men as does no other vagary. It creates more discussion and philosophical comment than any other problem. Compared with it the current location of the waist line, the cut of the neck or the presence or absence of sleeves are minor issues.

My interest in the matter is purely academic. As one of the sex which merely looks on and admires and wonders at the fickle changes of La Mode I have been tremendously struck by the vehemence with which the most recent edict of Fashion has been received. It was a rather scurvy trick of those mysterious authors of authoritative design, the hidden sources of inspiration in Paris, suddenly to knock the legs out from under the high skirt market. Perhaps it was not a trick at all. I have an idea that fashion is not the wilful arbitrary thing many people suppose it to be, but that it follows definite, immutable laws. We know that Gothic architects built their cathedrals higher and higher until, with Beauvais, came the great collapse. It fell down, and there was an end to it. So it was with skirts. They could go no further. They had nowhere to go but down. Of course, it is unfortunate for the lady who finds herself equipped for a long season with a legacy of shorts. As my friend Willie Aspinwall who is on the Exchange said of his cousin Margaret, "Poor Madge! She bought at the top. Now she is long on shorts and short on longs, and she can't cover." I'm not very well up on Wall Street patter but one look at lanky Margaret seemed to bear out Willie's statement.

Reading the various newspaper discussions and looking over a few sample exhibits on the Avenue I resolved to conduct a personal investigation. I decided to get the personal testimony of a varied group of people and compare their angles of observation. My first call brought me to the office of Mrs. Arnold Bemis, President of the Woman's Civic and Social Welfare League.

Mrs. B. is as formidable as her title. She stands, or sits, four-square to all the winds and it is easy to tell exactly what her opinions are on any subject. "This recent attempt of Paris dressmakers to foist their ridiculous standards on American womanhood will never be tolerated for a second," said Mrs. Bemis, angrily tearing a page from *La Gazette du Bon Ton*. "Look at that! Imagine a modern woman trying to cross Fifth Avenue wrapped up in eighteen yards of material like that. A few New York Society dames"—Mrs. Bemis's lip (the one with a slight moustache) curled scornfully—"may stand for it. It is all they can do. They can't walk. But not the sensible women of our League. Thousands of our members live in the suburbs. Tell me, how can a woman catch a train when she is already tangled up in one?"

Mrs. Bemis has a pretty epigrammatic talent if nothing else—admiring which I withdrew and sought my next victim, Dr. Eustace Willis, a young practitioner of my acquaintance.

"I have great hopes for the long skirt," said Dr. Willis. "My practise has picked up amazingly since our sidewalks have been systematically swept by a million or more ladies every day. Many homeless influenza germs have found permanent shelter in well-to-do establishments. This not only keeps our streets much cleaner but also makes possible an intensive study of colds, catarrhal troubles, sneezes and the insidious theater or concert-cough which has long baffled medical science. During the short skirt era people remained so infernally well that I thought I might have to go out of business. Now I am thinking of buying a new car. Put me down unmistakeably as a 'long'."

My next visit took me into the marts of trade where I found opinion curiously divided. The silk and fabric importers were unanimous in favor of the new style. An interesting contrary view was rendered by Mr. Isadore Klipsch, Strauss and Bendelmayer. "Where do stockings come off?" asked Mr. Klipsch with some heat. "Here ain't we spent thousands of dollars layin' in a stock of first class goods, y' see, an' what's gonter happen if a feller can't see 'em? Who cares about arms and necks an' waist lines? Such a fuss! Phooey! What the feller in the street wants is legs. Ain't I right, Strauss? An' what becomes of the new fency colors we make 'em, the apricots, the plum, the peach? Who's gonter eat all them fruits? Believe me, the only hope we got is in these here now side-doors they put in sometimes, these portieres they're wearin' so a feller can once in a while get a look-in, ain't it?"

I felt that there was much in Mr. Klipsch's point of view.

A rather pathetic view-point was disclosed by a young lady who must obviously be nameless. Let us call her Louise. Louise is the hat girl in one of our small, smart restaurants. She herself is both small and smart. She is not facially pretty—freckles and a slight cast in one eye prevent her competing in any beauty contests, but in other ways she is superb. "Yes, Monsieur," she murmured in her charming Gallic way, "eet is 'ard on some girls, ze long skairt. Eet hide sometime zeer only chances to attrac' ze attention. I myself, you know . . . I have not ze beauté of ze visage, but autrement . . . attendez moi, Monsieur, si vous pouviez voir . . ."

"Louise," I said, not wishing to prolong the interview, "what time do you leave here?"

"A dix heures," she answered.

Setting my watch, I departed.

Through a card from the manager I was fortunate in having a two minute interview with Vera Gilhooly just as she was leaving her dressing room at the Follies to go on to a supper party. She stood in the doorway dressed in a million dollars worth of ermine and delivered her opinion with terse decision.

"It's all or nothing with me, Boy. In the first number, the fashion review, of course, I wear skirts. But I don't have to. Some people think they look better in the short ones but there's a whole lot oughter be thankful for concealment. Honest, when I walked up Fifth Avenue a year ago I used to wonder where all the barrel hoops came from. But if you seen me in the last number, the Parade of the Perfumes, you'll know that I don't have to worry. And write this down in your little book, No matter what the square-toed highbrows say, they'll all be wearing just exactly what Paree tells 'em to inside of six months. Don't let 'em kid you about being independent. They're all hard-shelled conservatives and if there's anything they hate it's to be different. By-by!"

Vera swept off to her taxi leaving me astounded at her wisdom. She attempted no solution, to be sure, but showed such splendid common sense. After all perhaps it is purely idle speculation to attempt an answer to the question of what the well-dressed woman will wear. It would be simpler to say, what won't she?

THE EARLY DAYS OF PABLO PICASSO

MAX JACOB

FROM MAY 1923

A whole volume is needed when we try to speak of Picasso, and when he dies—which may God defer as long as possible!—we shall need many. Consider that here is a man who is only forty-one and who has modified the whole of painting. (He was born October 24, 1881, at Malaga.) Yes, all painting! for I defy the most distant to ignore the new demands he has made upon the art. And not painting alone: I have seen during fifteen years, first in the poor attic of Montmartre, 13 rue Ravignan, then in finer studios, 33 boulevard de Chichy, or 5 rue Schöl-chez, finer but always bare, for Picasso has that mysterious force, the spirit of poverty—I have seen workers in every art of this generation fired and tempered by his discriminating advice.

PICASSO'S SARCASM

A pleasantry of Picasso's would serve as guide-post for a whole life-time. He has a terribly sarcastic mind—his wonderful understanding of realities expresses itself in biting words which attack stupidity and folly in defense of his vast ideals of an entirely new art. I verily believe that he has even influenced the fashions in dress for men and women. On the days of "vernissage", great days on which all Paris gazed upon his faithful followers who, proud and envied, filled the exhibition rooms, the costumes of the women who surrounded him did more to mold the new spirit than did those of the smart women at the races. His genius is to uncover the first principles of art and to build upon them; thus he has made the fortune of several artists by creating a sculpture without stone, a sculpture which makes use of any material. The day that he applies himself to architecture or to designing furniture he will revolutionize them as he revolutionized the theater with his settings for *Parade*, the famous synthetic horse and the two cubiste managers; as he revolutionized dancing with the dance of the "Petite Américaine" in the same piece, made up of gestures taken from everyday life.

Apollinaire, that great exponent of the new poetry, often worked only to please him. Salmon would have torn up a poem, his best, at a joking criticism by Picasso. You perceive what this man was in his youth; today his field of action is enlarged; it is from the stage of the opera that he speaks to the artistic world and the settings which he sometimes consents to make for the Russian ballets are an education for the whole world, thanks to the illustrated papers.

Upon his first arrival in Paris, Picasso met with success. It was in '99. He came from Barcelona, where his father was Director of the Royal Academy of Painting. He seemed but a child; his great black eyes which have an expression so tense when he looks at one, so mocking when he speaks, so tender when he is moved, glowed with life under his low, wide, positive forehead; his hair was coarse, thick and smooth; today one or two silver threads shine in its blackness.

At that time he had a face of ivory, and was as beautiful as a Greek boy; irony, thought and effort have brought slight lines to the waxen countenance of this little Napoleonic man. He is today a dandy, albeit an unaffected one; he was then a Spaniard with wide hat and enveloping cloak. For a long time he wore the caps and sweaters of the sportsman; in fact, it was he who started this fashion in the world of art, as well as that of shaving oneself completely. When he came to Paris, he was accompanied by a manager who arranged for an exhibition at Vollard's. It was the manager who wrote me, in answer to a word of admiration, to come to the studio in the Place Clichy.

At that time, Picasso was living the life of the "provincial" in Paris; he wore a high hat and spent his evenings in the music halls. He had won fame there by his portraits of actresses in the public eye. Jeanne Bloch, Otero . . . all the stars of the Exposition. Ah, what changes, since, in him and about him! What an amazing evolution! It was a fortune; this fiery little boy of eighteen made two pictures a day, and the rue Lafitte paid a hundred francs apiece for them. Just think, two hundred francs a day before the war and for a child! Those paintings are priceless today; the intelligent museums have bought them.

I arrived, then, at the Place Clichy. I found a band of impoverished Spaniards sitting on the floor in the fine studio, eating white beans—for Picasso is profoundly kind, as he is profoundly honest, sensitive and sincere. There is much that is fatherly in this sarcastic dilettante, in this almost mystical knight. No one will ever know how much money he has given away, how many artists he has provided with success, nor how many have enriched themselves through but a single spark from his great flaming love of Art.

They kept me for the evening and half through the night—we were friends! That was in '99—we are friends still, I trust. Picasso, who now speaks French as well as an Academician and better, for his language has a color and a precision that might well be envied by the best French stylist, Picasso in those days spoke only Spanish. And yet we used to talk the whole night through; the manager slept, the Catalonians left—our enthusiastic youth found means of understanding each other. He made an immense portrait of me. Unfortunately, this genius has several times lacked canvases; one impecunious day he was forced to re-cover this masterpiece to create another.

THE "BLUE" PERIOD

One day he left Paris, perhaps because he had glimpsed new paths in art and felt the need of solitude to ripen reflection, perhaps because he had troubles which I do not remember. How many times Picasso has abandoned successes which have seemed too easy! Three times at least, to my knowledge.

All this was before the Exposition. When he returned from Spain he had his first taste of misery; it was in 1902, he brought back those celebrated blue paintings which were often done on wood. No one would buy them. A famous dealer who would be much vexed were I to name him, said to me literally—"Your friend has gone mad." The same man, one day when I was seeking to interest him in Picasso, who was ill, and in a landscape full of sublime melancholy, said—"The church is crooked." There are you experts! Very accurate connoisseurs, but prophets, no!—unless they are prompted. Poor child, he lived at the Hôtel du Maroc, in the rue de Seine, in a room whose ceiling sloped so sharply that his iron bed could hardly fit in. This bed was covered with drawings rather reminiscent of Puvis de Chavannes; no one wanted them. The house still stands; I think it is opposite the rue Jacob. How did he eat? The faithful few were as poor as he and Paris ignores those who will not follow her, until she begins to follow them. One day he succeeded in selling a pastel to a dealer for a hundred francs and went back to Spain. This picture represented a woman with a child holding an orange at the edge of the sea.

PÈRE VERNIN

When he returned in 1904, he settled down, if we can call it that, at No. 13 rue Ravignan. It is today the Place Émile Goudeau, a little sloping village square on Montmartre with crumbling benches under the trees. He took his meals at Père Vernin's in the rue Cavalotti, behind the Hippodrome, which was not yet the Cinéma Gaumont. The name of Père Vernin will be historic when all the young men to whom he has served his stew have attained celebrity; he was yet another whose fortune would have been made by Picasso if only the friends he attracted there had been any less hard-up than he, or as honest! That was the time of earnest meetings and gay insouciance. In the rue Ravignan and the rue Cavalotti, towards 1905 and later, poets, painters, musicians and actors flocked to Picasso. Montparnasse, which had only lately become a rival to Montmartre, came with Paul Fort. I used to see there Alfred Jarry, the douanier Rousseau, Georges Enesco, Jules Romains, Vildrac, Marie Laurencin, Fargue, Henri Hertz, Jean Richard Bloch, Georges Duhamel, Roger Allard, Mercereau and a hundred, a thousand others.

You understand that I am speaking of 1905; since then, Picasso has known almost every important artist in Europe. In those days he did not yet know the prodigious Jean Cocteau, nor Stravinsky, nor Satie. After the café of the Père Vernin, it was the turn of Azon's to be crowded. It was situated on the little square, just opposite the huge brown doorway of the studio. The studio was on the ground floor of a house which, from the square, seemed to have no upper stories, but seen from neighboring streets, revealed at least one. A veritable barn, Picasso's studio, with beams and walls of ill-joined boards and a crazy floor on which one could not tread at night without awakening the neighbors. I remember that a miserable vegetable-vendor, M. Sorrieul, complained that the chain of Picasso's dog, the admirable Frika, kept him from sleeping. In that house have lived many men, famous today—among them, Max Orlan, André Salmon, Pierre Reverdy, Van Dongen, Maurice Raynal, Juan Gris. Good Madame Coudray, the concierge, knew how to be kind when the rent was due, and how to tolerate noise. Oh! dear days of hardship, of work, of friendship and of joy. Several studios in the house were cellars, and the stairs were never swept. Everything was of wood.

GUILLAUME APOLLINAIRE

Of all the young and brilliant friends who came to the rue Ravignan, Picasso preferred Guillaume Apollinaire, that great lyric poet whom the war, alas! has killed. One day Picasso took me to a bar in the rue d'Amsterdam . . . to let me meet an extraordinary man. This is not the place to describe Guillaume Apollinaire—but how he dazzled us, how he charmed us! and what a place he held in Picasso's life. What a spectacle to see the friendship of those two geniuses who understood each other so well.

Apollinaire introduced him to Matisse, Derain, Picabia, Vlaminck and Braque. We used to dine often at Matisse's house, and I believe it was there that Picasso first saw a negro statuette. He grew to admire negro sculpture so much that he gave deep thought to the underlying principles of that art. Although Picasso has never taken me into his confidence as to the origin of his discovery of cubism, I have often thought that it was the application of the rules of negro sculpture which brought it about. He groped a long time toward this discovery, and his work absorbed him to the point of burying him in silence for hours at a time; "Go and amuse yourselves", he said, in the voice of the genius enslaved by himself, to Apollinaire and me, one evening when he was feverishly covering sheet after sheet of paper with signs and figures—sitting at the table which served also for his meals. Picasso "made" negro art as he "made" the work of Rousseau.

Picasso was also very fond of Salmon. He greatly likes clever people, and Salmon has in his cleverness a combination of tenderness and biting humor which gives great charm to his experience of Parisian life. It would need a volume, I repeat, to tell about Picasso and those who have sur-rounded him. He reigned on the Butte Montmartre as our Lord reigned in Palestine. Deaths, rivalries, removals, successes, have separated these hard-working young men, but I am persuaded that in his fine apartment on the rue La Boétie, Picasso never thinks without emotion of the friendly ties, the gaiety, and the discoveries of that poor and happy time. For a vivid picture of the life on Montmartre which centered about Picasso, one should read "La Négresse du Sacré Cœur", a novel by Salmon.

JAZZ: A BRIEF HISTORY

SAMUEL CHOTZINOFF

FROM JUNE 1923

very so often someone writes to a newspaper about Jazz. The writer, with an almost religious fervor, dissects the current popular tunes, assures us of their utter vulgarity, and finds in them the source of all sorts of contemporary degeneration. The spirits of all the great composers from Bach to Brahms are invoked; with a simple enumeration of these names the writer considers his case settled, and is content to remain, etc., "one who loves music" . . .

There is at once a rush to arms. The head of the Music department of a well-known college thanks the writer for his clarion admonition. It is about time, he thinks, that we return to a state of sanity. There are at present languishing any number of refined American composers whose only chance of a public hearing lies in the hands of a fashionable but ineffectual Society for the Encouragement of American Music. America, he goes on, does nothing for its native Music, while the smallest nation on the Continent builds opera houses, grants subsidies and altogether considers music an important enough business for governmental interference. The result is that, while the German peasant goes about his work whistling the *Andante* from Brahms's Fourth, the American man in the street goes about whistling "Stumbling" or "Yoo-Hoo" or whatever vulgarity is at the moment in the ascendant.

To this there is a stinging reply from the president of a popular music-publishing company, insisting that the music published by his house is clean entertainment for the masses. He points to the reverent treatment of the domestic virtues, the deification of parenthood and the little old homestead. To clinch the argument there soon appears an interview with a famous pianist who avers that he is just crazy about Jazz and finds it a great relaxation after a concert of serious music. This sort of thing recurs *ad infinitum* . . .

THE INVASION OF EUROPE

Meanwhile, the popularity of American jazz music, both here and abroad, is beyond dispute. As far back as 1920—and in the history of Jazz that is a long time—most of the large cities in Europe had succumbed. In the winter of that year I found in most of the cafés of Paris two orchestras: an American Jazz band and the usual French orchestra which played only tango and waltzes. While the French band played, most of the patrons remained at their tables; with the first crash of American banjo and snare-drum, there was a rising *en masse* and a rush for the floor. In London the better hotels and dance-clubs had imported American bands. In Berlin, though the music was entirely American, the orchestras were native, with a consequent loss, it must be added, of brilliancy and "pep".

It is not surprising that America and England, nations without a musical culture or tradition of their own, have embraced Jazz; but that France, with a peculiar and definite musical idiom extending over a period of several centuries, and that Germany—which has been to music what Italy has been to painting—have both succumbed so wholly to Jazz music, is astonishing. A serious analysis and appraisal of Jazz should reveal either a degradation of the artistic sensibilities of nations hitherto notable in the development of music, or new and unsuspected merits in the quality of the American creation.

The failure of America to develop a definite musical art is often explained from many points of view by economists, ethnologists, historians and psychologists. But from a musician's viewpoint, the chief deterrent is the absence of a comprehensive body of folk-tunes. That, as a basis and quarry yielding solid, earthy matter for the artist to weld into whatever form the combination of national and individual genius makes possible, seemed to be non-existent. I say *seemed*, because we are only now unearthing a mass of such folk-tunes under the name of Negro spirituals which have lain buried for half a century. In their stead we have had the negro paraphrases of Stephen Foster, a refined drawing-room emanation of these tunes. These have had a tremendous vogue here and have passed for indigenous negro tunes abroad. Though they have charm and a certain simplicity these paraphrases are pure white, and bear the same relation to the real Negro that a current Irish vaudeville song bears to a genuine, ancient Irish folk-tune, like "Molly Brannigan".

THE BIRTH OF "'LIZA JANE"

But the genuine Negro spirituals (first introduced here by Alma Gluck) are, in their way, comparable to the folk tunes of any European nation. They are the musical expression of a great group of American peasants, who became identified with the native soil through a century of compulsory labor on it. The music that arose from them was a confused mixture of vague African apprehensions, the breath of the fields and a crazy, devout Methodism which had become mystical through a realization that only in religion could they find escape from hopeless slavery. Thus many of these Spirituals attain a lyrical rapture in their adoration of God and their expectation of the promised comforts in Heaven compared with which even the psalms of David seem to lack fire. The sheer musical quality peculiar to these tunes is not less remarkable, and, strange as it may seem, it is this which forms the basis and salient peculiarity of present-day jazz.

The negro spiritual has two characteristics: one, an insistent and lively two-four rhythm which, being started, is carried along by the momentum of its start. This almost living beat is the base for every kind of sentiment and passion the negro slave felt and expressed. It is the frame for the naïve *I Got A Shoe* and the passionately mystical *I Couldn't Hear Nobody Pray*. It is this relentless pushing onward of the music that carries swiftly over sentimentalities and strengthens extravagant ecstasies. His confused reaction to a complex and alien religion is borne with a pathetic dignity on the stream of this throbbing mingling of time and sound.

The other characteristic of this music, of course an outgrowth of the first, is its physical effect on the listener. In the negroes themselves it produced a sort of rhapsodical epilepsy of which the lingering effects may be observed in street corner negro revivalists, and indeed in the antics of our own Billy Sunday, who not unwisely adopted the negro idea. The effect of this rhythm on the white race is not less marked, though less extravagantly so. There is an irresistible inclination to bodily time-marking: a lifting of shoulders, a rolling of eyes, a swaying of the head (the latter a conspicuous feature, I believe, of what is known as "collegiate" dancing). There is an inevitable longing to let this extraordinary rhythmic force take possession of one's body and work its will like the devils that were believed to enter the bodies of sinners in mediaeval or Puritan times. The reaction to this rhythm is universal and as compelling as a natural force.

THE TRIUMPH OF THE NEGRO

At the end of the eighties the negro who had come north discovered the commercial value of his own reaction to his own music. He went on the stage and delighted white audiences with dances of a character elemental, whole-hearted and extravagant, quite alien to the deliberate and lifeless gyrations to which the whites were accustomed. His native religious music could hardly have an appreciable effect on white people or even on the, by this time, free and equal Northern blacks. He retained the vital and living rhythm of his folk-tune as a foundation and lure and, on that, he erected a structure of entertainment that should represent and flatter the taste of the day. He danced the cake-walk, an elaboration of the courtly minuet, which he galvanized into life by a substitution of the two-four for the three-four beat. He "strutted". He jigged. Soon the demand for negro entertainers outgrew the supply, and white dancers and comedians found it profitable to cork their faces and imitate their more gifted colored competitors. The black-faced minstrel show became the vogue and earned large profits.

Meantime, it must be noted, the advance of the black entertainer in public favor imposed a corresponding deterioration in the quality of his stuff. The native element became threadbare; these shows became whiter and whiter until nothing remained but a rhythmical patter of feet.

THE IRISH MOVEMENT

The quality of the white American contribution to the gaiety of that same period was a mixture of vulgarity and sentimentality, unredeemed by any suggestion of vigor or health. At that time New York was Irish: the Irish immigration had reached its height and the Tammany Hall organization was in complete possession of the city. America was singing *Sweet Rosy O'Grady, Tammany* and numerous similar ditties. The languid waltz was in the ascendant and the average topical song was at heart a waltz.

The subject matter, when not Irish, sang of the beauties of a Sunday afternoon in the merry month of June and the boundless opportunities for a spoon in Central Park or at the Coney Island sea-'scape. The amorous effects of the waltz were celebrated in the famous *Waltz Me Around Again, Willie*. A deeper note was struck by things like *My Evening Star*, which the late Lillian Russell used to sing so devoutly, or in *The Mansion of Aching Hearts*. The victory over Spain was responsible for a plague of childishly patriotic songs, for the most part in waltz time. *Break the News to Mother* was both melting and danceable.

All this is not far removed from the present-day lyric; but the difference lies here: in the old songs, the meanness of the musical frame revealed piteously and starkly the utter puerility of the words, whereas the lyric of the contemporary popular song is apt to have a musical setting that is sufficient and altogether absolving.

In the period of which I have been speaking the music of the Broadway revue was a little less obvious than that of the popular song, a little bolder in invention. In the hands of trained musicians like Victor Herbert this music attained a kind of respectable distinction. But it lacked the inherent vitality to give it genuine popularity. The entertainments concocted by George M. Cohan were no better, though he advanced the metronome a few notches . . .

It is worth noticing that this conglomerate of popular art was unknown and unheeded outside America. Here musicians treated it with contempt. It never attained to the dignity of controversy. On the Continent, where there had evolved a lighter music of charm and distinction, it was quite unknown.

MISTER JAZZ HIMSELF

There were at that time in New York, and probably in other cities as well, a number of dance halls of a livelier character than the usual "Academies" frequented by the polite youth of the metropolis. These were in the negro quarter, run by negroes, at first, for their own race. Gradually, white folk, weary of the uninspired, insipid tum-tum-tum of their own dance orchestras, visited these questionable places and discovered a régime of the liveliest description. In smoke-filled back-rooms of saloons circulated dancers engaged in tortuous and unseemly evolutions to the blare of barbaric, blatant orchestras.

The instruments were as nondescript as the players. A piano stripped of its top and bottom coverings, the complete mechanism showing like the skeleton of a prehistoric monster. A few fiddles, a saxophone, a banjo, a drum and endless instruments for the making of sheer noise. Whistles, cymbals, cocoanut shells, rattles, all manipulated with amazing dexterity by the person at the drum. The entire orchestra behaved not unlike a party of dancing dervishes. They sang as they played, leaned forward, stood up in their chairs, moaned, flung instruments into the air and recovered them without missing a beat. This madness communicated itself to the dancers on the floor; they swayed and clung to one another in a manner then considered shocking.

The tunes played by these orchestras were, for the most part, negro improvisations but, also, they "ragged" the current tunes. That is to say, they subjected these tunes to a rhythmical metamorphosis. The erstwhile waltz or two-step, ambling sluggishly along, became, in their hands, a fervent quickstep. The familiar and anaemic complexion of these familiar melodies was charged and quickened with the old irresistible beat of the spiritual . . .

The thing caught on quickly and only waited on some astute person to secure its complete acceptance by toning down its racial extravagances. The transition must not be too abrupt. The new music was presented to the public by Mr. Irving Berlin, not directly as a complete invention of his own, but a sort of innuendo. In *Alexander's Rag-Time Band,* Mr. Berlin called universal attention to the quality of a mythical orchestra than which there was none better in the land. All must come and hear this paragon of bands which, in Mr. Berlin's description, resembled exactly the type of band I have just described. (A later and immensely popular song, *The Memphis Blues,* describes a band which is not mythical, but actual.) The musical setting of Alexander, although only a respectful paraphrase of a negro rag, was revolutionary. It was, in the current phrase, a riot; and it and its immediate prototypes had no trouble at all in completely replacing the then popular ballad. Moreover, this sort of tune made necessary new and more alluring dance steps, and the Negro walk and shuffle at once took the place of the waltz and two-step. The turkey and other animalian "trots" enjoyed an ubiquitous transplanting from the stuffy negro dens of their birth.

ALEXANDER'S TRIUMPH

Following closely on Alexander came a tune, *Everybody's Doing It*, which testified to the completeness of the revolution. They were, and still are. The Republic succumbed completely to the new dances and the new music. Mr. Berlin and his confrères were indefatigable and they were handsomely rewarded. Everything was "ragged". Old songs were exhumed. Even sacred ditties were not inviolable. Everything, from *"Home, Sweet Home"* to the scale, was grist for this syncopated, rhythmic mill.

In time the popular ear became ready for the complete assimilation of the undiluted music of the negro bands. One heard orchestras which erupted into climaxes of wailing trombones, shrieking whistles and farmyard noises of a chromatic sort, which resembled nothing that had ever been heard before. This was Jazz. The complete lack of restraint and the frequent degeneration of this music into mere noise made it impossible to listen to it for any length of time, and it enjoyed only a short and brazen popularity. Its points of excellence were abundant, however, and these were subsequently refined and developed into the extraordinary expression which is the Jazz of today.

In this development and refinement the trained executants played a significant part. The absorption in the new dances created a new situation for musicians. Heretofore the dance orchestras were recruited from among players of small talent whose equipment was inadequate to the demands of a Symphony Orchestra, or even of a good theater or hotel. The demand for good jazz bands and the inability of the old-time dance musicians to satisfy the yearning for more piquant rhythms and more variety in the accompaniments and middle voices, inevitably brought a better class of musicians into the field. These organized bands of their own. On the material at hand they lavished the resources of executants well-trained in the musical classics.

The printed music was found to be less complex than the skill of the players. The men began to ornament the melodies, to fill in the inner voices. Unconsciously, they aimed at a presentation approximating the ingenuity and complexity of a symphonic performance. The raucous brasses, though not deprived of their chromatic setting, were muted to a silver pianissimo. Drums and all noisy accessories were discarded and the business of the old, inflexible, Negro-spiritual rhythm, which remained, as ever, the foundation, was given to banjo and piano and the profound double-bass. The oboe, clarinet and saxophone roamed in rich freedom the wide area between the melody and the bass, enveloping and clouding the angular frame in suave, elastic, melodious counterpoint, while muted horns blew a soft contour, like a wind which fills a sail . . .

New and startling rhythms were essayed and seemed to confuse the accustomed steps of the dancers not at all. Though alarming at first, these excursions were found not to interfere with the recurrent one-two beat. As it shuffled along, the public ear was assailed by bizarre and exotic harmonies. People danced along in a sensuous dream to music tricked out in a haunting splendor which had no musical counterpart. The inflexible negro rhythm, a freedom of treatment unheard of in a dance form, and a diabolical ingenuity in orchestration, had achieved a beauty in form and presentation, if not in content, quite new to musical art.

MUSICAL EDUCATION

Through the development of dance music—the evolution I have described covered somewhat over twenty years—the American people acquired what may be termed a musical literacy. Through it they became aware of rhythm, and rhythm is the life of music. Secure on this basis they were free to assimilate the strange harmonies, the sudden modulations, of contemporary jazz. The man in the street, transplanted suddenly from the Palais Royal to Carnegie Hall, where a symphony was in progress, would experience a sense of familiarity with the external, the structural form of the symphony, hitherto possible to trained musicians only.

Not long ago, the harmonies of Debussy, Ravel and other modern extremists, outraged the sensibilities of a formidable number of excellent musicians. These harmonies now sound quite natural and almost simple to the habitués of dance-halls and the owners of phonographs! A person who can hum *Stumbling* for example, with its difficult alternation of violently contrasting rhythms, will find no difficulty with Brahms. Of course I mean technical difficulty; the same person will not therefore be able to surmise the emotional content of a Beethoven quartette. But there his limitation is only that of the performer who has sufficient technique to play a great concerto but is lacking in the mental equipment to envisage the ideas in it. Brahms's *Wiegenlied* is simplicity itself compared to *Everybody Step*, yet the former is beautiful music while the latter is only extremely clever jazz . . .

It is an interesting indication of the pervasion among the masses of this sort of musical sophistication, a musical literacy, that the virtuoso bands of the hotels and dance-salons are now used as "acts" in vaudeville houses. People are happy just to sit and listen. And these are really virtuoso bands: they produce a tone often mellower and richer than one hears in the concert halls. The audiences that listen to these bands are acquiring more than a sophisticated musical idiom; they are beginning to sensitize their eardrums, a difficult and subtle educational process.

OUR CONTRIBUTION TO MUSIC

But this music needs no apology. Created—and recently again stimulated—by the musical talent of the negro, it constitutes the musical contribution of this country and it is a genuine and legitimate contribution. In *Shuffle Along* its verve, simplicity and ardor have again rejuvenated the spineless and degenerate American musical-comedy. Besides the usual negro rhythmic buoyancy, the music of this show revealed lyric and dramatic qualities of a high order. The setting of *Kiss Me*, for example, is amazingly dramatic, passionately sincere. (These qualities are totally absent, of course, from the crude lyric.)

That large body of songs known as "The Blues", of infinite variety, is an interesting by-product; they reflect the various reactions of the soul to a not altogether perfect Universe. They have here an emotional, as well as the rhythmic, kinship with the old negro spiritual. The rhythm is distinct, though languid; the "blue" state is indicated by an appropriate monotony of melody.

The negro genius has been chiefly responsible for whatever musical development America can boast. It is that genius which has produced the American jazz, the only distinct and original idiom we have. It, and not the music of MacDowell and Foster and a host of imitators of the German and French, is the musical speech of this country.

POEMS

T. S. ELIOT

FROM JULY 1923

MORNING AT THE WINDOW

They are rattling breakfast plates in basement kitchens,
And along the trampled edges of the street
I am aware of the damp souls of housemaids
Sprouting despondently at area gates.

The brown waves of fog toss up to me
Twisted faces from the bottom of the street,
And tear from a passer-by with muddy skirts
An aimless smile that hovers in the air
And vanishes along the level of the roofs.

SWEENEY AMONG THE NIGHTINGALES

ὤμοι, πέπληγμαι καιρίαν πληγὴν ἔσω.

Apeneck Sweeney spreads his knees
Letting his arms hang down to laugh,
The zebra stripes along his jaw
Swelling to maculate giraffe.

The circles of the stormy moon
Slide westward toward the River Plate,
Death and the Raven drift above
And Sweeney guards the horned gate.

Gloomy Orion and the Dog
Are veiled; and hushed the shrunken seas;
The person in the Spanish cape
Tries to sit on Sweeney's knees

Slips and pulls the table cloth
Overturns a coffee-cup,
Reorganized upon the floor
She yawns and draws a stocking up;

The silent man in mocha brown
Sprawls at the window-sill and gapes;
The waiter brings in oranges
Bananas figs and hothouse grapes;

The silent vertebrate in brown
Contracts and concentrates, withdraws;
Rachel *née* Rabinovitch
Tears at the grapes with murderous paws;

She and the lady in the cape
Are suspect, thought to be in league;
Therefore the man with heavy eyes
Declines the gambit, shows fatigue,

Leaves the room and reappears
Outside the window, leaning in,

Branches of wistaria
Circumscribe a golden grin;

The host with someone indistinct
Converses at the door apart,
The nightingales are singing near
The Convent of the Sacred Heart,

And sang within the bloody wood
When Agamemnon cried aloud,
And let their liquid droppings fall
To stain the stiff dishonoured shroud.

A COOKING EGG

En l'an trentiesme de mon aage
Que toutes mes hontes j'ay beues . . .

Pipit sate upright in her chair
Some distance from where I was sitting;
Views of the Oxford Colleges
Lay on the table, with the knitting.

Daguerreotypes and silhouettes,
Her grandfather and great great aunts,
Supported on the mantelpiece
An *Invitation to the Dance.*

. . .

I shall not want Honour in Heaven
For I shall meet sir Philip Sidney

And have talk with Coriolanus
And other heroes of that kidney.

I shall not want Capital in Heaven
For I shall meet Sir Alfred Mond:
We two shall lie together, lapt
In a five per cent Exchequer Bond.

I shall not want Society in Heaven,
Lucretia Borgia shall be my Bride;
Her anecdotes will be more amusing
Than Pipit's experience could provide.

I shall not want Pipit in Heaven:
Madame Blavatsky will instruct me
In the Seven Sacred Trances;
Piccarda de Donati will conduct me . . .

. . .

But where is the penny world I bought
To eat with Pipit behind the screen?
The red-eyed scavengers are creeping
From Kentish Town and Golders Green;

Where are the eagles and the trumpets?
Buried beneath some snow-deep Alps.
Over buttered scones and crumpets
Weeping, weeping multitudes
Droop in a hundred A. B. C.'s

THE BOSTON EVENING TRANSCRIPT

The readers of the *Boston Evening Transcript*
Sway in the wind like a field of ripe corn.

When evening quickens faintly in the street,
Wakening the appetites of life in some
And to others bringing the *Boston Evening Transcript*,
I mount the steps and ring the bell, turning
Wearily, as one would turn to nod good-bye to Rochefoucauld,
If the street were time and he at the end of the street,
And I say, "Cousin Harriet, here is the *Boston Evening Transcript*."

LA FIGLIA CHE PIANGE

o quam te memorem virgo . . .

Stand on the highest pavement of the stair—
Lean on a garden urn—
Weave, weave the sunlight in your hair—
Clasp your flowers to you with a pained surprise—
Fling them to the ground and turn
With a fugitive resentment in your eyes:
But weave, weave the sunlight in your hair.

So I would have had him leave,
So I would have had her stand and grieve,
So he would have left
As the soul leaves the body torn and bruised,
As the mind deserts the body it has used.
I should find

Some way incomparably light and deft,
Some way we both should understand,
Simple and faithless as a smile and shake of the hand.

She turned away, but with the autumn weather
Compelled my imagination many days,
Many days and many hours:
Her hair over her arms and her arms full of flowers.
And I wonder how they should have been together!
I should have lost a gesture and a pose.
Sometimes these cogitations still amaze
The troubled midnight and the noon's repose.

AN ESSAY ON BEHAVIORISM

BERTRAND RUSSELL

FROM OCTOBER 1923

Although the word "Behaviorism" has grown familiar during the last few years, the ordinary layman has no very definite idea as to what it means. Behaviorism is in the first instance a method in psychology, and only derivatively a psychological theory. It is possible to accept the method without accepting the theory, although the one leads by a natural development to the other.

There are few full-fledged behaviorists; the chief is Mr. John B. Watson, formerly a professor at Johns Hopkins University. But many men who are not prepared to go the whole length are willing to go a considerable distance with the behaviorists, and to admit that their contentions are very important. The present writer is among those who are sympathetic to behaviorism, without accepting it in its entirety. In considering it, it will be well to begin with the method.

As a method, behaviorism is distinguished by the fact that it rejects "introspection" as a special source of knowledge about mental processes. Whatever various philosophers may have believed, it has been customary in scientific practice to suppose that there are two different ways in which we become aware of occurrences: there is the way of the senses, which tells us what is going on in the world about us, or in our own bodies, and there is the way of introspection, which tells us what we are thinking or feeling or desiring. We know our own "thoughts", so it seems, directly, whereas we can only guess the thoughts of others by what they do or say. We can remember our own dreams, but we only know what other people have dreamed when they tell us. We know when we feel pleased or displeased, but if we choose to behave so as to conceal our feelings, other people cannot know them.

In this way there comes to be a world of private knowledge apparently open to each one of us about himself, but not directly accessible about other people. This private inner world we think of as our "mind". It is supposed to be the distinctive business of psychology to study "minds", and its distinctive method is supposed to be that peculiar knowledge of our own mental processes which is called "introspection".

The behaviorist does not, of course, deny that we know things about ourselves which we do not know so easily about other people. We cannot help knowing when we have a toothache, whereas it is easy not to know when other people's teeth ache. What the behaviorist denies is not the fact of this knowledge but the supposed peculiarity of the method by which it is acquired. Our senses tell us more about what is happening in a room in which we are than about what is happening at a distance; but the knowledge is of the same kind in both cases. Similarly, our senses tell us more about what is happening in our own body than about what is happening elsewhere. We have not only the senses of sight and hearing and so on by which we become aware of external things, but also organic sensations which have specially to do with our physiological "inside". But all the knowledge we obtain in this way may be regarded as knowledge of something physical, not of something "mental". It may be said that it is our bodies which we come to know by means of physiological sensations, only that the knowledge is fuller than in the case of external bodies.

The behaviorist denies that there is any knowledge of a different *kind* from our knowledge about tables and chairs. And he holds that everything we can know about ourselves could, theoretically, be known by an external observer, provided he had suitable instruments for observing and adequate skill in drawing inferences. He rejects altogether the special method of "introspection", as being fallacious and misleading. Psychology, he maintains, should be concerned with the "behavior" of a human being or an animal (as the case may be), that is to say, with something displayed in actions which are visible to the onlooker, or at least may be so if he is a sufficiently skilled observer. Hence the name "behaviorist". This name denotes a person who thinks that behavior, rather than mental states, should be studied by the psychologist.

Considering this question practically, without troubling ourselves about possible metaphysical implications, it must be admitted that there is a very great deal to be said for the view that the psychologist should confine himself to behavior. There is first of all the wide field of animal psychology, which is very instructive in regard to the psychology of human beings, and also full of interest on its own account. It is clear that animals cannot tell us the results of their introspection, even supposing they indulge in it. We can only know about animal psychology what is to be discovered by observing how animals act. It is a mistake, scientifically, to state the results of our observation in language involving inference to mental processes. We know that a dog wags his tail when he sees his master, but we do not *know* that he feels pleased. We see that cats spit and arch their backs in the presence of dogs, and we infer that they hate dogs, but the inference is not very well founded. Nothing is really added to our knowledge by such inferences, which are always precarious. It is better to confine ourselves to observing and correlating the external facts of animal behavior, which we can ascertain with scientific precision, rather than to indulge in doubtful dramatic interpretations of their acts, which may be as misleading as they would be in the case of an actor on the stage, whose object is to simulate emotions which he does not feel.

How much more fruitful the behaviorist method is than the method of mental interpretation, at least where animals are concerned, may be seen in the experimental study of the process of learning in animals, which practically begins with [Edward L.] Thorndike's *Animal Intelligence*. A cage or a maze is constructed, the animal is put inside and food outside, or *vice versa*, and its attempts to get at the food are observed. Its first attempts are entirely random, and only succeed by accident; but after a certain number of trials with the same cage or maze, the animal learns exactly what to do, and becomes as expert as a trained acrobat. Of course the task must be sufficiently easy for the first accidental success to be achieved before the animal is weary of trying, but provided this condition is fulfilled, any animal of an intelligent species will gradually achieve perfection. If it is then allowed to forget, it learns again much more quickly than the first time. These experiments on learning are of great importance, and may in time throw light on the best methods of human education.

The study of animal instinct is another important branch of comparative psychology which is much more fruitful when conducted by behaviorist methods than when entangled in discussions as to what an animal "foresees" or "desires". These discussions lead nowhere, because we have no means of testing the various hypotheses. Observations of behavior, on the contrary, yield definite results, and give whatever genuine knowledge is possible as to the instincts of animals. These instincts are much clearer and more definite than those of human beings, and yet they are the source from which human instincts have developed. For all who wish to understand human instincts, accordingly, animal instincts are very enlightening. A book such as [W. H. R.] Rivers' *Instinct and the Unconscious* shows how they throw light even upon such a subject as the nervous disorders caused by the war, many of which were of the nature of a throw-back to some more primitive form of the instinct of fear.

This brings us to the matters dealt with by psychoanalysis, which is primarily a method of understanding and airing certain kinds of nervous disorders. It is undoubtedly a very valuable method, representing an immense advance. But the subject has been obscured by the emphasis laid on the distinction between the conscious and the unconscious. There was formerly a notion that we ought to be "conscious" of all that goes on in our "minds", and when this notion had to be abandoned, people resorted to "unconscious" mental processes as something rather strange and mysterious.

In fact, however, everybody—whether layman, psychologist, or philosopher—has had the very vaguest ideas as to what was meant by "consciousness". William James threw out a challenge in his essay called Does "Consciousness" Exist?, but the effect of this challenge was less than it ought to have been. It seems to be the rule that our mental processes are unconscious, and the exception when they are conscious; and even when they are conscious, this is a quite unimportant characteristic of them. What is more, the unconscious desires with which Freudians operate appear to be, not mental states at all, but merely tendencies to a certain kind of behavior. When this is realized, and psychoanalytic material is re-stated in the language of behaviorism, the mystery surrounding "unconscious wishes" disappears, and the facts concerned cease to be surprising. Thus, in regard to the "unconscious" or "sub-conscious", behaviorism as a method has advantages quite as great as in regard to animal psychology.

As a method, however, it is not obliged to claim that it can cover the whole field of psychology; when it advances this claim it ceases to be merely a method and becomes a psychological theory. It is time to consider it from this point of view.

Behaviorism as a theory holds that none of the facts upon which psychology is based are essentially private to one observer. This involves the view that there is no such thing as "thought", as opposed to bodily movements; for bodily movements can be observed by others, but my thoughts, if they exist, can only be observed by myself. We are thus faced with the question: Do people think? And, if so, what happens when they think?

To this question Mr. [John B.] Watson gives a very radical answer:

People do not think, they only talk. What is called "thinking" consists of talking to oneself. He maintains that, if we had suitable instruments, we could discover incipient little movements of a man's throat and tongue when he "thinks", and that these are the movements of beginning to pronounce the words to himself. A person who can "think", according to this view, is merely a person who has learned to pronounce words in the right order, like a rat which has learned to take the right turns in a maze. Freud relates somewhere that, when he was lecturing in America, after he had explained that dreams are always egoistic, a lady got up and said that might be true in Austria, but was not true in America, where dreams were often full of virtue. I hope nobody will retort by maintaining that Mr. Watson's view of thinking may be correct in America, but is not correct in Europe.

Mr. Watson's view of thought is not so easily disposed of as some might be inclined to suppose. To begin with: we only know the thoughts of others through their behavior, and especially through what they say or write, so that any evidence that thinking is more than talking must be derived from observation of ourselves. Now, obviously something goes on when we think. Is this of the nature of small bodily movements? Or is it of some quite different nature? Before going into the question, I recommend the reader to think concentratedly about a bubble with his mouth open. Nine people out of ten will feel an almost irresistible impulse to bring their lips together so as to form the letter B. This little experiment will show the reader that Mr. Watson *may* be right.

There are, however, great difficulties in the way of accepting his view as the whole of the truth. To begin with, many people are "visual" types; they "think" mainly in visual images, and even words are represented rather by the look of them in print than by the pronunciation of them. Most of their "thinking" is not in words at all, but in more or less vague images. This seems to be true of the bulk of the human race, and only untrue of writers and orators, to whom words as such are specially important. If so, Mr. Watson's theory of thinking may be true of "thinkers", but not of ordinary mortals. Purely verbal thinking may be the highest stage, not the lowest. In that case, what happens when the rest of us think? Or, for that matter, what happens in sensation, for example when we see something?

The traditional view is that when we look at an object something occurs which is called a "perception", and that when afterwards we remember the object or imagine a similar one, something occurs which is called an "image". Both of these *seem* to be radically different occurrences from matter in motion. Mr. Watson denies the "image" altogether; that is to say, he denies that what we take to be images are anything radically different from sensations or perceptions. They may be fainter, and they may have no proximate cause external to the nervous system; but they are not a different kind of entity. This is a difficult question, upon which there has been much controversy. Let us, for the sake of argument, concede Mr. Watson's contention as to images. What, then, shall we say of perceptions?

It is, of course, admitted by the behaviorist that we perceive things. This is essential to his position. In acquiring physical knowledge, we are all supposed to perceive the same things; this is the advantage of physical knowledge over the psychological knowledge supposed to be derived from introspection, which no other observer can directly verify. But the question arises: How does the behaviorist know that he perceives things? Does not this knowledge involve that very introspection which he professes to discard?

It is a perfectly possible hypothesis that animals, although they perceive objects just as well as we do, are quite unaware that they do so. A cat, we may suppose, can have the knowledge which we should express by saying "there is a mouse", but not the knowledge "I see a mouse". Perceptions are fleeting occurrences, which do not have the persistence believed to belong to physical things. You may open your eyes for a moment, see the things in your room, and then shut your eyes again. You believe that the things in your room have not existed only during the moment when your eyes were open, but something did exist only during that moment. This something is what is called a perception. It is impossible to deny that we have knowledge of fleeting occurrences of this sort. And it is impossible to identify these fleeting perceptions with the movement of the eyelids or the stimulus to the optic nerve or the disturbance in the brain caused by this stimulus.

And the odd thing is that, when we come to reflect, we find these fleeting perceptions to be what we really *know* about the external world. The permanent objects of traditional physics and common sense are inferred from what we perceive. And the publicity of physical observation is only a matter of degree, because no two people, looking at the "same" object, have precisely similar visual impressions. The momentary perception, moreover, is more like what the most modern physics requires as its substratum than is the permanent "thing" of common sense. Matter and bodies, which used to be thought to persist through time, have been dissolved by Einstein and Relativity into series of "events", each brief and evanescent like my perception when I open my eyes for a moment.

It seems, therefore, that what occurs in this moment is the sort of thing to be taken as the ultimate reality out of which both mind and matter are constructed. If so, we shall require new categories and new modes of thought. The behaviorist may remain justified as against traditional psychology, but not as against the revolutionary physics of our time. The physicists have undermined our belief in "matter" at the same time that the psychologists have undermined our belief in "mind". Therefore, the work of the psychologists cannot be used to further the cause of matter, but must be placed to the account of a "tertium quid", which the American realists, following a suggestion of Dr. H. M. Sheffer [the logician], call "neutral stuff". But this opens a very large question, which cannot be dealt with as an appendix to a discussion of Behaviorism.

THE WOMAN BEHIND THE MASK

COLETTE

FROM NOVEMBER 1924

He gazed abstractedly at the foaming torrent of masqueraders streaming past him, vaguely disturbed by the vivid colours and by the dissonances produced by two orchestras that were placed too close together. The hood of his monk's gown was too tight across his temples and his mask made his nose twitch irritably. Nevertheless he savoured this mood, half of unrest, half of pleasure, which made the passing of the hours almost unnoticed. He had wandered through all the corridors of the opera house, had tasted the golden dust of the ballroom floor, had recognized some rather bored friends and had found the indifferent arms of a very fat girl—whose fancy had impelled her to represent a sylph—wound about his neck. Embarrassed by his domino, tripping in the manner of all males suddenly encumbered with skirts, this doctor in the monk's garb did not dare to remove either his mask or his domino on account of the rather college-boy sort of prank that he was perpetrating.

"I shall spend the night at the Nogents," he had said to his wife. "They've just telephoned me and I'm afraid the poor old lady . . . but, do you know I had an almost childish desire to go to that ball. It's ridiculous, don't you think, for a man of my age never to have seen a fancy dress opera ball?"

"Yes, dear, absolutely absurd! If I'd known, perhaps I shouldn't have married you."

"But you—don't you want to go to this—this green and violet ball? Even without me . . . if you would enjoy it, dearest?"

She had shuddered—one of those long shivers of disgust in which one could see her hair and her delicate hands tremble and her throat quiver as if at the touch of a slimy creature or the sight of something repulsive.

"I! Can you see me in that mob? delivered into all those hands? I'm not a prude—but I am—I am fastidious—and I can't help it!"

Leaning against the balustrade of a box just over the grand stairway, he thought of that trembling doe, his wife, while he stared at the bare back of a sultana squeezed by two enormous hands with long dirty nails. Crowding out of the sleeves of a Venetian signor, these hands left their impress on the soft white feminine flesh. Because he was thinking of his wife, he started perceptibly when he heard at his side a little "ha-hum", a ghost of a cough that was habitual with her. He turned and saw, mounted on the balustrade, what was clearly a Pierrot from the flowing sleeves, the wide pantaloons, the skull cap, the chalky whiteness of the bit of skin that was visible under the lace ruffle of the mask. The thin stuff of the costume and of the cap, shot with threads of violet and sil-ver, shone like the iridescent-salt-water eels that you catch at night, spearing them from a boat to which they have been attracted by a pine torch.

Overcome with surprise he waited for the little "ha-hum" again; but in vain. The eel-like Pierrot, seated nonchalantly, beat with one swinging heel on the marble balustrade and revealed of herself only two satin shoes, and a black gloved hand resting on one hip. The two slanting slits in the mask, carefully veiled with tulle, allowed only a smothered flash of indis-tinct fire from her eyes.

He had to speak—

"Irene!"

Then he stopped, remembering his own deception. But little used to making believe, he had forgotten to disguise his voice. The Pierrot scratched herself with a movement free and rather common.

The husband breathed again. "Ah, it is not she!"

But the Pierrot drew from a pocket a golden box and opened it to take out a stick of rouge; and the anxious husband recognized an ancient snuff-box with a little mirror inside of it, his present to her on their last anniversary.

He pressed his hand to his heart with a movement so sudden and so unconsciously theatrical that the eel-like Pierrot noticed it.

"Is that a declaration, Violet Domino?"

He did not answer. Half choked with astonishment, suspense, and dark forebodings, he listened for a long, long moment to the scarcely disguised voice of his wife. The eel looked at him, perched lightly, with her head on one side like a bird.

Then she shrugged her shoulders, jumped to the ground and moved away. The movement released the anxious husband, who, becoming actively and normally jealous, became once more capable of thought. He rose and followed her, very deliberately and without haste.

"She is here with someone," he thought. "In less than an hour I shall know all."

A hundred dominoes, violet or green, showed that he need not fear being either noticed or recognized. Irene walked carelessly ahead of him. He was thunderstruck at noticing that she swayed her hips, and dragged her feet a little, as if she were wearing mules.

A Byzantine, in emerald and gold brocade, seized her in passing, and she drooped into his arms, her slender figure swallowed up in his embrace. Her husband ran towards the couple and reached them just in time to hear Irene cry coquettishly—"You brute, you!"

She moved away with the same relaxed and easy step, stopping often, gazing in at the open doors of boxes, scarcely ever turning round. She hesitated at the foot of a staircase, turned abruptly, went back to the entrance of the orchestra, and insinuated herself adroitly, into a noisy group of people, with a movement like that of a sword gliding into its sheath. Ten pairs of arms imprisoned her. A wrestler, almost naked, thrust her against the edge of the lowest tier of boxes and held her there.

She yielded under the weight of the man, turned her head for a laugh that was matched by the laughs of the others; and the man in the violet domino saw the teeth of the wrestler shining under the flap of his mask.

Then she extricated herself lightly and sat down upon the steps which led to the ball-room. Two steps behind her, her husband watched her. She fixed her mask, smoothed her rumpled jacket and readjusted her close-fitting cap. She seemed as calm as if she were alone. Then after a few minutes rest, she set forth again.

On the dance floor, she put her arm on the shoulder of a warrior who asked her, without words, to dance. She danced with him, pressed close to his side.

"He is the one!" said the husband to himself.

But she did not exchange a single word with the warrior and left him, calmly, at the end of the dance.

She went and drank a glass of champagne at the buffet, then a second glass, paid for them, watched, motionless, the beginning of a fight between two men, surrounded by a crowd of shrieking women. She amused herself also by putting her little black impish hands on the white throat of a woman dressed as a Hollander, in a gold headdress. The latter cried out nervously.

At last the anxious husband, following her, saw her stop, as if compelled, beside a young man, seated panting and out of breath on a bench, fanning himself with his mask. She bent and, taking his beautiful, fresh but rather brutal face mockingly by the chin, kissed his half-open mouth.

But her husband, instead of throwing himself upon them and tearing the two apart, lost himself in the crowd.

Stupefied, he no longer feared—he no longer *hoped*—that she was deceiving him. He was sure, now, that she knew neither the dance-intoxicated youth whom she was kissing, nor the warrior with whom she had danced. He was certain that she was not waiting or looking for anyone, and that, abandoning the lips that she held with her own, like a flower drained of honey, she would set off one instant later in search of another—to forget and to taste until she should finally become satiated and go home—the strange pleasure of being alone, free, really herself, in her native animalism, of being unknown, in the solitude absolute and inviolate conferred upon her by a fancy dress costume and a little mask.

WHEN CALVIN COOLIDGE LAUGHED

E. E. CUMMINGS

FROM APRIL 1925

Calvin Coolidge laughed.

Instantly an immense crowd gathered. The news spread like wildfire. From a dozen leading dailies, reporters and cameramen came rushing to the scene pell-mell in highpowered aeroplanes. Hundreds of police reserves, responding without hesitation to a reiterated riot-call, displayed with amazing promptness a quite unpredictable inability to control the ever-increasing multitude, but not before any number of unavoidable accidents had informally occurred. A war veteran with three wooden legs, for example, was trampled, and the nonartificial portions of his anatomy reduced to pulp. Two anarchists (of whom one was watering chrysanthemums at Salt Lake City, Utah, while the other was fast asleep in a delicatessen at the corner of Little H and 12 1/2 Streets) were immediately arrested, lynched, and jailed, on the charge of habeas corpus with premeditated absence. At Lafayette Square, a small dog, stepped on, bit the ankle [of] a beautiful and highstrung woman who had for some time suffered from insomnia, and who—far too enraged to realise, except in a very general way, the source of the pain—vigorously struck a child of five, knocking its front teeth out. Another woman, profiting by the general excitement, fainted and with a hideous shriek fell through a plateglass window.

* * *

On the outskirts of the throng, several nonogenarian members of the Senate, both Republican and otherwise, succumbed to heart-trouble with serious complications. A motorcycle ran over an idiot. A stone-deaf night-watchman's left eye was extinguished by the point of a missing spectator's umbrella. Falling seven stories from a nearby office-building, Congressman N. G. Knott of Tennessee (Dem.) landed in the midst of the crowd absolutely unhurt, killing eleven persons including the ambassador to Uruguay. At this truly unfortunate occurrence, one of the most promising businessmen of Keokuk, Iowa, Aloysius Q. Van Smith (a member of the Harvard, Yale, and Racquet Clubs) swallowed a cigar and died instantly. Fifty plainclothesmen and two policewomen with some difficulty transported the universally lamented remains three and three-fourths miles to a waiting ambulance where they were given first-aid, creating an almost unmentionable disturbance during which every-body took off everybody's hat and the Rev. Peter Scott Wilson, of the Eighteenth Anabaptist Church of Paragould, Ark., received internal in-juries resulting in his becoming mentally unbalanced and attempting to undress on the spot.

Needless to say, the holy man was prevented by indignant bystanders from carrying out his ignominious intention, and fell insensible to the sidewalk.

Calm had scarcely been destroyed, when a lovesick sailor from the battleship Idaho was seized with delirium tremens. In still another part of the mob, a hydrant exploded without sufficient warning, causing no casu-alties and seriously damaging an almost priceless full-length portrait of ex-President Theodore Roosevelt kissing ex-Admiral Hashimura Togo on both cheeks by John Singer Sargent in the neighboring chapel of the Y.W.C.A. Olaf Yansen, Klansman and plumber, and a floorwalker, Abraham Goldstein, becoming mutually infuriated owing to some prob-ably imaginary difference of opinion, resorted to a spontaneous display of physical culture, in the course of which the former (who, according to several witnesses, was getting the worst of it, in spite of his indubitably superior size) hit the latter with a brick and vanished. Mr. Goldstein is doing well.

While quietly playing with a box of safety-matches which his parents, Mr. and Mrs. James H. Fitzroy, of 99 Hundredth Street, Omaha, had given to their little son James Jr. to keep him quiet, the infant—in some unaccountable manner—set fire to forty one persons, of whom nine and thirty were burned to ashes. A Chinese, Mi Wong, who exercises the profession of laundryman at 17 Sixteenth Street, and Signor Pedro Alhambra, a millionaire coffee-planter, who also refused to be interviewed but is stopping at the New Willard, are the survivors. Havoc resulted when one of the better-liked members of the voting married set (whose identity the authorities refuse to divulge) kissed Tony Crack, iceman extraordinary to the White House, on the spur of the moment, receiving concussion of the brain with two black eyes. In the front rank of onlookers, a daughter of the people became so excited by the Chief Executive's spectacular act, hereinbefore referred to, that before you could say Jack Robinson she presented the universe with twins.

B ut such trivial catastrophes were eclipsed by a disaster of really portentous significance. No sooner had Wall Street learned what Mr. Coolidge had done, than an unprecedented panic started, and Coca-Cola tobogganed in eight minutes from nine hundred decimal point three to decimal point six zeros seven four five, wiping out at one fell swoop the solidly founded fortunes of no less than two thousand two hundred and two pillars of society, and exerting an overpowering influence for evil on wheat, and sugar, not to mention that ever mobile commodity, castor oil, all three of which tumbled about in a truly frightful manner. At Detroit, Mich., the president of the India Rubber Trust Co., hatless and with his white hair streaming in the wind, tore out of the Soldiers and Sailors' Savings Bank at a snail's pace carrying in one hand a hat belonging to the president of the latter institution, James B. Sears, and in the other a telephone which the famous first had (in the frenzy of the moment) forgotten to replace on the distinguished second's desk.

A hook-and-ladder, driven by Augustus John at an estimated speed of sixty eight miles an hour, passed over the magnate longitudinally as he crossed Edsel Avenue and left a gently-expiring corpse whose last words— spoken into the (oddly enough) unbroken mouthpiece of the instrument, only to be overheard by P. Franklin Adams, a garbage-man—were: "Let us then, if you please—"

So unnerved was the Jehu of the Henry Street Fire Station by this totally unexpected demise that, without pausing to consider the possible damage to life and limb involved in a purely arbitrary deviation from the none too ample thoroughfare, he declined the very next corner in favor of driving straight through the city's largest skyscraper, whose one hundred and thirteen stories—after tottering horribly for a minute and a half, during which negligible period several thousand suspicious characters left town—thundered earthward with the velocity of light, exterminating every vestige of humanity and architecture within a radius of eighty leagues including one billion six hundred and forty nine million five hundred and thirty eight thousand two hundred and seven Ford sedans.

This paralysing cataclysm was immediately followed by a fire of stupendous proportions whose prodigiously enormous flames, greedily winding themselves around monuments, cyclone-cellars, and certain other spontaneous civic structures, roasted by myriads the inhabitants thereof, while generating a heat so terrific as to evaporate everything evaporable within an area of fourteen thousand square miles not exclusive of the Missouri river—which, completely disappearing in fifteen seconds, revealed a giltedged submarine of the U-C type containing (among other things) William Jennings Bryan, William J. Burns, William Wrigley Jr., Strangler Lewis, the Prince of Wales, Senator Richard O. Thimble of California, Babe Ruth, Major Arthur B. Good, Humphrey Ohm, emeritus professor of radio at Johns Hopkins University, Rear Admiral George

Monk, K. C. B. etc., Nichola Murray Butler, Sir Arthur Conan Doyle, T. S. F., Harold Bell Wright, Clive Bell, the honorable Robert W. Chambers, the Amir and Amira of Afghanistan and their hosts, Mr. and Mrs. Harold S. Packingbox of Philadelphia and Newport, Al Jolson, Luther Burbank, Ben Ali Hagin, Alfred Stieglitz, Howard Chandler Christy, Daniel Chester French, Paul Manship, George Gershwin, Houdini, Thomas A. Edison and Dr. Frank Crane, the last of whom (being only incompletely intoxicated) promptly shuffled off this mortal coil with the Star Spangled Banner upon his lips and was buried by six or seven stalwart bootleggers on the exact spot where he did not fall.

A moving picture of the preceding historical catastrophe was thereupon instigated by the usual genius of Mr. [D. W.] Griffith who, with unerring judgment if not tact, invoked Rudolph Valentino at a salary of two hundred and seventy-five thousand dollars per week, less nineteen cents war-tax, to impersonate simultaneously both George Arliss and Napoleon, whereas Lillian Gish played to imperfection the thankless part of the old mother who—after being bitten by sharks—kills the villain with a knitting-needle on horseback and escapes out of the crater of Vesuvius in a brown paper bag, causing a strike among the white paper bag manufacturers, which spread all the way from Tuscaloosa to Yazoo.

Suddenly—unexpectedly—in the midst of all this infrahuman and ultranational pandemonium, compared with which such trivial incidents as solar eclipses, earthquakes, the battle of Aegospotami, Sheridan's ride, the fall of Babylon, the Declaration of Independence, and Pepy's Diary, were as an inelegant globule of H_2O beside the tempestuous entirety of the Dead Sea—in the centre of doom, debauchery, and dissolution—in the naked heart of tintinnabulous chaos—a miracle, a thing unknown, unanalysable, a phenomenon irremediably acatalectic, indubitably unbelievable, and totally indescribable, occurred.

Over the whole country there swept (as sometimes sweeps, o'er the sickbed of some poor delirious sufferer, a spontaneous sweetness—purging the spirit of its every anguish, uniting the multifarious moods and aspects of the human heart in a triumphant arch through which, with flags flying and bugles blowing, the glorious armies of the soul go marching as to war)—there thrilled—there burgeoned—a mysterious and invincible ululation of utter, absolute, unperforated silence.

So stunning, so irrevocable, was this silence, that the beasts of the field, the fowls of the air, and the fish of the sea, felt, and (each in his own peculiar and characteristic way) responded to, its thunderous intensity. The prairie-dog of Kansas and the armadillo of Texas emerged from their burrows hand in hand, bent on satisfying at all costs an unquenchable curiosity as to its occult cause—united by a common inquisitiveness, the moose of Maine and the codfish of Massachusetts (abandoning simultaneously their respectively foliate and aqueous habitats) put their heads together, and listened—the versatile mocking-bird of Kentucky started from his sleep and mingled his mellifluous pæons of inquiry with the more staccato queries of the cynical rose-breasted nuthatch—even the mayor of Kankakee, Ill., fired by an overwhelming curiosity, leaned out of a superb gothic aperture in the pre-romanesque I. O. O. F. hall, dropping a half-smoked Chesterfield into the exact middle of a passing load of hay, with the remark: "Is cigarette taste changing?"—in short, all America, which (but a moment before) had been convulsed to its very roots by unparalleled spasms of massacre, machination, and mayhem, closed its weary eyes . . . and sank suddenly into a profound swoon of unadulterated ecstasy, a delicious coma of inexpressible bliss . . . as through the entire nation, from sea to sea, completely surged that sublime and unmitigated titillation of telepathic tranquility, of rapturous reintegration, of perfect peace . . .

Calvin Coolidge had stopped laughing.

WHAT, EXACTLY, IS MODERN?

ALDOUS HUXLEY

FROM MAY 1925

At a café in Siena I once got into conversation with an Italian medical student. Like most of his compatriots, he was very open and confiding. We had not known one another half an hour before he told me the whole story of his life. Among other things he informed me that he had spent a year as a student at the University of Rome, but that he had been compelled to remove to Siena because it was impossible for him to learn anything at Rome; there were too many distractions in the capital, too many feminine distractions in particular. He knew that he would never get a degree if he stayed at Rome. "In a little town like Siena," I said, "I suppose there are no distractions of that sort?" "Not so many," he admitted, "as at Rome. All the same," he added, and smiled a smile of male fatuity, "you'd be surprised by the young women of Siena. They're really very modern." And he went on to tell me of his adventures with the local shop girls.

I laughed, not at his stories, which were exceedingly tedious and commonplace, but at his peculiar use of the word, "modern". It was the first time I had heard it employed in such a context. Since then I have heard it similarly used, more than once. I remember, in London, hearing one of those scrubby camp-followers of the arts who make their "artistic temperament" the excuse for leading an idle, sordid and perfectly useless life, loudly and proudly boasting that he was absolutely modern: anyone might have his wife, so far as he was concerned. And he gave it to be understood that the lady in question thought just as little of promiscuous infidelity—was, in a word, just as modern—as he.

Now, as a grammarian and a literary pedant, I strongly object to the improper use of words. Every word possesses some single, definite meaning. It should always be used in its accepted sense and not forced to signify something it was never meant to signify. Thus, when one wants to say of a person that he or she is lascivious and insensitive to the point of indulging promiscuously in what is technically known as "love", one should state the fact in so many words and not say that he or she is "modern". For such a person is not modern, but on the contrary, antique and atavistic. To behave like the Romans under Caracalla, the Asiatic Greeks, the Babylonians, is not a bit modern. In point of historical fact it is monogamous love and chastity that are the modern inventions. My Italian friend and the young camp-follower of the arts were terribly old-fashioned, if only they had known it. They were eighteenth-century in their outlook, they were Roman-Empire, they were Babylonian. Really modern people love like the Brownings.

My Italian friend and the camp-follower of the arts had, it is true, a certain justification for their employment of the epithet, "modern", in this particular context: the state of mind which they thus qualified does happen to be fairly common, in certain circles, at the present time. But a thing may be fashionable without necessarily being modern. There is a great difference between mere fashionableness or contemporaneity on the one hand and modernity on the other. For things and ideas which were fashionable in the past may become fashionable again. Crinolines and clinging draperies, waists high or low, tight or loose, alternately come and go. But it would be absurd to call any one of them modern merely because it happens to be in vogue at the particular moment when you are speaking. Only that which is really new, which has no counterpart in antiquity, is modern. Thus, our mechanical civilization, with the conditions of life and the ideas begotten by it are modern. But sexual promiscuity is not modern at all, it is a very ancient and anachronistic habit which happens, at the moment and in certain limited circles, to be fashionable.

We talk of modern art just as loosley and inaccurately as we talk of modern manners. Some contemporary art is genuinely modern, inasmuch as it is typical of our civilization alone and different from ancient art. Much, on the other hand, is not modern, but merely something old, *réchauffé*, which we call modern only because it happens to be in voyage. Thus, the barbaric music of Stravinsky is fundamentally not modern at all. It is merely an ingenious, scholarly and more efficient development of the noises made by savage people to work themselves up into a state of emotional excitement. Those who heard the transcriptions of Tibetan music brought back by members of the Everest expedition must have been struck by the close resemblance which this savage music bore to Stravinsky's. Without excessive vanity we can say, I think, that the Tibetans are several thousand years behind us in mental development; the music of Stravinsky and his imitators is therefore only a cultured and conscious atavism. In their intellectuality and idealism, Bach and Beethoven are incomparably more modern than Stravinsky. Among contemporary musicians Schoenberg may be regarded as modern for unlike the fashionably atavistic Stravinsky, he is doing something which our savage ancestors could not do—appealing to the intellect and the spirit, not to the primary emotions and the nerves. Schoenberg, though not, perhaps, a greatly inspired artist, is at any rate moving forward in the direction of all human development—towards more and more mind and spirit. Stravinsky is going backwards, away from mind; toward physiology.

In speaking of the visual arts, we make a somewhat similar mistake. For we are accustomed to call "modern" almost any picture or sculpture which happens to be unlike the object which it is supposed to represent. Now distortion as such is not at all modern. All primitive art is nonrealistic. So is all incompetent art (which does not mean, of course, that all non-realistic art is incompetent). Non-realism in itself is no criterion of modernity. It is only an accident that we happen to be living in an age when many artists cultivate a deliberate naïvism, when the technical practice (though not the subject matter and the symbolism) of the primitives is freely imitated and art is simplified and conventionalized to the utmost.

There is obviously nothing remarkably modern in imitating the primitives. What is modern—and deplorably so—is the contemporary habit of
emptying the primitives of their content and significance. Art for art's
sake and the theory of pure aesthetics are modern products, due to the
divorce of art from religion. The majority of contemporary painters, one
feels when looking at their works, haven't the faintest notion what to paint.
They exercise their art in the void, so to speak, making no contact with
the life and the ideas around them. Plenty of admirable artists have
shown, in the past, that it is possible to combine pure aesthetics with story
telling and the expression of ideas. Few of the most talented artists of the
present day make any attempt to accomplish this union or there would be
more really modern art.

It is the same in literature as in painting and music. What is commonly called modern, by journalists and other thoughtless people, is either trivially eccentric, like the literature of the dadaists; smartly cynical
and heartless in a minor eighteenth-century way, like the novels of Mr.
[Ronald] Firbank; or obstreperously gross and blasphemous, like *Ulysses*,
which is simply the reaction of its author against his mediaeval catholic
education. The blasphemies in *Ulysses* are precisely like those of Marlowe
in the sixteenth century and the grossnesses are those of a Father of the
Church, who, having emerged from his hermitage, enlarges on the hor-
rors of the sin-ridden world. None of these literary manifestations are
modern. For they are not new; they do not represent what is most typical
of our civilization; they are off the main line of progress, which is towards
increasing subtlety of mind, increasing sensitiveness to emotion, increasing toleration and understanding. An enormously enhanced mental elas-
ticity and freedom distinguish this age from past ages. The most modern
work of literature is the most intelligent, the most sensitive and spiritual,
the freest and most tolerant, the most completely and widely comprehending. Thus, the most modern novelist who ever wrote is certainly
Dostoievsky. That he happened to die in 1881 makes no difference to his
modernity. His subtlety, his sensitiveness, his intelligence and compre-
hension remain unsurpassed and hardly approached. His novels are still

the most complete and characteristic product of the modern mind. It may be hoped, it may even be expected, that, in the course of evolution, the mass of human beings will grow to be as intelligent, as deeply and as widely comprehending, as exquisitely sensitive as was Dostoievsky. He has been dead for more than forty years. But he was so excessively and abnormally modern that it will probably be several centuries before the rest of us have come abreast with him.

To distinguish what is modern in recent literature from what is not modern requires only a little reflection. Thus, Anatole France, however delightful an author, is not modern; he is a contemporary ancient, a sort of Lucian brought up to date. Marcel Proust, on the other hand, is decidedly modern; his sensitiveness and his acute, though somewhat limited, understanding of character, are things to which we can find no parallel in antiquity. D. H. Lawrence is partly extremely modern, partly atavistic, in the manner of Stravinsky. As a poet, Thomas Hardy, in spite of his age, is a great deal more modern than, shall we say, Jean Cocteau. It would be easy, but tedious, to multiply such examples. They would all point to the same conclusion: not all that is fashionable is modern. Let us not, therefore, abuse a very useful and significant word by applying it indiscriminately to everything that happens to be contemporary.

POEMS

LANGSTON HUGHES

FROM SEPTEMBER 1925

angston Hughes' poem, *The Weary Blues*, was awarded the first prize in the contest for Negro writers recently instituted by *Opportunity*. The judges were John Farrar, Witter Bynner, James Weldon Johnson, and Clement Wood. In January 1926, Alfred A. Knopf will publish a book of his verse. . . . The work of this poet is informed with a sensitivity and a nostalgia, racial in origin, for beauty, color, and warmth. His subjects are extraordinarily diversified. A lyric simplicity marks his sea pieces; his cabaret verses dance to the rhythm of Negro jazz; now he mourns for the hurt of the black man; again he celebrates the splendor of the women of Mexico or the savage beauty of the [inhabitants] of the African coast.

Although still a very young man, Langston Hughes has crowded more adventure into his life than most of us will experience. Born February 1, 1902, in Joplin, Mo., he has lived in Mexico, Topeka, Kansas, Colorado Springs, Charlestown, Indiana, Lincoln, Illinois, Cleveland, Ohio, New York City, Staten Island, Pittsburgh, the West Coast of Africa, Holland, Paris, Desenzano, on Lago di Garda, Verona, Venice, and Genoa. His occupations have been as various as his peregrinations. He has acted as paper boy, hotel porter, soda-fountain boy, waiter, cook, errand boy at a florist's, sailor, farmhand, advertising solicitor, pantry-man in an oyster house, book agent, and even as a beach-comber!

— CARL VAN VECHTEN

CABARET (FROM "THE CRISIS")

Does a jazz-band ever sob?
They say a jazz-band's gay;
Yet, as the vulgar dancers whirled,
And the wan night wore away,
One said she heard the jazz-band sob—
When the little dawn was grey.

TO MIDNIGHT NAN AT LEROY'S

Strut and wiggle.
Shameless gal.
Wouldn't no good fellow
Be your pal?
Here dat music . . .
Jungle night.
Here dat music . . .
And the moon was white.
Sing your Blues song,
Pretty baby.
You want lovin'
And you don't mean maybe.
Strut and wiggle,
Shameless Nan,
Wouldn't no good fellow
Be your Man?

FANTASY IN PURPLE

Beat the drums of tragedy for me.
Beat the drums of tragedy and death,
And let the choir sing a stormy song
To drown the rattle of my dying breath.
Beat the drums of tragedy for me,
And let the white violins whir thin and slow,
But blow one blaring trumpet note of sun
To go with me to the darkness where I go.

SUICIDE'S NOTE

The calm,
Cool face of the river
Asked me for a kiss.

THE EDUCATION OF HARPO MARX

ALEXANDER WOOLLCOTT

FROM MARCH 1926

Nightly now in the performance of *The Cocoanuts* at the Lyric Theatre—a Broadway playhouse built years ago by Reginald DeKoven but given over this season to the jauntier tunes of Irving Berlin—there comes a moment when a mute and ineffably comic clown stops his antics, cuddles up in a pool of light to a great, golden harp and plays it with a caressing stroke that is all his own. Nightly the hilarious audience, of which you would have sworn that each member would rather die then and there than listen to anyone play anything pays him the tribute of an abrupt and breathless hush. Even the commuters forget all about that 11.25 for Mamaroneck and when his turn is done, the applause is an avalanche.

His name is Marx—either Adolph or Arthur according to the date of the record you consult. But this fascinating question is of purely academic interest. For he lost both names somewhere in the shuffle of the two-a-day. There he and his brothers were celebrated for many years before Broadway graciously discovered them, and, in its infuriatingly parochial way, proceeded to assume either that they had just gone on the stage or, more plausibly had been in confinement somewhere for a generation.

So now in the program of the Lyric, as well as in the croquet world (where he might be described as ambitious but no more than adequate) and also in the weekly shambles of the Thanatopsis Pleasure and Inside Straight Club [the regularly scheduled poker game organized by the members of the Algonquin Round Table], Arthur Marx is known only as Harpo.

With the patiently educated musicians who shudder at his technique, I have the greatest sympathy. It is, indeed, one of the more annoying phenomena of the American theatre that a man should become known from coast to coast by the name of an instrument which, properly speaking, he cannot play at all. Like Berlin, whose *Remember* he has been twanging sweetly every night, he is musically illiterate. Professors of the harp assure me with tears in their eyes that his heresies in fingering are so deplorable that it would be too late now even to begin teaching him a correct attack upon the inscrutable strings. Why, say the professors, this zany even tunes his harp in a fashion so preposterous that if a really good harpist should try to pluck a melody from his strings, the result would not only be painful. It would not even be recognizable. Smouldering at the recurrent statements that he cannot play the harp at all, Harpo appears at least to have fixed his own so that no one else can play it.

Early in life he suffered from similar disparagement of his musicianship. When he was a youngster living in a third avenue tenement, he was afflicted by the fact that whereas his older brother, Chicco, had been taught to play the piano expertly he himself could play only two tunes. These were *Love Me and the World is Mine* and *Waltz Me Around Again, Willie*, and whereas he played them with great spirit and no little feeling, listeners affected after a time to find his performances monotonous.

Fortunately, there was at that time a striking resemblance between these two of the brothers, so striking, in fact, that the mild, innocent Harpo had his hair pulled on several occasions by enraged women who explained later that they had mistaken him for the devastating Chicco. But the likeness had its conveniences as well. Whenever one of the nickelodeons with which the town was beginning to break out in a rash, would advertise for a pianist to tinkle pleasantly during the Biograph, Chicco would apply for the job, dazzle the management with his wealth of melodies and agree to go on duty that night at six. Not once did the guileless management detect the fraud when, at six, Harpo would come around and go to work. After a time when he *would* persist in accompanying the custard pie battles with *Love Me and the World is Mine* and would firmly attend the burning of a great factory in Peoria with *Waltz Me Around Again, Willie*, a puzzled manager used to always throw him out. But after all a week's pay is a week's pay.

His subsequent turning to the harp can be traced to the fact that there was one which stood always in the corner of their house when he was growing up. It had been his grandmother's in Germany. The grandfather who died in Chicago at the age of 101 was for many years a wandering magician journeying from one Hanoverian town to another in a wagon which was big enough not only for his bag of tricks but for his children, his wife and her harp.

When the old man and his tribe came to America, the daughter went to work in a lace factory but the memory of those barnstorming days in Germany clung to her and the notion that her family were show folks persisted even into the period when she was a mother of five boys, no one of which betrayed the slightest inclination to go on the stage. Her inner determination that they should do so whether they wanted to or not was only whetted by the triumphs of her brother who, not content with being known as the fastest pant presser south of Rivington Street, had forsaken trade for art and was doing well in vaudeville. The more ancient among the patrons of the two-a-day will remember the Manhattan Comedy Four of which he was a prankful member and many more will recall the insidious ditty entitled *Mr. Gallagher and Mr. Shean* with which this land was cursed a few years ago. Well, that Mr. Shean was the Marxes' Uncle Al.

When Mrs. Marx grimly made a vaudeville act out of her own struggling offspring, her instinct for the difficulties of the game called Pigs-in-Clover made her discreet enough to employ only two of the boys at first. There seemed to be no place for Harpo who led a dissipated existence as bellhop at the Hotel Seville, where his only connection with his seven arts lay in his not particularly remunerative contract to take Cissie Loftus's dog for an airing in Gramercy Park every day.

The thought of him left behind when the act should go on tour proved too much for the ample heart in the bosom of that combined mother and manager, Minnie Marx. At the last moment, she appeared dramatically on the steps of the Seville, flung him into a cab, rushed him to Coney Island where the act was booked for the week and fairly pushed him onto the stage. As there had been no preparation, he had nothing to do and, like the House of Peers throughout the war, he did it very well. It has been ten years since he has spoken a word on the stage (except one New Year's Eve when he grew garrulous and spoke two) and now there is no one who can say more with no words at all except a fellow named Chaplin. *He's* a good comedian, too.

The history of the Marx Brothers in the vaudeville halls of the South and the Middle West is an exhilarating chapter in the story of American vagabondage. For years they were billed as The Four Marx Brothers except on the rare occasions when they would be joined by an aunt or two. Then they would appear in the program as The Six Nightingales or The Five Tomtits as the case might be. I think Mrs. Marx's most magnificent gesture was her rising to the crisis presented to her when, after the war, Gummo Marx came out of the army determined not to go back on the stage at all. Without batting an eyelash, this great lady announced (with an exaggeration amounting almost to perjury) that her fifth and last was ready to take his place.

So her set is still unbroken in *The Cocoanuts* but eighteen years had to slip by before her dream came true. She had always dreamed that she should see "The Four Marx Brothers" picked out in lamps on the Broadway night. It was not until the Spring of 1924, however, that the workmen began to erect such a sign over the portals of the old Casino Theatre. For this occasion, Mrs. Marx felt that nothing short of a new gown would do, for she intended to sweep majestically to the proscenium box on the opening night. In anticipation, she was standing on a chair while the dressmaker fluttered about her when the chair failed basely at its not inconsiderable role and Mrs. Marx broke an ankle. Of course she attended the première just the same but it is admittedly difficult to be carried in majestically.

The next day the New York papers admitted the Marxes to the ranks of the elect and, while whole families were rent in twain by the great debate as to whether Groucho Marx was funnier than Harpo, the latter grew pensive and decided to begin taking harp lessons after all. He went to the most celebrated Maestro in the city, found that the lessons would be $10 for each half hour, decided he could make the Thanatopsis pay for them and started in. But the Maestro, having heard him play, swore there would be no way of his unlearning all the shockingly wrong things he knew about the harp.

"Why," said the Maestro, "there are one or two things you do I never saw any one even attempt before."

Indeed there was one trick of Harpo's with the strings that quite baffled him. Harpo showed how he did it. The Maestro practised for ten minutes and mastered it. Then there was another. Harpo showed him that one too. The Maestro used up another ten minutes.

"Well, well," said the professor, cheerily. "Your half hour's up. Gracious, how the time does fly!"

And Harpo, much impressed with the big man's art, paid his ten dollars and went his way. It was after he got to thinking about it next day that the course began to strike him as unpromising. So he never went back.

HELLO, BIG BOY

**An Inquiry into America's Progress During
One Hundred and Fifty Years
*(appearing in the magazine's special issue on
the country's sesquicentennial)***

SHERWOOD ANDERSON

FROM JULY 1926

Nations are like people. It takes a long, long time for one of them to grow up. Most people, I am sure, never get beyond about twelve years of age. No one gets very old or very wise. The great problem is to get intellectually and emotionally beyond twelve, well, just a bit beyond twelve.

Thank Heavens we in America have begun to hear less and less of the good old days, and of the spotless virtue and wisdom of the makers of America. In Abraham Lincoln's day you had to breathe softly when you spoke of "The Fathers". Certain men, being ambitious, managed to get up a row between the American colonies and Mother England. For a long time our historians had to be very careful in speaking of all that period. Such a sacred lot of men, doing such a sacred thing. Everyone noble and grand—doing noble, grand things—out-nobling all the rest of mankind. It makes your bones ache to think of it. Nowadays anyway we can be a bit more careless and human when we speak of the early days of the Big Boy, America. It is being done. First-rate histories are now being written about the whole affair.

* * *

We are finding out something of truth about the Adamses, the Jeffersons, the Madisons and the rest. I think we respect them none the less but they get a bit nearer our own level. That's a help. We are what we are and we aren't so bad. No need to twist the British Lion's tail any more. The Irish vote doesn't cut the figure it did. When you quit being afraid you can be more gentle, more human. America is far and away the strongest and richest nation in the world now. If we can learn to be gentle without being too patronizing we'll be O. K. A hundred and fifty years since we pulled that little party on King George—well, well. How the time passes. If we hadn't pulled it how many grand titles we might have had over here by now. Think of it—Sir Charles of Kalamazoo, Count Albany, Duke Schenectady, Viscount Reno, Lord Pittsburgh and Wheeling. It makes your mouth water to think of it. Thinking of it almost makes a royalist of a man. Do you know I have several friends who think there should be a royalist party in America. And it isn't a bad idea. I like a parade myself. If we only had a Pretender I believe I'd get in line. Well, we got started, running our own house and, of course, we had to go on. There was another little scrap with Mama England later but we were lucky to get out of that as well as we did. She came near slapping us good—that time. What we got out of it was the beginning of the reign of the people.

There was one Andrew Jackson who fought a battle in New Orleans after the war was all over and no battle needed—and won it too. It was about the only thing we did win, that time.

It made Jackson, made the common man politically conscious. When Jackson went in, the old Eastern and Southern crowd, who had been running things, were in a bad way.

It's rather dangerous business this talking all the time about what a wonderful fellow the common man is. He may believe it.

After the second war with England we got a trial of the common man in power. That ended in Lincoln. A lucky ending. No nation ever gets a poet in power more than once.

*   *   *

But I am not trying to write, even briefly, of the political history of America during these hundred and fifty years. I am trying to think where we have got in another way. After all being politically-minded may be but a sign of immaturity.

Such faith in politics and in politicians all during that long middle period of our history, after we had fought our way through to recognition as a nation. For a long time the State was to the average American, what God was to the man of the Middle Ages.

Pass laws and make men happy. Solve the problems of life by passing more laws. Ten thousand new laws by 1928. Onward and upward.

For a long time Americans thought the power of the state would work down into individual lives—remake individual lives—but that faith is being lost now. No one hangs on to it now but the Anti-Saloon League, the Watch and Ward Society and the K. K. K.

A big, fat, rich country, the land stretching away westward, on and on. Great rivers, forests, mines to be opened, railroads to be built, immigrants pouring in. Had England managed to hold on, this might have been an English country now. We do speak that language, after our own fashion. That is a confusing fact.

What a conglomeration of peoples from all over the old world, coming here, raising their sons and daughters here, speaking our American language, making songs in it, writing stories in it.

It must be confusing to the English mind. You still hear an occasional Englishman referring to us as one of the Lion's cubs. We aren't, of course, anything of the sort. In any American town or city nowadays, there are more descendants of any one of a dozen European nations than of England. After we kicked loose the young bloods of England began going out to their own colonies. Why not?

We got out of our row with England the chance for a trial at the making of something new in the world. Who wants another England this side of the water? That's been done once.

* * *

You see I'm only trying to sum things up after these hundred and fifty years in my own fashion, as a present day American man, a man glad he is an American.

Surely we don't deserve so much credit, being so rich and grand and all. We do deserve some credit for being so amusing and we are amusing. We have made of America a lively, amusing place in which to live. At least, they must give us credit for that.

It must have been a long time to wait here for something to begin, but it did begin—in my time too. I'm glad of that.

Sophistication began, civilization began.

From the point of view of the arts, and I am speaking here somewhat from that point of view, being one of that sort and being very American; from the point of view of the arts I say, we are beginning to get on a bit. There is evidence of it on all sides, in the buildings in our cities, in the cities themselves, in the rapidity and boldness of our development in all forms of expression.

As a nation we are still young. It has only been a hundred and fifty years. What's that? Well, we may still be wearing short pants, but we are walking down past the clothing stores on Main Street and looking at the spring styles in long pants almost every day now.

Such a job we tackled—whew!

The only reason we ever hung together as one nation was because the mechanical age came along at the same time we did. The machine is the only thing that made it possible for us to be one nation, spreading ourselves out over an entire continent. The very thing that made us stands in the way of our development as a civilized people.

The machine itself isn't a civilizer. As a people, for a time it looked as though we were going to be a nation of machine-worshippers, but I've a hunch we are going to escape that.

Civilization, sophistication, depends, I should say, upon the opportunity offered in a country for the development of individual expression of life, through work. The machine and the natural wealth of the country did away with much drudgery, but it tended also to destroy individuality. We had a lot of that at the beginning. In the early days, when the towns and cities were widely scattered, when it was a difficult slow job to get from one place to another, when the forests spread away on all sides, men lived in comparative isolation and were thrown back upon themselves. Those who were able to bear such a life at all became strong individuals. They were bold, half mystics, believing divinely in themselves and their own dogmas, thought out in lonely places, who infected other men with their dogmas because they were strong men.

Then the machine, the herding of men into towns and cities, the age of the factory. Men all began to dress alike, eat the same foods, read the same kind of newspapers and books. Minds began to be standardized as were the clothes men wore, the chairs they sat on, the houses they lived in, the streets they walked in.

For a long time here the only individualistic expression of life in the arts or in architecture were European fragments, accidentally overlooked in the swift march of the standardizing machine. There was the *Vieux Carré* in New Orleans, fragments of Spain on the West Coast, English and German fragments in New York City and in New England—leaking over into the Middle West.

The machines had promised America much and had delivered. All of American life is unbelievably more comfortable, more liveable, than it was in the days of our more rampant early Individualism.

And individual life here, being more comfortable, has also aesthetic values it did not have before the machine came. The crass, tobacco-chewing, cock-fighting, quarreling life led by the men of the middle period of American history is unknown now, except in a few isolated regions of the South, where the railroads, the automobiles, the radios and the aeroplanes have not yet done their work.

You get all of this standardization of the trappings of life—cheap comforts—and you pay for it. We are paying for it.

Democracy is itself, I am quite sure, but an expression of the notion of the standardization of life. The majority is right. It is the duty of the minority to conform. What an absurdity—really. We see the absurdity very clearly in the effect upon us all of the passing of our prohibition amendment—the State more and more losing its grip on men's imaginations, the State, as a controlling factor in lives, becoming constantly more and more ineffective.

Is this loosening of the grip of the State necessarily a destructive sign? I think not. To the men of the middle period of our hundred and fifty years it would have seemed terrible. It may be only a way of pulling the State in its proper position in our scheme of living. Putting it somewhere near where the French put it after their debauch of state worship. Surely, for citizen Anderson, the State should be a servant, not a master. It should clean and police the street in front of his house, arrest violent men who disturb or annoy him. The State should never be permitted to say what he shall eat and drink, what he shall think, what he shall say to his fellows.

My own central interest is in human life, getting all I can out of my own life and the lives about me—not in the growth of the power of the State. I believe that with the coming of civilization, comes also the international mind. I want more sophistication myself. I need it. I admire some primitive arts but I do not want to be a primitive. I believe also that I am a pretty typical American.

However, I am talking in the dark now, being pretty heavy and serious. You would never guess I was in *Vanity Fair.* Excuse me please. This is the first time I ever tried to talk about such a big thing as America. I am confused and a little puffed up. I feel like a President writing a State Paper and really cannot think politically. Besides, if I were a President, I would have a secretary to do all this. There was a man I met once. His name was Randolph Bourne and he had a perfect scheme of government, had all of the functions of government properly arranged in the scheme of living. I used to sit hearing him talk and his words were like music to me, but he is dead now and I cannot remember the details of his scheme.

I am just a man going about. Since I was a child I have seen that life was unfair to some men, more than fair to others. I'm a lucky man myself. All the Negroes tell me so. I've got the power of making passes. I cure warts. I have no idea that laws will change anything. Life is like that, has always been like that. There is a kind of natural compensation always at work.

What I conclude is that in America life is better now for the individual man than in another place in the world I know about. And that isn't due to any special virtue in us, as Americans, but to the fact that our country is so big and so rich.

We present day American men live in flush times and I'm glad we do. I consider myself lucky, being born when I was. In another three or four hundred years we may be as crowded and hard up here as men are in older lands.

By that time, I dare say, our tone as a nation will have become fixed. The French, the Germans, Italians, English, Spaniards, all of the older peoples of Europe, were once a mixed people as we are now, but none of them ever had such a grand garden to play in.

They became fixed as a type, as a people, because new peoples from the outside quit pouring in and because, gradually coming to know each other, living a long time together in one place, accepting themselves for what they were, they developed artists who gave expression to their lives.

As I have already gone so far as to suggest, a nation is at the beginning like a newborn child. If England was the mother of the Big Boy, America, she was, I fear, a woman of questionable virtue. No one knows for certain who the father was. It is what a woman gets for trying to live in so many houses.

The child got out of the mother's arms and tried to walk and talk for itself. For a long time it talked the mother's tongue, rather unchanged, thought the mother's thoughts.

The child had been left alone in a big place and was afraid. It is the frightened child who brags, blusters. That was the tone of American thought and of American art for a long time. Boasting of our own inferior efforts at national expression and secretly imitating the very people we pretended to scorn.

All of our early literary efforts, our painting, architecture, music was imitative. When I was a boy there used to hang, in almost every Middle Western house, framed pictures of Whittier, Longfellow, Holmes and Emerson. None of these men expressed anything distinctly American. They were not motivated by the life in which they lived.

Whitman came, a windy gusty sweet singer but his voice was not heard.

Followed Poe, such men as Bret Harte and Howells.

To the modern man there seems in all of these men a kind of death, they were like men living and working in a vacuum. O. Henry was in the same mood.

Twain broke away. He wrote *Huckleberry Finn*, but they caught him and suppressed him. Boston and Respectability put him to sleep.

What went on in writing went on in all of the arts. One might have thought that life in our own towns and cities meant nothing. It did not mean much.

The fear was on us still. We had the inferiority complex.

Fear of what England would think, of what Germany and France would think. The arts are for older peoples. Younger peoples should be seen and not heard. Not so very long ago that the most second-rate of English novelists, coming to our shores, was met down the bay by representatives of all the big metropolitan newspapers. "What do you think of us? What do you think of America?"

People everywhere reading what such men had to say as though it mattered. If we have been brutally patronized it is our own fault. We sure laid ourselves open.

We have begun getting a somewhat different feeling in America now. Of course we still bend the knee some but not as abjectly as we did. We are beginning to build our own cities, love our own towns, respect ourselves as artists and as a people. When I was a boy there used to be a saying, "when he dies every good American goes to Paris". Now he goes to New York and I don't blame him. It's a better town, more majestic, terrible and wonderful.

San Francisco is something, too, and New Orleans and Boston and Chicago.

What has helped more than anything else is the dying out of the old belief, held so strenuously by the so-called Fathers, and carrying on through all the middle period and until well after the Civil War, the belief that in America all the problems of mankind were to be solved, because this was a special, God-made country, inhabited only by men up to the special mission of showing mankind how to solve its problems.

You can't get over that belief until you have artists who spring up naturally in a country, who get their inspiration as story-tellers, painters, singers and builders, out of the life of their own country and out of the people directly about them.

Artists who look upon themselves as men with missions, are pests, but all real artists do serve some such purpose indirectly.

Believing in the life directly about them, these men begin to give it forth so that all may a little love and understand.

My notion is that things do not begin at the top and work down. Things work the other way. My own life begins in the house in which I live. It goes from that out into the street, begins a little to comprehend the life of the street, of many streets, of a town, of a city.

What nonsense for me to say I love my country, if I do not love my own house, my own street, my own town. If I am not interested in the life of the neighbour across the fence I am not interested in life at all. Living, emotionally and imaginatively in another place, in Europe or in some place far away, living in books or pictures primarily, I am nothing. When

I want to reform or change the life about me, because of some fancied superiority in myself, I am a pest and a bad citizen.

Personally I think that America is getting somewhere and has been getting somewhere in my time. I like it here. The Puritans, the reformers, are still with us, but they are on the defensive now.

We get on. Today, in America, no man does good work in the arts without it being recognized. The artist here may not be widely acclaimed but good work never was very quickly or widely acclaimed anywhere.

We get enough. Being Americans we are lucky dogs. It may not be any special merit in ourselves that we live in the most prosperous country in the world, in what is, perhaps, its most prosperous period, but I am not one who dislikes the good things of life because I do not deserve them. I rather like things better for not deserving them.

I may not deserve to be an American, in America, in 1926, after a hundred and fifty years, but I'm sure glad I am one.

A WESTERN REUNION

In Which a Pleasant House Party Is Disrupted by Some Marital Jealousies

GEOFFREY KERR

FROM AUGUST 1926

Palm Beach 21 January
Mrs Henry Dumm
51 East 51 Street New York

HOW ABOUT COMING DOWN FOR FEBRUARY AND
MARCH

Ethel Wrisk

* * *

New York 22 January
Mrs Arthur Wrisk
Champagne Villa Palm Beach

DARLING I DONT SEE HOW I CAN AS OUR HUSBANDS
ARENT SPEAKING TO EACH OTHER

Anne Dumm

* * *

Palm Beach 23 January
Mrs Henry Dumm
51 East 51 Street New York

ITS QUITE ALL RIGHT WITH ARTHUR WHAT ABOUT
HENRY

Ethel

* * *

New York 24 January
Mrs Arthur Wrisk
Champagne Villa Palm Beach

IS CHARLEY KNECKER STAYING WITH YOU

Anne

* * *

Palm Beach 25 January
Mrs Henry Dumm
51 East 51 Street New York

OF COURSE DARLING THATS THE INDUCEMENT

Ethel

*   *   *

New York 26 January
Mrs Arthur Wrisk
Champagne Villa Palm Beach

IN THAT CASE NO GOOD ASKING HENRY BUT I
WILL COME

Anne

*   *   *

Palm Beach 27 January
Mrs Henry Dumm
51 East 51 Street New York

HURRAH WHEN

Ethel

*   *   *

New York 28 January
Mrs Arthur Wrisk
Champagne Villa Palm Beach

HENRY GOES TO PITTSBURGH MONDAY FOR TWO
DAYS SHALL LEAVE TUESDAY

Anne

* * *

New York 1 February
Henry Dumm
William Penn Hotel Pittsburgh

LEAVING TOMORROW FOR TWO MONTHS HOLIDAY

Anne

* * *

Pittsburgh 2 February
Mrs Henry Dumm
51 East 51 Street New York

WHERE AND WHY

Henry

* * *

New York 2 February
Henry Dumm
William Penn Hotel Pittsburgh

YOULL HAVE TO GUESS

Anne

* * *

Pittsburgh 2 February
Mrs Henry Dumm
51 East 51 Street New York

I INSIST ON KNOWING

Henry

*   *   *

New York 2 February
Henry Dumm
William Penn Hotel Pittsburgh

I AM GOING TO THE GEORGE TOANS IN CHICAGO
BECAUSE I AM BORED

Anne

*   *   *

New York 2 February
Mrs Arthur Wrisk
Champagne Villa Palm Beach

STARTING NOW LOVE

Anne

*   *   *

New York 2 February
Mrs George Toan
105 Blair Avenue Chicago

ON MY WAY TO ETHEL WRISKS AT PALM BEACH FOR
TWO MONTHS FUN HAVE TOLD HENRY I AM STAYING
WITH YOU IS THAT ALL RIGHT AND WILL YOU
FORWARD THINGS

Anne Dumm

* * *

Chicago 3 February
Mrs Henry Dumm
51 East 51 Street New York

MR AND MRS TOAN LEFT MONDAY FOR EUROPE
Dawson

* * *

Pittsburgh 3 February
Mrs Henry Dumm
Care George Toan 105 Blair Ave Chicago

ARRIVING ELEVEN TOMORROW MORNING TO STOP
ALL THIS NONSENSE
Henry

* * *

New York 8 February
Mr John Knecker
816 Park Avenue New York

DO YOU KNOW WHERE YOUR SON CHARLEY IS
Henry Dumm

* * *

New York 8 February
Henry Dumm
51 East 51 Street New York

YES HE IS WITH THE WRISKS AT PALM BEACH
John Knecker

* * *

New York 9 February
Arthur Wrisk
Champagne Villa Palm Beach

IS ANNE STAYING WITH YOU

Henry Dumm

* * *

Palm Beach 9 February
Henry Dumm
51 East 51 Street New York

I THOUGHT WE WERENT SPEAKING

Arthur Wrisk

* * *

New York 10 February
Arthur Wrisk
Champagne Villa Palm Beach

I DID NOT SPEAK I WIRED KINDLY ANSWER

Henry Dumm

* * *

Palm Beach 10 February
Henry Dumm
51 East 51 Street New York

THAT IS A PURE TECHNICALITY I REFUSE TO ANSWER

Arthur Wrisk

* * *

New York 11 February
Mrs Henry Dumm
Care Arthur Wrisk Champagne Villa
Palm Beach

ARE YOU THERE

Henry

* * *

Palm Beach 12 February
Henry Dumm
51 East 51 Street New York

NO

Anne

* * *

New York 14 February
George Young
Everglades Club Palm Beach

IS ANNE STAYING WITH THE WRISKS

Henry Dumm

*   *   *

Palm Beach 15 February
Henry Dumm
51 East 51 Street New York

FRANKLY YES STILL MORE FRANKLY SOMEONE ELSE
IS TOO

George Young

*   *   *

New York 15 February
Mrs Henry Dumm
Care Arthur Wrisk Champagne Villa
Palm Beach

I FIND YOU ARE THERE PLEASE DONT STAY THERE

Henry

*   *   *

New York 17 February
Mrs Henry Dumm
Care Arthur Wrisk Champagne Villa
Palm Beach

DID YOU GET MY WIRE

Henry

*   *   *

Palm Beach 17 February
Henry Dumm
51 East 51 Street New York

YES

Anne

*   *   *

New York 17 February
Mrs Henry Dumm
Care Arthur Wrisk Champagne Villa
Palm Beach

ARE YOU COMING HOME

Henry

*   *   *

Palm Beach 18 February
Henry Dumm
51 East 51 Street New York

NO

Anne

*   *   *

New York 18 February
Mrs Henry Dumm
Care Arthur Wrisk Champagne Villa
Palm Beach

DISAPPROVE STRONGLY OF YOUR PRESENT VISIT
PLEASE TERMINATE IT IMMEDIATELY

Henry

*   *   *

New York 20 February
Mrs Henry Dumm
Care Arthur Wrisk Champagne Villa
Palm Beach

DISAPPROVE VERY STRONGLY OF YOUR HOST AT PALM
BEACH AND HIS OTHER GUEST WILL YOU PLEASE DO
WHAT I ASK AND COME HOME

Henry

*   *   *

New York 22 February
Mrs Henry Dumm
Care Arthur Wrisk Champagne Villa
Palm Beach

MY DISAPPROVAL IS EXTREME INSIST THAT YOU
RETURN AT ONCE

Henry

* * *

New York 24 February
Mrs Henry Dumm
Care Arthur Wrisk Champagne Villa
Palm Beach

VERY WELL THEN

Henry

* * *

New York 26 February
Arthur Freeman
Knickerbocker Club New York

WILL YOU DO ME A FAVOUR

Henry Dumm

* * *

New York 26 February
Henry Dumm
5l East 51 Street New York

PROBABLY NOT WHAT IS IT

Arthur Freeman

* * *

New York 27 February
Arthur Freeman
Knickerbocker Club New York

WILL YOU PLEASE WIRE ANNE AT THE WRISKS AT
PALM BEACH AND TELL HER I AM MISBEHAVING

Henry Dumm

* * *

New York 27 February
Henry Dumm
51 East 51 Street New York

WHY NOT TELL HER YOURSELF

Arthur Freeman

* * *

New York 28 February
Arthur Freeman
Knickerbocker Club New York

SHE WOULDNT BELIEVE ME

Henry Dumm

* * *

New York 28 February
Henry Dumm
51 East 51 Street New York

ALL RIGHT

Arthur Freeman

* * *

New York 28 February
Mrs Henry Dumm
Care Arthur Wrisk Champagne Villa
Palm Beach

SAW HENRY AT COLONY LAST NIGHT DINING WITH
PETITE BLONDE

Arthur Freeman

* * *

Palm Beach 1 March
Henry Dumm
51 East 51 Street New York

BEST WISHES

Anne

* * *

New York 1 March
Arthur Freeman
Knickerbocker Club New York

PLEASE MAKE IT STRONGER

Henry Dumm

* * *

New York 2 March
Mrs Henry Dumm
Care Arthur Wrisk Champagne Villa
Palm Beach

HENRY INVARIABLY AT COLONY WITH PETITE BLONDE

Arthur Freeman

* * *

Palm Beach 2 March
Henry Dumm
51 East 51 Street New York

CONGRATULATIONS

Anne

* * *

New York 3 March
Arthur Freeman
Knickerbocker Club New York

STRONGER

Henry Dumm

* * *

New York 3 March
Mrs Henry Dumm
Care Arthur Wrisk Champagne Villa
Palm Beach

BLONDE REPORTED TO BE IN RESIDENCE

Arthur Freeman

* * *

New York 3 March
Henry Dumm
51 East 51 Street New York

IVE DONE MY STRONGEST

Arthur Freeman

* * *

New York 7 March
Arthur Freeman
Knickerbocker Club New York

THANK YOU ANNE IS BACK

Henry Dumm

LIBERTY, EQUALITY, FRATERNITY:

Why Rights for Women Have Brought About the Decline of Some Notable Institutions

CLARENCE DARROW

FROM DECEMBER 1926

I am not one who objects to change, but there are some innovations that I resent. For instance, prohibition annoys me; not because I ever cared much for alcohol, but because prohibition has taken so much good feeling and colour out of life. Then there are the barber shops. I have always liked barber shops; true, in common with many others, I got the safety-razor habit years ago, and this kept me out of barber shops except on those rare occasions when I visited them to get my hair cut. I liked the red, white and blue stripes winding down the barber pole. Somehow they seemed to be a symbol of liberty, even after the reformers began to discredit and curtail freedom, and women began to be emancipated.

The barber and his shop have a history. And because the degeneration of the barber shop proves an important point, I shall tell what I know of their history. In the olden days the barber was the surgeon, and some of them to this day continue to let blood. The barber shop was not only the place to get a shave and haircut but it was likewise the social centre. In fact, historians tell us that in the Eighteenth Century in England the barber shop was the favourite resort for "idle persons", and in addition to its attraction as a focus for news, a lute, a viol, or some such musical instrument, was always kept for the entertainment of waiting customers.

The musical instruments had disappeared before I began to frequent the places, but the "idle fellows" were still there. These always seemed to have leisure and were found sprawling comfortably over the big chairs— never too busy to wait for a shave. They were good conversationalists and spoke without restraint, discussing in an easy and colourful way the topics of the times. They were well posted on race horses, chorus girls, prize fighters, elections and other interesting and manly topics. Their language was not always grammatical nor their stories chaste. The barber shop frequenter had a rich "lingo" of his own that seemed to fit the place. It vied with the Pullman smoker as a centre for the distribution of droll stories.

I was raised in a small town in the middle West where democracy was real and social intercourse was easy. On Saturday nights when the "hired men" came in from the country they gravitated to the barber shop. In those days conversation was still an art; the barber shop promoted and cultivated this art in its own way. Altogether it was an important social centre and was, in effect, a community club where neither initiation fees nor dues were demanded, and, best of all, it was for men only. Its precincts were never invaded by women, and so its votaries knew but few inhibitions.

Of course, in the early days the barber shop was not the only man's club. The automobile had not then driven out the horse, and the livery stable was a common *rendez-vous* for men on Saturday afternoon. Here, too, would foregather the good fellows of the town and country round. It was especially the headquarters for local statesmen. Amid flies and pungent odours political fortunes were made and lost, and the Constitution was defended against its foes.

And then there was the saloon of grateful memory. This, too, was an institution where men could gather by themselves. Under the influence of stimulants they grew sociable and even loquacious. Leaning over the bar with one foot resting on the brass rail, they discussed politics and religion, horses, and men and women, and argued and conversed and loved each other to their hearts' content.

On rare occasions the polls had much the same atmosphere. But after the advent of "Woman's Suffrage", with "lady" clerks and "lady" judges, the lounger disappeared from the precincts on election day and conversation grew restrained. The men stopped telling stories, they took off their hats to vote, and left their cigars and pipes outside the door. Voting became almost as solemn and silent as a religious rite. Men no longer went to the polls for social intercourse, to tell stories, to discuss their neighbours, the women and the candidates. The place was clean and shiny and uncomfortable and no man cared to linger. They came in solemnly, deposited their votes and went back to work.

Alas—the livery stable, the saloon and the polls lost their pristine charm. Men were driven from pillar to post and the barber shops alone remained as the last fortress for their vanishing fellowship and freedom. Women still wore long hair and long skirts, and there was no excuse for them to intrude themselves into this last sanctuary. For a time men made the best of what was left. The barber himself was an institution. He had long since forgotten that his ancestor was a surgeon and he never "put on airs". He was a master of conversation. He was always loquacious; he could discuss religion and politics and all the other questions of the day. His observations were not only enlightening and interesting but were likewise discreet. He always had views about debatable subjects but he never intruded them. While he slowly stropped his razor, made his lather, and soaped your face, he skillfully drew you out on these important subjects. He never expressed his opinion until he heard from you and he then, invariably, agreed with what you said. The barber never gave the impression that he was greedy for your money. He did everything with the leisure which marked the true gentleman. While you reclined restfully in his beautiful plush chair he generously lathered your face, then carefully washed it off, and covered it with hot and cold towels in turn. After the second or third shaving there were no end of lotions for your skin. He wound up his gentle ministrations by combing your hair in the most meticulous way, and let you go out happy and looking better than you had since the last visit, or would again until you came back for another shave.

During this performance he regaled you with stories of race horses, giving you fresh and private tips from "God knows where". Often, too, he led up discreetly to the information that he could place a bet on the races if you wished him to. No objectionable people ever came to the place. One never met a clergyman or a deacon there, or any person whom you had to "look out for", or who took away your comfort or your ease. For a brief hour the place was yours and you felt perfectly at home. Somehow the barber shop was the only place you visited where you never seemed in a hurry to get away. If you were not "next" it did not matter. There was literature, and colourful pictures on the wall. These pictures generally portrayed chorus girls, horses, dogs and sporting men, wearing red coats and riding on horse-back following the hounds. In the way of literature there was always the *Police Gazette* with its pictures of lovely actresses wearing tights, a novelty in those simple days. There were pictures, too, of thoroughbred dogs and race horses, together with stories telling their ages and pedigrees and their marvellous exploits. If literature and art failed to interest you, there were sociable and congenial fellows lounging in the chairs, and the formality of an introduction was never needed to make you friends. The barber shop made all men kin. In the middle of the floor was a battered brass cuspidor, shiny in spots, or a square box filled with sand or sawdust. In front of the barber chairs was a large mirror covered with fly-netting in the summer time. You could loll back and see the barber "come at" you with his sharp knife. You could watch your changing face and head slowly emerging under his magic touch until it became a thing of beauty, and almost made you a stranger to yourself. By the side of the mirror was a rack filled with shiny mugs. On these were blazoned the names of the wealthiest citizens of the place. The mugs were the special property of the men whose names they bore. They were supposed to be kept private for sanitary purposes. Still, since there were no special razors nor individual brushes, one gathered the impression that the private mugs were there because the leading citizens wanted to show off, or because the grocer, merchant or hardware man wished to keep in the public eye.

On account of my safety razor, and because I generally had my hair cut at one of the big hotels, I had quite forgotten the old time barber shop. I had, of course, realized that in many ways the world was changing; that new machinery and a modified social life were making their inroads everywhere. With all the rest I knew that the Nineteenth Amendment, bobbed hair and women's clubs were "ladyizing" the world. I had never realized that the barber shops, too, were suffering from the blighting touch of new ideas and social customs. I had never seen a woman in a barber shop, except now and then a "manicurist" who was sophisticated and unobtrusive, and not much in the way. These I had seen only in the big cities in the large hotels.

A visit to my old home town brought to me the revelation that nowhere was man any longer safe from the inroads of "refinement" and "civilization". I needed a shave and I went to the barber shop. Alas, it was not the old time barber that I knew and loved. His voice was modulated to a lower key. He was not talking. He was a solemn, quiet and respectful man. He did not even look like a barber. He looked and dressed like the secretary of the Y. M. C. A.—at least he looked as I have always fancied that these secretaries ought to look. He told me that I would have to wait a few minutes,—"would I kindly take a seat." He did not even tell me that I was "next". I looked around and lo—in one of the barber chairs was a young lady, and seated in another chair, waiting her turn, was a middle aged, kindly looking woman patiently reading the *Christian Science Monitor*.

I would have fled in dismay but I needed a shave. As I was obliged to wait, I looked for a *Police Gazette*—but to my utter amazement there was no *Police Gazette*. On the table was a *Woman's Home Companion*. My eyes sought for the familiar pictures on the wall. But gone were the dogs and horses and the red coated men. In place of the old time decoration was a solitary picture and, to my amazement and horror, where I once would have beheld a highly coloured lithograph, I saw Whistler's *Mother*. When I went into the shop I was smoking a cigarette. Automatically I took it from my mouth and prepared to flip it towards the cuspidor which should have been in the middle of the room; but there was no cuspidor, not even a box of sawdust or sand in its wonted place. In fact, there was no cuspidor anywhere in the shop. The floor was covered with a neat mat. It was spotless and antiseptic. Bewildered, I threw my cigarette out of the door and sat down to wait. I did not even try to read. I had no objection to the *Woman's Home Companion*—but I felt that its place was in the home and not in the barber shop. I looked for the old time rack of cups bearing the names of the *Who's Who* citizens, but it, too, had disappeared like a far-off dream. In its place was a cupboard, and as the barber opened the door I saw, to my dismay, powder lip-sticks, rouge and what not. The cupboard was barren of everything that belonged to a barber shop. Pensively I waited for my turn. The young lady was giving directions to the barber: "Cut the ends just a little bit at a time so we can tell when we strike the outline that I want. Don't go down too deep at the back of my head, where it's flat, you know."

"Yes, yes—I remember," answered the obliging young man; "you'd look good with a swell new wind-blown touzle."

In the mean time the lady who was observed reading the *Christian Science Monitor* had taken another barber chair which had been vacated by the occupant. She held fast her *Monitor* as she settled back in the seat. "This time you can trim me down to—well, on account of my years, let's call it a mannish, instead of a boyish bob." It seemed a pity to sheer off her lovely, becoming curls, but—"There," she exclaimed, "now no more fortunes will be spent by me for permanent waves."

The younger woman admired and patted the whisk-broom effect bristling over her ears, chummily asking, "Would you have a hot oil shampoo, if you were me, or would you wait until I have my next marcel?" The barber hesitated, thoughtfully, before replying, "Well—for your style of coiffure I'd advise only water-waves. We have just got in a Ritzie line of

water-wave comb-sets, in that big show case next to those 'Vanity Razors.'"
"Oh, razors remind me," confidingly whispered the pretty patron, "this is
the day—"

The door opened abruptly and a man and woman entered the shop. I
realized that again and again I must give my turn to "Ladies First"—that
no matter how long I waited I might never be "next"; that woman has
taken all the so-called advantages that man once had and yet clings fast to
her old time privileges as well. I realized that for some years past man has
been slowly losing his place as "next". In fact I doubt if he had ever been
really "next". This idea was probably only apparent,—a delusion like most
of life.

I waited no longer, but fled from the shop. As I went away I pondered
over the long steady invasion of women into what was once man's domain
and what this invasion means to both. Is not the so-called "Woman's
Awakening" taking the colour and freedom from the world? Is it not slowly
and surely destroying the illusion and the romance which lure the born
and the unborn alike in the prime venture of living?

SOME AMERICAN EXPATRIATES

FORD MADOX FORD

FROM APRIL 1927

Editor's Note:—Ford Madox Ford, collaborator and biographer of Joseph Conrad, nephew of Dante Gabriel Rossetti and grandson of Ford Madox Brown, attempts in this article to explain to America why so many of its votaries of the arts are voluntary expatriates. Mr. Ford, who has recently made his tenth visit to the United States, discusses, specifically, Ernest Hemingway, whose most recent novel, The Sun Also Rises, *has become a best-seller; George Antheil, the modernist composer who is now playing in concert in America; and Ezra Pound, the American champion of futurism in poetry. Mr. Ford analyzes these men as artists, as friends, and particularly as Parisian-Americans.*

Sir Henry Wotton, the inconveniently witty envoy of James I, incensed his royal master by stating that an ambassador was a man sent to lie abroad for the good of his country, and I am frequently reminded of his epigram when in this country I hear—as I constantly do—comments on those fortunates or unfortunates who go to Europe in order to live whilst they paint pictures, write books, compose music or do such other things as make Europe respect the United States. For Big Business may make the United States envied, or detested, or ignored, or avoided, by Europe in general and France in particular; respect it cannot earn. It is long since France discovered that a country's books are its best ambassadors.

But such Americans here as talk to me about the American artistic colony in Paris call them expatriates *coram publico* and have the air of secretly gloating over their supposed exploits with the bottle and other implements of bliss or of forgetfulness. I do not know that Mr. Ernest Hemingway's admirable novel *The Sun Also Rises* or the fame of the uproars that arise when Mr. George Antheil gives a public concert have not added to or confirmed these rumours of riotous lives led in the greyer and more mouldering streets of Paris. Now, as the gentleman says in *Major Barbara*, there is a great deal of tosh about this and the last gentleman who leeringly interrogated me as to the habits of American-Parisian expatriates was considerably drunker than I have ever seen any of his compatriots across the water. Mr. Hemingway's book is certainly finely alcoholic and irregular, but it is not a balanced record of life in Paris, any more than the newspaper records of crime in New York give a balanced impression of the quiet metropolitan existence that life in New York really is. And when Mr. Antheil gives a concert, representatives of the French, Polish, Russian, Hungarian, Czecho-Slovak and Lithuanian *jeunes*—but not too *jeunes*—attend and throw things, emit catcalls, wave their arms and demonstrate from the galleries of the concert hall. Then the music comes to a stop and Mr. Ezra Pound arises in his place and shouts "Dogs! *Canaille!* Unspeakable filth of the gutter!" and French enthusiasts for the music of Mr. Antheil exclaim with tired voices: *"Oh, Taisez-vous!"* and *"Laissez-nous écouter!"* and it is all very gay and revives the demonstrations that have always attended the births of new forms of Art in Paris . . . But that does not make Mr. Antheil a riotous figure.

On the contrary, during these demonstrations, he sits at his piano on the platform and patiently grins at the footlights, waiting to go on with the *Ballet Mécanique* or a Symphony. And Mr. Pound is a patriot, championing American music, a very Ajax; and the rest of the Colony in their best bibs and tuckers modestly applaud the fulminant chords with a well-drilled unanimity and so the cause of American art is advanced in the most art-loving city of the world.

I select a concert of Mr. Antheil's, rather than any other festivity of the American Latin Quarter, for adumbration because these are the most riotous social functions that I ever there attend, and because they pretty well attest my text of the moment—that there is a good deal of tosh about these Paris-American legends.

And if you think it out for yourself you will see that that must be the case. Mr. Hemingway writes extremely delicate prose—perhaps the most delicate prose that is today being written; Mr. Antheil composes music that, besides being very advanced, is of an extremely—I had almost written excruciatingly—learned nature. I know this because not only have I studied his scores with attention, but I have turned over for him whilst he played, so that I have seen and heard the exact relation of the sounding music to the written page. And Mr. Antheil's eccentricities are of the sort that is born of knowledge; he is carrying the old music of tradition a stage further, not merely making an irresponsible row on tin canisters.

Now it is an extremely difficult thing to write delicate prose, and perhaps almost more difficult to write scholarly music that is also advanced. You as lay reader may not believe this. There is a tendency amongst members of the public to think that, if they turned their attention to it, they could easily write books as good as those of—oh, whoever is your favourite author; and that with a little attention they could write music as complicatedly beautiful as the four- or eight-part fugues of Bach. But they could not. Try it and see.

Well, you cannot write delicate and beautiful words, still less can you compose advanced and very complicated music, in what is here, I believe, called a state of hang-over. It cannot be done. Try it and see. Art—any art by which you may become famous—is a tiresome and laborious affair; if it were not, famous painters, musicians and writers would grow on every blackberry bush. They do not. Then it is mere common sense to assume that the artist is not a candidate for *delirium tremens* or the other things that men fear. Of course there are gentlemen who take studios for purposes of debauchery—but it is done more often in New York than in Paris. There is more money in New York. And New York is much the more amusing city—for people who have such tastes. At any rate the South Side of Paris is less amusing than New York, for it is a place of hard work and precious little money. How it may be with Montmartre I do not know; the readers of this journal probably know better than I, for I have been there only twice in the last thirty years and then did not much like it.

The South Side—the Latin Quarter, I know very intimately and have known it all my life. I studied there as a boy and live there now. It is a region of professors, doctors, judges lawyers, students, some artists, some musicians, some writers and except for a notorious *carrefour* rendered disagreeable by foreign tourists of all nations, it is about as quiet as the British Museum. To that cross-roads the tourists of all nations go to make as near beasts of themselves as they dare, and other tourists of all nations who are less courageous go and play the rubberneck from cheap tourists' cars, their eyes sticking out of their heads, so attractive is "vice". But the resident American colony avoids these *parages*. It really does. So do I. One has to be at work at a decent hour of mornings.

But the queer thing is that a constant warfare wages between the American colony of the North Bank and that of the Quarter—or rather, the American Colony of the *Quartier de l'Etoile* is constantly making raids on the Americans of the *Quartier Montparnasse*. Why Americans cannot let each other alone I could never understand. I do not know that my own countrymen in Paris are especially gay or attractive or interesting, but at least they never try to uplift *me*. But the resident Americans of Commerce, Industry, Finance and the rest are never easy but when they are trying to improve the morals of their unfortunate artistic compatriots on the South of the Seine. A little time ago they were seriously proposing—the serious proposal appeared in the local Press—to go in bands and, either by persuasion or by appeals to the police *de bonnes mœurs,* to make the South Side of Paris a little, if not brighter, then better, than they found it.

There is no end to these activities. The other day I was applied to furnish a character for Mr. Antheil—not of course by Mr. Antheil himself, but by an American organization. Now I do not know Mr. Antheil, so very well as all that—but if there were anything against his morals I should know, for though Paris is not as much of a whispering gallery as New York, it can do its bit in that way too. So I replied in words to that effect, adding that whenever I had been in his company on social occasions his conversations and behaviour had been of the most impeccable and that his music was wholly admirable. (I may make the note that the other day in Chicago I heard M. Darius Milhaud speak complimentarily of Mr. Antheil's music, and if you know anything at all about French composers, you will know what *that* means.)

Now my "character" of Mr. Antheil was quite sufficient to secure for him the travelling scholarship or whatever it was that the American Organization desired to bestow on him. It was more than sufficient. But what happened? This: An ornament of sorts of the commercial resident American Colony, occupying some sort of minor official position, took it upon himself to write to that American Organization imploring them as they value the purity of America's daughters and the spotless folds of Old Glory—imploring them not to honour Mr. Antheil. And why?. . . . Because Mr. Antheil was a friend of Mr. Pound!. . . . Now I ask you!

As I have said, I do not know Mr. Antheil very well. But I meet him in drawing rooms where he would not be admitted if there were anything against him. That is enough for me and for any sensible human being. But Mr. Pound I know very well indeed—as well as it is possible for one man to know another. And I will vouch for it that no more sober, honest, industrious and wholly virtuous American is to be found on this, or the other side of the Atlantic. To know him is to know that—and to know him is an honour. That that minor American official does not know that, is due to the fact that Mr. Pound does not suffer fools gladly. That is perhaps a fault.

But I think the United States ought to do something to stop that sort of imbecility, which renders it ridiculous in foreign eyes. The American artistic colony of Paris—and, heaven knows, of New York too—do a great deal to dignify the United States in the eyes of the world. Let the testimony of myself, a foreigner, bear witness to that. Then the non-artistic part of the United States should at least let them alone. The reason why large numbers of American artists live in Europe is almost entirely economic. They are very badly paid; they can live in Paris for almost nothing. There is no conspiracy against the United States, or even against hundred per cent Americanism. They are hundred per centers all right. They make me tired with it most times. And that any obscure and ignorant minor official commercially occupied, should have the power to interfere with the destinies of an artist whom the rest of the world considers to adorn this country . . . well, it makes the whole of Paris and the Russians and Czecho-Slovakians and Lithuanians and Spaniards and the Ruthenians and the Wallachians and Armenians, cackle.

I don't know exactly what is to be done about it—except that Americans should read the poems of Mr. Pound and see that the works of Mr. Antheil are performed often and with applause. That is bound to come some day. It would be well if it came soon—for that would really be the New World redressing the balance of the Old.

BLAZING PUBLICITY

WALTER LIPPMANN

FROM SEPTEMBER 1927

The publicity machine will have become mechanically perfect when anyone anywhere can see and hear anything that is going on anywhere else in the world.

We are still a good long way from that goal, and the time has not yet come when the man in quest of privacy will have to wear insulated rubber clothing to protect himself against perfect visibility. That is something for posterity to worry about. It may even be that when men have lived for a few more generations in the modern apartment house they will have become so habituated to sharing their neighbors' joys, their neighbors' sorrows, their neighbors' jazz and the odours of their neighbors' cooking, that the race will no longer have any prejudices in favor of privacy. They may enjoy living in glass houses.

We can see this promised land, but we shall not enter it. Yet we have made great progress in a somewhat different direction. We can transmit sound over great distances. We can transmit photographs. We can make moving pictures. We can make moving pictures that talk. Tomorrow we shall have television. The day after tomorrow we shall have a combination of the radio telephone and television. These inventions combined with the facilities of the great news gathering organizations have created an engine of publicity such as the world has never known before. But this engine has an important peculiarity. It does not flood the world with light. On the contrary it is like the beam of a powerful lantern which plays somewhat capriciously upon the course of events, throwing now this and now that into brilliant relief, leaving the rest in comparative darkness. The really important experiments with the modern publicity machine have been made since the war. During the war itself the machinery was not yet sufficiently developed, and the censorship was too active, to allow more than a few trials of its possibilities. The war, therefore, was never reported to the people at home as we now understand reporting. The non-combatants never knew the war as they have since had an opportunity to know the precise behavior of Judd Gray when he testified in the Snyder case. The epoch-making events in the experimental stage of our modern publicity machine have been, if I remember correctly, the visit of the Prince of Wales, the death of Rudolph Valentino, the channel swimming of Gertrude Ederle *et al*, the amours of "Peaches" Browning, the Hall-Mills case, the Dempsey-Tunney fight, the Snyder case and the reception to Lindbergh. These events have really been *reported*, in the modern sense of the word.

No one can say we have not been neutral in our choice of the subjects on which we have cast the full brightness of the publicity machine. It is after all a mechanical device. It does not have and could not have an automatic governor to regulate its use according to accepted standards, or any standards, of good taste and good policy. The machine can no more be made so as to regulate itself in a civilized fashion than an automobile can be made which will refuse to run if there is a drunken driver at the wheel. Our publicity machine will illuminate whatever we point it at. If we point it at the "Peaches" Browning affair, it will ruthlessly and efficiently flood the consciousness of men with swinishness. Point it at Lindbergh and it will transfigure the mundane world with young beauty and unsullied faith.

The machine itself is without morals or taste of any kind, without prejudice or purpose, without conviction or ulterior motive. It is guided by men. More specifically it is guided by newspaper men. They are the watchers who scan the horizon constantly looking for the event which may become the next nine days' wonder. They set the special writers and the batteries of photographers hurrying to the scene of action. If their judgment has been good, that is to say if they have picked a sensation which the public finds fascinating, the lead is taken up by the auxiliary services, the moving picture people, the managers of the chains of broadcasting stations, and the Mayor's committee on the reception of distinguished visitors. In the providing of these sensations many are offered and few are chosen. The public interest works somewhat mysteriously, and those of us who serve it as scouts or otherwise have no very clear conception as to just what will go down and what won't. We know that the best sensations involve some mystery, as well as love and death, but in fact we work on intuitions and by trial and error. We know that sensations have to be timed properly for the public cannot concentrate on two sensations at the same time. It is no use trying to tell the public about the Mississippi flood when Ruth Snyder is on the witness stand. These excitements have to be taken in series with a certain interval of quiet during which public attention can relax and refresh itself for the next exertion. The opening of the Hall-Mills prosecution had to be delayed two weeks, I believe, until the front pages could be cleared of the clutter of news about a subway strike. Chamberlain and Levine, for example, flew too soon after Lindbergh, even if they had been as charming and had had fewer relatives, to arouse the interest which their exploit would otherwise have justified.

The search for subjects on which to employ the new publicity machine is conducted under highly competitive conditions. This is a matter of business. As a result of this competition we have seen the development of some weird devices for stimulating the interest of readers whose imaginations do not soar unaided. For the literate who cannot quite translate words into visual images there is now the synthetic photograph made by scissors, paste, and hired models. It tells a story, if not *the* story, almost without words. But above all there is the personal narrative which gives the illusion of intimacy and inwardness. This personal narrative is, of course, rarely written by the person involved: by the ladies who are still dripping wet from their channel swim, by the ladies waiting for the electric chair, by the flyers caught in a jam of kings and prime ministers. Even journalism is not produced under such conditions. And as for the recently published memoirs of Rudolph Valentino from the spirit world, even the most trusting smile as they read eagerly about his love-life there. The competition is fierce, and the rules are few. The go-getters of the publishing world set the pace.

But in those enterprises where they run foul of such critical public opinion as still exists they are usually aided and abetted by the law and its officers. The worst cases, the ones which have really aroused protest, are almost invariably based on court proceedings. It is here that we have all gone mad. On the theory that any act involving a public official may legitimately be published in a free country by a free press we have made the divorce courts and murder trials a privileged source of material for these sensations. The ordinary rules of libel and laws about decency do not prevail apparently where the pretense can be employed that only matters of record are being published. It is here, if anywhere, that some attempt is likely to be made to control the whole business.

The suit against Charlie Chaplin furnished a striking example of how abominable the thing can become. The unproved allegations of his wife's lawyers, having become a matter of record, could be published to the world without fear of punishment for the outrage, and without the possibility of adequate remedy to Mr. Chaplin himself. Fortunately in this instance friends of Mr. Chaplin in the responsible press rose in their wrath and mitigated the outrage. But that is exceptional. The whole proceedings in divorce cases are essentially private matters, certainly as to details, and if it is not possible to adopt some sort of self-denying ordinance against the exploitation of divorce cases, we may be driven to experiment with some law like the recent English law which forbids the publication of all the juicy scandal, and confines the report of a divorce case to the barest legally relevant facts.

In murder trials the thing has also gotten altogether out of hand. The

Snyder trial was conducted by Mr. Justice Scudder with extraordinary dignity inside the court room. Yet the trial was a scandal by every established standard of justice. No doubt the pair were as guilty as Satan. It was nevertheless a scandal to have the trial conducted to an accompaniment of comments by celebrities seated in the bleachers who took the case out of the hands of the judge and the jury, and rendered a daily verdict at so much per column on the precise guilt of the two defendants. Justice cannot be done if this is to be the normal atmosphere of great trials, and some day I believe a courageous judge will have us up before him for that contempt of court of which we are unquestionably guilty. Some judge will have to do this, I am afraid and hope, before the bench can restore that atmosphere of deliberation to which the most contemptible criminal is entitled.

The modern publicity machine will not be destroyed by such regulation as this. It will still have a world of excitements on which to work. There is no way of imagining where it will take us. We do not, for example, know how to imagine what the consequences will be of attempting to conduct popular government with an electorate which is subjected to a series of disconnected, but all in their moments absolutely absorbing, hullabaloos. There is no apparent logic in the series; once it is like a peep show with vast multitudes looking through the keyhole of the bedroom door; and then again it is like a religious festival with the multitudes worshipping sublime youth. We observe that through it all the important and prosaic affairs of mankind, government and diplomacy and education are rather completely ignored by the participating crowd. It would be idiotic to pass judgment on something about which we know so little. And yet one wonders, I at least with some anxiety, what would happen if some day the lights of this engine were suddenly set blazing upon our sectional and our sectarian irritations; or upon some great and delicate controversy with a foreign power. For once the machine is running in high, it evokes a kind of circular intoxication in which the excitement about the object of it all is made more furious by fresh excitement about the excitement itself.

The old adage of our salad days about the curative effects of publicity under popular government seems rather naive in this age of publicity.

The light we now throw on events can burn as well as heal, and somehow we shall have to learn to apply it gingerly. The question is whether we can. The perfecting of the machinery will not wait upon our acquiring the wisdom to use it. In all probability we shall only very slowly acquire the wisdom we need by trial and error in the use of the machine itself. The human mind is not prophetic enough to pursue the problem and solve it theoretically in advance. There is no use grumbling then about the character of some of our hullabaloos. They should be regarded frankly as experiments.

The philosophy which inspires the whole process is based on the theory, which is no doubt correct, that a great population under modern conditions is not held by sustained convictions and traditions, but that it wants and must have one thrill after another. Perhaps the appetite was always there. But the new publicity engine is peculiarly adapted to feeding it. We have yet to find out what will be the effect on morals and religion and popular government when the generation is in control, which has had its main public experiences in the intermittent blare of these sensations. There is something new in the world of which we can but dimly apprehend the meaning.

That it means the turning away of popular interest from a continuing interest in public affairs seems fairly clear. Whether one is to regard this as a good thing or a bad depends, I suppose, at least upon one's feeling about how desirable it is to have the people take a direct part in public affairs. I am inclined to ask myself whether in view of the technical complexity of almost all great public questions, it is really possible any longer for the mass of voters to form significant public opinions. The issues are not understandable to anyone who will not give extraordinary effort to studying them. The usual rhetoric of politics has in the meantime gone stale, and it cannot begin to compete in vividness and human interest with the big spectacles of murder, love, death, and triumphant adventure which the new publicity is organized to supply. The management of affairs tends, therefore, once again to rest in a governing class, a class which is not hereditary, which is without titles, but is none the less obeyed and followed.

A PRIMER OF BROADWAY SLANG

WALTER WINCHELL

FROM NOVEMBER 1927

Noah Webster, the big verb and adjective man, who is remembered for his famous corner on words, tossed off without a break in his lexical stride this definition of the word "Slang":

"Slang: To use abusive language, to use slang, an insulting word, a new word that has no just reason for being. Origin: Cant of thieves, gypsies, beggars, etc.; new language or words consisting either of new words or phrases, often of the vagrant or illiterate classes, or of ordinary words or phases in arbitrary senses, and having a conventional but vulgar or inelegant use; also the jargon of a particular calling or class of society; popular cant."

All of which any Broadway "peasant" might dismiss with: "Mebbe so, but it sounds like a lotta applesauce because that mug Webster certainly don't know his groceries." But Mr. Webster, it seems, knew his dictionary. Slang, briefly speaking, is verbal short hand, a language coined by various groups to crystallize in one word or phrase a frequently needed and complicated meaning. There is army slang, hobo slang, railroad slang, circus slang, stage slang, underworld slang and countless other kinds of argot, but the slang of the show business has, perhaps, more colour and certainly a wider currency than any other.

Probably because Broadway is where the theatrical business begins (and ends for most of its followers) it is the slang capitol of the world. It is difficult to imagine any other spot on the globe where the citizenry takes so readily to slang, and one suspects that the reason why the articulations of the show business are chiefly in slang, is that most actors were "born in a dressing room" or neglected their schooling to go on the stage. Consequently they are naturally more accomplished in the art of mimicry than they are in the three R's and even the youngsters whose parents are stars and can afford special tutors for them, are exposed to the idiom of the theatre long before they begin kindergarten.

It is not, therefore, unjust to assume that the majority of show people are no more than semi-literate. The terms in which they evaluate their fellow-men are sufficiently indicated in the line: "Look at that guy enjoying life. I'll bet he's so ignorant he can't even do a handstand!"

The average member of the show business (and one speaks quite naturally of all Broadway natives in the same breath) would rather perfect his "personality," his specialty, or his stage style than achieve an education. When he has developed a dance routine distinguished by some hair-raising steps or is able to arouse an audience to gratifying applause with his songs or stories it does not matter very much whether he can swap conversation with what he calls "highbrows". Hence his daily commerce is accomplished in the language he understands—slang.

He doesn't hope that he "makes good". He hopes that he "clicks". He trusts that he doesn't "flop" or "brody" meaning that he hopes he will not fail. And when he "wows 'em" or "panics 'em", he has been a "hit", and, when a person snubs him he doesn't call that snob "a high-hat" or "a ritzy person". He merely decides that he has been "up-stage". The greatest distance from the "apron" back to the rear wall is "up-stage" or as far away as you can get from the footlights. The word "up-stage" is commonly used today by all groups.

Perhaps, *Variety*, known as the Bible of the theatrical profession, is responsible for most of the show business slang. What it does not actually invent is eventually recorded by it. The staff of *Variety* consists of men who started their careers in the theatre either as ushers or players and one of them, Jack Conway, who also served the baseball team at first base, is conceded to be the ace "slanguage" hurler in the world. At least many authorities so report of him.

For the vaudeville branch of the show business *Variety* coined such famous colloquialisms as "Big Time" and "Small Time", differentiating the first rate circuits from the second rate. Several years ago the paper was ineffectually urged by the B. F. Keith Circuit to cease labelling the three-a-day houses "small-time", but *Variety* could not be persuaded to abandon its foundling.

To this day the B. F. Keith chain call the small-time "The Family Time" but the players still string along with the theatrical paper. Mr. Conway's adroit word-coining was the subject of a recent article in *The American Mercury*. Although Conway is now concerned with motion pictures in Hollywood, his contributions to slang still make up most of the current Broadway tongue. Among some of Conway's more famous expressions are: "Bimbo" (for a dumb girl); "They got belly laughs" (an act that aroused hearty abdominal laughter); "She has plenty of S. A." (a girl with a lot of sex-appeal); "That's a lotta boloney!" (I don't believe it); "It's a pushover" (a "cinch"; easy to accomplish); "High-Hat" (swell-head); "Arab" (A Jew); "Laugh That Off!" ("Put that in your pipe and smoke it"); "Peasants" (People); "Stems" and "Gambs" (legs); "Play the chill" (putting on airs); "Meet the Headache" (the wife).

There are numerous other Conway word claims. One—not too well known—was employed in a play last year by John V. A. Weaver. It was "she wears round heels". Conway declares that the expression was used to describe a woman who was easy to make a date with, but others contend that "a round-heeler" was applied to street-walkers many years ago. However, Conway's "That's the pay off!" is swiftly making the rounds. It is employed when one enthusiastically describes anything that is first-rate: the acme, the last word!

T. A. Dorgan (Tad), the eminent cartoonist, has contributed gracefully to "slanguage". In his newspaper cartoons he invariably offers a new one, but his most famous was "Yes, We Have No Bananas". Two obscure song-writers fashioned a comedy song around the expression and collected over $100,000 royalty on it. Tad never drew a penny or even recognition for inventing it. Another of his famous hits was "ball and chain" (for wife).

Nationally famous is "He's a great big butter and egg man". There are various versions of how that was coined. A New York columnist once requested a Broadwayite to furnish its origin and the Broadway lad told how Texas Guinan created it when a stranger in her café ordered drinks for the house and wouldn't give her his name when she asked him for it, so she might introduce him. To hear the veterans of Broadway argue it, Texas Guinan did nothing of the kind. The credit, "the howl," belongs to Harry Richman, also a café entertainer, who so described a big spender while officiating as master of ceremonies at the Shelbourne Hotel, Coney Island, five years ago.

The spender was "Uncle Sam" Balcom, who represents a butter and egg firm. His accounts include most of the New York cabarets and he returns some of the profits to the cafés by being liberal with his expense money. One night at the Shelbourne he was in an unusually generous mood. He ordered *champagne* for every one in the house. Richman broke the happy news in this fashion: "Folks, I have a treat for you. You're all going to drink *champagne* on a friend of mine. I can't think of his name off-hand, but he's a great big butter and egg man!" Cheers followed the announcement and some of the merry-makers gathered about Balcom, toasting him. From then on Mr. Balcom was known wherever he went as "That great big butter and egg man".

Later the phrase became a synonym for heavy spenders and rapidly circulated through the country. And most of the night club managements assert that its constant use in the newspapers to identify visitors to New York who spend money in cafés was chiefly responsible for last year's disastrous slump in Broadway night club patronage. These strangers, it seems, felt that they were being overcharged, and since they were merely out for a good time, they could not in justice be termed "suckers".

The slang expression "Hello, Sucker!" constantly used by Texas Guinan in her night club was first employed by a Denver newspaper publisher and circus owner who greeted everyone, friend or foe with "Hello, Sucker!" Wilson Mizner brought it East. Miss Guinan will confess that her abuse of both expressions was responsible for a marked decrease in night club business. The visitors began to resent her slapping them on the head with a clacker—a procedure invariably followed by the greeting "Hello, Sucker!" In the old days, a spender or "sucker" was "a John", but that phrase is *passé* now.

Perhaps, the slang word that attained the greatest international significance was "Jazz". Walter J. Kingsley, a press agent claims that he first exploited it, when he represented Reisenweber's, a onetime popular rendezvous near Columbus Circle, in New York. The "Paradise Room" at Reisenweber's, then conducted by Margaret Hawkesworth sought a new attraction. They sent for a traveling crew of musicians who featured a style of music, new to Broadway. Their try-out captivated Miss Hawkesworth and Mr. Kingsley.

"What sort of music is that?" queried the press agent. "What do you call it?"

"Oh, I dunno," responded the director, "we just jazz up the arrangement, plenty of clarinet and brass variations".

"Well, what do they call it in Chicago?" asked Kingsley.

"They calls it jazz, I guess. Some calls it jass and some spells it jasc."

"Well, sir," beamed Kingsley, "it will be Jazz here in New York" and he immediately wrote a display advertisement featuring JAZZ Music. He had to keep advertising the name for a while and it was some months before it caught on. Then it went into general use after an invasion of jazz outfits from Chicago and its adoption by Paul Whiteman.

Jazz comes from the idea that a score is jazzed into an arrangement that is jasbo—a slang expression used many years ago by minstrels who resorted to cheap stuff for laugh material. Jazz, in other words, is musical hokum entertainment. "Hokum", in case you haven't heard, is low-down stuff. Actors who redden their noses, and wear ill-fitting apparel, and take falls to get laughs, are "hokum comics" *a la* "skid" in Mr. Arthur Hopkins' successful play *Burlesque.*

The word "hoofer" is show business for dancer. Entertainers who "hoof" used to "hop the buck". When Bonnie Glass, the wife of Ben Ali Haggin, danced at the Palace Theatre in New York she was described on the billhoards as a "high-toned hoofer".

"And so's your old man!"

Maybe you've heard the alleged origin of that one. The legend is that one night the Duke of M—was being driven about London for air. After a long taxi ride he told the driver to pull up at the Bachelors' Club. "How much is the fare?" asked the Duke.

"I leave it to yer lordship," said the cabman.

"In that case here's a shilling," countered M—, who likes to pull a nifty now and then.

The veteran cabman weighed the shilling in his palm and asked:

"Are you a member of the Bachelors' Club?"

"Yes, for many years."

"So's your old man!" chirped the vindictive driver as he motored away.

That story was repeated by the Duke himself and swiftly made the London rounds and finally reached the stage. The comedian Arthur West, in England at the time, brought the yarn to America and employed it in a *Ziegfeld Follies.* The rest is history.

James Gleason, who won fame as a player in *Is Zat So?* which he wrote a season or so ago contributed to "slanguage". Damon Runyon, the sports writer, Johnny O'Connors, Rube Goldberg, the cartoonist, Wilson Mizner and hundreds of other "wisecrackers" on Broadway are credited with many of the famous bits of slang. Among the newer expressions is: "He's a phoney!" meaning "he isn't on the square or on the level", a fourflusher. "What's your racket?" meaning "What do you do for a living?". "To beef" or "squawk" is to complain. "Flicker" is a "movie"; "I've got the needles" is "My nerves are bad". "The Heebie-jeebies", ditto. "Take it on the lam" is making a quick getaway or hurried disappearance. "Flivver" which is a synonym for a Ford car was first used to describe a show that failed. "A turkey" is a third rate production. "Taking him for a ride" is underworld for enticing a person to death. A "rat" or a "heel" is a double-crosser or a worthless person. To be "burned up" is to be angry. A "flame" is a fellow's sweetheart. A "femme" is a girl. "He's gahgah" means "he's crazy over her". "Rolled off my knife" is being "hardboiled" or indifferent to trouble. "The run-around" is stalling or failing to keep a promise. "In your hat" is equivalent to "applesauce", "boloney", "hooey", or "banana oil".

When a fellow "carries the torch" it doesn't imply that he is "lit up" or drunk, but girl-less. His steady has quit him for another or he is lonesome for her. "Sing a torch song" is commonly used in Broadway late-places as a request for a ballad in commemoration of the lonesome state. Tommy Lyman is said to have created the slang and he announced one night: "My famous torch song: 'Come To Me, My Melancholy Baby'."

"That's hot!" or "She's hot!" describes a girl who has a great deal of personality, charm or "It". Elinor Glyn coined "It", now commonly known as Sex-Appeal. A New York newspaper, *The Morning Telegraph*, boasts in its columns that it is "The only newspaper in the world with 'IT'." Broadway is known as "The Main Stem". Abel Green, a theatrical reporter calls it "Mazda Lane" and others refer to Broadway as "The Incandescent District"; "Tungsten Territory", "The Big Artery", and "Coffee Pot Canyon".

To "crash the gate" is getting into a place without paying. "Paper" is a pass. "And How!" is an ejaculation. For instance: "Did you meet Her?" "Did I? And How! ! !"

There is a current gag fashioned after it: "What two Generals crossed the Delaware?" "I give up." "George Washington—and Howe!"

When a person is "all wet", he's a "flat tire", a "wash-out", a "dud", a "false-alarm"—meaning "He's not my type" or "no good". In the underworld a "V" is a five dollar bill, a "saw-buck" is a ten spot, a "yard" is one hundred dollars, "two-bits" is twenty-five cents, a "grand" is a thousand dollars. A "poker-face" or a "dead-pan" is a lifeless facial expression. "He has a good poker face" meaning that he can be holding four aces and you wouldn't suspect it. Eddie Sullivan, a sports writer, so called Helen Wills, the tennis champion, which appellation still clings to her because she seldom smiles.

When a patron in a night club is "clipped" he isn't punched, he's "taken" or "gypped" out of some currency or he is overcharged. "He got a fast count" means the same. To put on "the nosebag" is to eat. "Giving a guy the works" is handing someone a raw deal. "The sticks" are the small towns. "The Grouch bag" or "boodle bag" is the purse that actors wear pinned to the underclothing. To "die standing up" is to fail miserably. A "kibitzer" is some one who watches card players and offers suggestions. A speak-easy is a "whisper-low", a "hush-house" or a *sotto voce* parlor".

"On the cuff" is "on the house" or "free" . . . "Coasting" is a kibitzer who "mooches" meals and drinks on others until payday . . . "the ice" is jewelry . . . "Give me the ice" is "ritzed me" or "chilled me" or "hi-hatted me" (to be snubbed) . . . To "bump off" is to murder or otherwise to get rid of a person . . . "Coffee and cake money" is small salary . . . A "bozo" is a bum . . . "Ankling" is walking . . . A "nance" is an effeminate man . . . A kootch or hootchie kootchie dancer is a "torso tosser", a "thigh grinder" or a "hip-flipper" . . . "to milk an audience" is to overdo anything . . . "the top shelf" is the gallery . . . "Ace-deuce" is "nothing better" . . . to "hold up the exits" is to stop the show . . . an act that is "full of larceny" is an act that has stolen its material from many others and people who infringe on others' style or material, are not plagiarists, but "echoes".

Most of the argot that Broadway invents is relished and rolled on the tips of "Main Drag" tongues, but little of it is comprehensive west of the Hudson River, or north of Harlem.

Some wiseacre once said that a nation without its slang is in the period of decadence. The glory of Greece and the heights of the Roman civilization never left slang to posterity. Perhaps if they had, Caesar's *Commentaries* might not be so difficult to swallow. If the greatest Roman of them all ever said that Cleopatra had "a mess of S. A.", history carries no record of it. But hundreds of years later Will Shakespeare dug up the whole affair and was panned by the critics because he delved into the argot of his day to put it over.

And today, Shakespeare's slang is the classic of literature. So it may be with Broadwayese.

RUSSIA: THE GREAT EXPERIMENT

THEODORE DREISER

FROM JUNE 1928

*Editor's Note: In this paper Theodore Dreiser, the greatly cele-
brated American novelist whose conscientious industry and acu-
men in observing and judging nations and men have been
sufficiently established, presents a picture, several conclusions
and an opinion of present-day Russia, whence he has lately
returned. The mammoth, almost impudent, attempt of the Soviet to abolish all distinctions of class, private property, economic ambition and everything associated with them, in the
face of all history and established institutions, is the magnificent theme of Mr. Dreiser's article. Famous as an observer of life,
his name stands behind his reporting of facts, but* Vanity
Fair *must emphasize the fact that the opinions expressed in the
article are not its own, but Mr. Dreiser's.*

Vladimir Lenin, [who died in 1924, was] the greatest of all modern leaders, I think. . . . The New Economic Policy [of 1921] as introduced by Lenin was not a retreat in the face of victorious capitalism, but rather the real beginning of the economic struggle against it. A new weapon for a new aim.

This new weapon has now been in action for almost seven years, and its results can already be judged to a certain extent. In these seven years Russia's shattered economic system, as I found in my [recent] tour, has been rebuilt until today *the pre-war level of production has been reached and passed.* (Data in support of this fact is furnished in volume by the current heads of all departments in Russia and is rather easily substantiated.) At any rate, with change a new period opened up for the Russian government, the period termed by them the period of the building up of socialism.

And now comes the difference between Russian industry as it existed before the war and as it exists today. Large-scale industry, the immense electrical schemes, the harnessing of Russia's immense water power, etc., are to the extent of almost ninety percent State undertakings. Foreign commerce is to the extent of a hundred percent under the control of the State through the State monopoly of foreign commerce. Transport is almost completely, if not completely, under the control of the State and the Co-operatives. In the commercial world alone, (and that to an ever-lessening degree), does that economic thing known to us as private initiative play any rôle, and even here it is a subordinate one. Something like seventy percent of all commerce, both wholesale and retail, is now in the hands of the State and co-operative organizations. The influence of the business man (the NEPman, as he is called in Russia), is limited almost exclusively to commerce, and he is strongest in retail trade. But even here, as anyone can see for himself in Russia, the course of development is gradually eliminating him. The private shops are the poorest of all. Those of the state and of the Co-operatives (unions of buyers) are the best. *It is the aim of the State organizations and above all of the cooperatives, to eliminate the private trader entirely, not with administrative measures, i.e., not at the point of the bayonet, but by producing better goods at a cheaper price.*

The figures in all branches of industry and commerce for recent years show that the share of the State and co-operative organizations in the economic system of the country is steadily increasing, both relatively and absolutely, both with regard to turnover as well as invested capital. The last stronghold of the NEPman is, of course, in the villages. Here the land is officially the property of the State loaned out to the peasantry for usage. There are three types of peasantry—the well-to-do (for Russia), known as the Kulaks, the middle-scale peasantry and the poor peasantry and direct land-workers. *It is the alliance of the factory workers and soldiers with these two latter categories, i.e., the middle-scale peasantry and the poor peasantry and land-workers, which forms the basis for the present government in Russia.* The break-up of this alliance would make it impossible for any purely proletarian government to maintain itself with only the support of the workers. The policy of the government in Russia is now, therefore, directed towards maintaining this alliance by sharing the achievements of the development of industry and agriculture between the workers and peasants and reducing the distance between the two classes of those who work, and by making the peasant a participant as well as the worker in the building up of socialism. This latter is achieved by the growth of the co-operative idea amongst the peasantry, by the rational re-distribution of the land, by the establishment of direct connection between the workers in the towns and the peasants on the land through so-called adoptions, etc., i.e., the workers of one factory or one industrial district adopt a special agricultural district, collect money to buy tractors and farm implements for this district, distribute literature, make special journeys at the week-end, as far as this latter is practically possible, etc., etc. Thus, the peasants observe their share in the advance of industry in the ever-increasing number of tractors and modern agricultural machinery making their way into the country, also in the coming of the radio, telephone, electric light, phonograph, bus, street car, rural free delivery, etc., etc.

Take the manifesto issued by the Central Executive Committee of the Soviet Union, i.e., the supreme governing organ of the country, in connection with the tenth anniversary of the 1917 revolution, which was celebrated while I was there. This manifesto promised the workers the introduction of the seven hour day, and instructed the executive organs to commence with the gradual carrying out of this decision within the space of one year. This decrease of working hours is not to be accompanied by any reduction of wages. A further concession to the workers was the sum of fifty million roubles for the building of workers' dwellings, in addition to an equal sum already set aside for this purpose in the State Budget for 1927–28. Today, the peasants, in practice, receive still greater immediate benefits. Before the manifesto referred to, twenty-five percent of the peasants were totally freed from the necessity of paying the single agricultural tax. Yet that manifesto ordered that a further ten percent be also freed; that is, that thirty-five percent of the peasantry from now on be further freed from the necessity of paying the agricultural tax. Further, the manifesto freed the peasants from the necessity of repaying the loans received as a credit from the State in connection with the bad harvest of the year 1924–25. The poor peasantry were declared freed from paying their outstanding taxes, and the middle-scale peasants were furnished favourable conditions for repayment of what they used. More, the State also agreed in this manifesto to take over the complete costs for supplying the poor and middle-scale peasants with land, and a further sum of ten million roubles was laid aside for this purpose. A scheme for old-age pensions for poor peasants was promised and is to be put through. Incidentally, the death sentence for all crimes with the exception of crimes against the State, military crimes and armed banditry, was abolished, and the sentences of all prisoners with the exception of those sentenced for any of the above crimes, plus that of malicious defalcation, were to be reduced.

From this manifesto, issued when I was in Moscow, one can see, I think, that the peasant class is neither downtrodden nor exploited. My subsequent travels confirmed me in this. If anything, my general impression was that the Central Government was trying to do more than the industries and the labour of the people would warrant at this time.

But now as to the people who actually rule Russia. The actual mechanism of the soviets I need not go into. It is rather well known by now, I think. Sufficient to say that the main principle of the franchise in Russia is votes for all those who are working for the aim of the government, i.e., the building up of socialism, and none for those who are not, such as NEPmen working for their own personal profit. In other words, modern Russia presents us with a class State almost in pure culture, a class State where one class openly dominates, if you will, in contradistinction to other States where the dominance of a class is concealed by the normal methods of democratic liberalism. The men who are the leaders of the State are poor. When they die, as all men must, they leave no estate behind them. This is a most tremendous fact for an outside observer. Whatever one may think of the present-day rulers of Russia, one cannot deny their honesty and, as measured by all our tests, their selflessness with regard to the good things of this world. During the latter part of his life, Lenin, in my opinion the greatest personality of our generation, lived with his wife and sister in two small rooms in the Kremlin. With the exception of that last part of his life when he lived as a reconvalescent at Gorki. The rooms of Lenin in the Kremlin have been maintained intact, with everything in them, as far as I know. They offer perhaps a classical example of the simplicity and frugality of the present-day rulers of Russia. Lenin, however, was not alone in this. Most of the leaders live in simple hotel rooms or in single rooms in the Kremlin, and the actual wage of all officials and leaders from Stalin down is 225 roubles a month—about $112. There is no question of personal accumulation of wealth. There can be none, save by graft and outside hoarding, and the men I met did not look like grafters. As a matter of fact, compared with our political leaders and those of some other countries that I have chanced to meet in my time, I rank them as high as any—more earnest, more thoughtful and sincere, more capable of thinking—and that is the highest compliment I can pay them.

There is then, of course, the problem of the Party. The Communist Party is openly the yeast of the revolution, or, as Lenin termed it, the locomotive of the revolution. Through this Party and its nation-wide organization, the hegemony of the working class is maintained, the soviets influenced, (controlled if you like), but once again, not at the point of the bayonet but by organized work among the masses, the communist agents or workers winning the confidence of the latter and acting as their leader. In every working class of peasant organization there is a communist fraction with its members and officials and leaders who definitely and openly work in an organized fashion to guide the policy of the whole organization. So it is in the soviets themselves and in the soviet congresses which finally elect the government of the country. The Party, of course, has a monopoly and it tolerates no other party at its side. Hence the recent ousting of Trotzky and his followers who wished to organize a second or rival party and so wrest the power from the present group. The regime which now exists in Russia is a dictatorship, openly, a dictatorship of the proletariat, as it is termed. No oppositional parties are tolerated, no bourgeois press and no bourgeois organizations. This dictatorship is a weapon for a particular end—the bringing of that classless, brother-loving society in which no dictatorship will be needed.

And now, as to the final aim of all this, the establishment of the classless society, the abolition of the dictatorship and the State. The aim of this workers' dictatorship is not to perpetuate the working class as we understand it today, indefinitely. The aim is to abolish it. This class is the first class in history that set out to abolish itself. It intends to do this by abolishing all classes. That is its future aim.

As to the result or end, we have the privilege of watching this huge experiment. For that is what it is. Personally, I am dubious of the result because I cannot even conceive of a classless society any more than I can conceive of life without variations and distinctions. It is these same which give us our sense or illusion of reality and without these no reality. As a matter of fact in the Russia of 1928 with private property practically abolished there are as many classes—or almost as many—as ever. The Communists say not. And in their schools they teach the children that the day of a Classless society, brotherly love, all for one and one for all is at hand. But step forth into the streets, the offices, the factories, the stores, universities—what or where you will and see. Is the ditch-digger any less a ditch-digger or any less unimportant for being one in Communist Russia than would elsewhere be the case? Never believe it. Nor the beggar or the servant either. All appear to function as before—not oppressed of course—better taken care of than elsewhere in the world may be, but still ditch-diggers, servants, beggars and looked upon as such by all the superior intellects. Whereas the Communist official, with his assistants, his official car or cars, his offices and authority is as much if no more a bigwig than he was before the revolution. Certainly he is as much kowtowed to and respected as any other official in any other part of the world. I could not see any difference in his state here from elsewhere.

Similarly the learned doctor or professor is still the learned doctor or professor looked upon as such—and as superior mentally and by training to one who lacks the capacity for such a development. Similarly the manager or director of a great store or factory or hotel—or the chemist or physicist or scientist of any of the important institutions or universities of Russia. All are looked up to as being above the common worker or servant and so they will continue to be, I fear. On the contrary the working man or servant or beggar, except for the security of life, shelter and food which the new system affords them are still workers, servants, beggars, and the Communistic system does not seem to help them much. True, with native ability they can rise—but what laborer or servant or beggar anywhere today cannot do as much. But the class sense remains. I am a doctor, you are a beggar, and as such we can scarcely mingle on equal terms, can we? And communism cannot remedy that, I fear, any more than it can make a brilliant brain associate with a dull one.

On the other hand one result of all this effort has been to shake up the whole country, to generate such tremendous stores of energy in a whole people that the whole world is talking about and looking towards Russia. And much in the way of improvement is certain to come of it. Communism may not work, but if it does not some form of democracy or improved dictatorship on the part of such people as wish to better things will. Under the circumstances I am not inclined to complain but applaud. What is more I would like to see Russia as it is now, recognized and aided financially in order that this great impetus to something better may be strengthened. For here is a thinking people. And out of Russia, as out of no other country today, I feel is destined to come great things mentally as well as practically, or such is my faith at least. And with such a possibility in so troubled and needful a world as ours it is only common sense to aid it to do the best it can.

DO WOMEN CHANGE?

D. H. LAWRENCE

FROM APRIL 1929

They tell of all the things that are going to happen in the future—babies bred in bottles, all the love-nonsense cut out, women indistinguishable from men. But it seems to me bosh. We like to imagine we are something very new on the face of the earth. But don't we flatter ourselves? Motor-cars and aeroplanes are something novel, if not something new—one could draw a distinction. But the people in them are merely people, and not many steps up, if any, from the people who went in litters or palanquins or chariots, or who walked on foot from Egypt to Jordan, in the days of Moses. Humanity seems to have an infinite capacity for remaining the same—that is, human.

Of course there are all kinds of ways of being human; but I expect almost every possible kind is alive and kicking today. There are little Cleopatras and Zenobias and Semiramises and Judiths and Ruths and even Mother Eves, today, just as there were in all the endless yesterdays. Circumstances make them little Cleopatras and little Semiramises instead of big ones, because our age goes in for quantity regardless of quality. But sophisticated people are sophisticated people, no matter whether it is Egypt or Atlantis. And sophisticated people are pretty well all alike. All that varies is the proportion of "modern" people to all the other unmodern sorts, the sophisticated to the unsophisticated. And today there is a huge majority of sophisticated people. And they are probably very little different from all the other sophisticated people of all the other civilizations, since man was man.

A nd women are just part of the human show. They aren't something apart. They aren't something new on the face of the earth, like the loganberry or artificial silk. Women are as sophisticated as men, anyhow, and they were never anything but women, and they are nothing but women today, whatever they may think of themselves. They say the modern woman is a new type. But is she? I expect, in fact I am sure, there have been lots of women like ours in the past, and if you'd been married to one of them, you wouldn't have found her different from your present wife. Women are women. They only have phases. In Rome, in Syracuse, in Athens, in Thebes, more than two or three thousand years ago, there was the bob-haired, painted, perfumed Miss and Mrs. of today and she inspired almost exactly the feelings that our painted and perfumed Misses and Mrses. inspire in our men.

I saw a joke recently in a "modern" German weekly—a modern young man and a modern young woman were leaning on a hotel balcony at night, overlooking the sea:

HE: "See the stars sinking down over the dark, restless ocean!"

SHE: "Never mind that nonsense! My room-number is 32!—"

That is supposed to be very modern: the very modern woman. But I believe women in Capri under Tiberius said "Never mind that nonsense!" to their Roman and Campanian lovers, in just the same way. And women in Alexandria in Cleopatra's time. Certain phases of history are "modern". As the wheel of history goes round women become "modern", then they become unmodern again. The Roman women of the late Empire were most decidedly "modern"—so were the women of Ptolemaic Egypt. True modern never-mind-that-nonsense women. Only the hotels were run differently.

Modernity or modernism isn't something we've just invented. It's something that comes at the end of civilizations. Just as leaves in autumn are yellow, so the women at the end of every known civilization—Roman, Greek, Egyptian, etc.—have been modern. They were smart, they were chic, they said "never mind that nonsense", and they did pretty much as they pleased.

And then, after all, how deep does modernness go? Even in a woman? You give her a run for her money: and if you don't give it to her, she takes it. The sign of modernness in a woman is that she says: "Oh, never mind that nonsense, boy!"—So the boy never-minds it—never-minds the stars and ocean stuff.—"My room-number is 32!"—Come to the point!

But the point, when you come to it, is a very bare little place, a very meagre little affair. It's not much better than a full-stop. So the modern girl comes to the point brutally and repeatedly, to find that her life is a series of full-stops, then a mere series of dots. Never mind that nonsense, boy! . . . . . Then she comes to being tired of dots, and of the plain point she's come to. The point is all too plain and too obvious.

And so the game begins again. Having never-minded it, and brought it down to brass tacks, you find brass tacks are the last thing you want to lie on.

No, women don't change. They only go through a rather regular series of phases. They are first the slave: then the obedient helpmeet: then the respected spouse: then the noble matron: then the splendid woman and citizen: then the independent female: then the modern never-mind-it girl. And when her edict has been obeyed, the mills of God grind on, and, having nothing else to grind, they grind the never-mind-it girl down, down, down—back to—we don't know exactly where—but probably to the slave once more, and the whole cycle starts afresh, on and on, till, in the course of a thousand years or two, we come once more to the "modern" never-mind-it girl.

And the modern never-mind-it girl of today has just come to the point where the fun leaves off. Why? For the simple reason that the modern boy *doesn't* mind it. When men and women start cutting all the nonsense out of one another, there's pretty soon nothing left. There is certainly very little left of the love business. So that when the boy begins leaving out all the stars and ocean nonsense, he begins leaving out the girl too. As the process continues, and he leaves out the moonlight and the solitude and even the occasional bouquet of flowers, the girl dwindles and dwindles in his feelings, till at last she does become a mere point in his Consciousness, next to nothing. And not until she is a blank, blank, blanketty nothing to him, emotionally (except perhaps a residual irritant) does she wake up and realize that it has happened. In urging him to cut out all the nonsense she has cut herself out, completely. For in some strange way, she herself was the very nonsense she was so anxious to eliminate. When a woman gets into a critical mood, all a man's feelings about her will seem to her nonsense, sickening nonsense. She amputates herself from the boy's consciousness, and then stares at the blank where she ought to be. She stares at it helpless and paralysed, and has not the faintest idea what to do about it. She has reached the point where she is nothing, blank nothing to the man. The eliminating process has been so complete. And then, she begins to be nothing to herself.

For the bitter truth of a woman is that if she is nothing, or as good as nothing, to any man, she soon becomes nothing to herself. She becomes nothing to herself, and turns into one of these bitter women who assert themselves all the time, with a hammering self-assertion because they are nothing; or she hitches on to a job, and hopes to justify her existence in work, or in a cause; or she repents, not in sack-cloth and ashes, but in the prettiest frock she can find, and sets out once more in the hope that some boy will feel a bit of nonsense about her. And this time, she is not going to cut out all the nonsense. She is pining now to be treated to a little stars and ocean stuff, to be mixed up with the moon, and given a bouquet of flowers.

For after all, there is a difference between sentiment and sentimentality. And if the boy is sufficiently moved by the presence of the girl really to feel an emotion at the sight of the stars sinking over the ocean, that's one to the girl. It's a piece of flattery. A woman has a hold over a man, in the long run, not by her power of brutally and pointedly coming to the point and cutting all the rest out, but by her power of calling up in him all kinds of emotions which to her are perhaps irrelevant and nonsensical—have nothing to do with *her*—but which in the boy are just the natural reaction to the presence of the woman who really touches him. The more associations a woman can evoke in a man—associations with stars, ocean, moon, violets, humanity, the future, and so on—the stronger is her hold.

But women are not fools for very long. They soon learn their lesson, and the moment they have learnt their lesson, they change. The girl who was so smart cutting out all the nonsense of stars and ocean, in the boy, will change like a shot, and be considerably more humble about stars and ocean, once she realizes that she has reduced herself to a nonentity. And the moment she realizes it, she will begin the cycle all over again.

IF YOU ARE GOING TO ANTIBES

ALEXANDER WOOLLCOTT

FROM JULY 1929

They tell me there is a woman living in a small frame house in a Montana village who has expressed no intention whatever of going to Antibes this summer. I have heard no explanation of this bizarre uniqueness of hers, have received, as yet, no details to account for what does seem at first blush a somewhat too studied effort to be conspicuous. Perhaps she has a morose aversion to human society. Then again she may be merely destitute. Or, haply, bedridden.

The tendency of the aforesaid human society to gather each summer in a kind of hilarious, moist and irresponsible congestion at that once obscure point on the Riviera is a quite recent deflection in the drift of peoples over the face of the earth. Of course the Azure Coast has long been a favourite picnic ground for the idle. For generations the Russian gentry would leave their cherry orchards to shift for themselves and hide on the Riviera from the unkindness of the Muscovite winters. Even now, the Blue Train from Paris discharges their grandchildren onto the station platform at Nice, but, in the whirligig of time, these come to go on as extras in one of Master Ingram's movies.

Then, in his day, the foxy grandpa of the present Prince of Wales so relished this eternal playground that his memory still haunts the Esterel, and a singularly depressing statue of him adds just the needed note of ugliness to the pleasing prospect at Cannes. But these, mind you, were always winter visitors. Indeed, the momentum of the tradition that the Riviera is peculiarly a Winter resort is still so strong that not until December does Monaco really bestir itself, flinging wide the doors of the opera house, stripping the shrouding dust-cloths from the tables in the Sporting club, and extracting a little something from the till at the Casino to subvene the Imperial Russian Ballet, which is now, alas, neither imperial, Russian, nor (according to its sterner critics) a ballet.

But two or three years ago it dawned abruptly on the world's floating population that whereas the Riviera was pleasant enough in Winter—preferable, certainly, to Archangel or Sitka, or even Utica, New York—it is incomparably more agreeable in the Summer, when the skies are always smiling and the malachite green of the Mediterranean invites you to the most delightful swimming to be had anywhere in the world. How abrupt this discovery was, I myself can testify, for when I was in Antibes in June, 1925, some six guests—people like Roland Young and the progeny of Robert Benchley and other persons of no social importance whatever—rattled around in the vast spaces of the *Grand Hôtel du Cap*, their footfalls echoing hollowly in its deserted corridors. Only three years later I lived to see the once abject management explaining patiently to one Bernard Shaw that they had no room for him.

I never did understand why anyone ever went in the Summer months to the northern coast of France, where the only sound is the ceaseless complaint about the weather, pierced from time to time by the shrieks of discomfort from those foolhardy enough to go swimming in the Channel, which is about as suitable for that purpose as a pool of iced tea. I suppose they continued supinely to go there because, having been to the Riviera in the Winter, they assumed that they must go somewhere else in the Summer. How they chanced upon the dazzling discovery that there really was no law compelling them to do so, remains one of the minor mysteries of our time. For centuries they had deserted the mid-Summer loveliness of the Riviera for no other reason than the interesting and incontestable, but somewhat irrelevant, fact that it was also a pleasant spot in Winter. I doubt if any generalship was employed in creating the recent stampede in the other direction. Indeed, I am quite sure that neither the startled and unprepared hotels nor the *Départment de Tourisme* had anything to do with deflecting the crowd. That deflection, which appears to have been self-starting, therefore throws no light on the art of propaganda. It really belongs, rather, in a footnote to the volume called *The Manners and Customs of Sheep.*

I feel I shall fail ignominiously in any attempt to tell you what you—all of you, that is, except the aforesaid Montana recluse—will find as ingredients of an Antibes Summer. I glance back over the weeks in June, July and August that I spent there last year and wonder which bright-coloured piece out of the rag-bag of my experiences would best serve as an illustration of an Antibes day.

A mphibious days they are, in a land where bathing suits are *de rigueur* until sundown, and luncheon guests bring with them only a pair of pajamas to change to coyly behind the nearest rock or syringa bush. Then come cool, fragrant nights of moonlight and nightingales, with whizzing motor rides along the Middle Corniche to Monte Carlo, and low traffickings with the door man at the Casino for the loan of a necktie wherewith to conceal one's base intention to violate the Casino's solemn rule against gambling in a sport shirt. I seem to remember libations served to guests still dripping from the sea under the willow trees at Charles Brackett's villa—libations of Black Velvet, a sinister potion compounded of champagne and stout, and so inflammatory of one's sense of power that, after only three glasses, I challenged a passing mass of peasant strength to a wrestling bout, and spent the next ten days nursing a broken rib.

Or mint smashes, served at a cozy bar in the Street of the Marble Cross in Nice, where the *patron*, as he crushes the mint leaves, reminisces of the eighteen years he spent as steward of the Whitehall Club in New York.

Or perhaps you would rather savour the sight of that eternal miracle, Mary Garden, casually riding an aquaplane over the turquoise sea as the easiest way of running over to luncheon at Somerset Maugham's, whose white Moorish villa on the Cap Ferrat is so built against the side of a hill that you can step from the swimming pool onto its roof, and peer into the study with the Gauguin window, brought all the way from Tahiti.

Then I seem to remember tea with Frank Harris in his flat at Nice—a Frank Harris grown gentler with age and a little bewildered that the world is not remuneratively interested in his amorous memoirs, but still defiantly dressed like a river-boat gambler of the 70's, and reciting in his matchless voice the lovely scraps of Shakespeare which he seems to clink fondly in his hand as a miser clinks his gold pieces.

Or luncheon with Shaw, the latter finding the wordless, saucer-eyed and uproarious Harpo Marx an ideal listener for his anecdotes, but confessing next day to a slight embarrassment. Frank Harris, Maugham, young Michael Arlen and Lloyd Osborne, Rebecca West and Scott Fitzgerald—such Riviera fauna were sufficiently docketed in his mind. But Harpo Marx? What had *he* written?

Or little dinners up in the hills at Saint-Paul-du-Var, with the Alpine foothills turned amethystine in the sunset, with wine-stains on the red-checkered table-cloths, with pigeons wheeling unceasingly overhead, and dogs dozing dreamlessly on the terra cotta tiles.

Or big dinners at the Cap itself, hellishly frequent dinners given by hostesses giddy with the new grandeur of having enough servants for once in their lives. The last one I went to—a vast, jostling convention of tables set upon the riparian rocks—comes back to me in odd, freakish wisps of memory. There is Elsie de Wolfe, for instance, summoning her car and departing in medium-high dudgeon just as the cocktails are being served. She had been asked for 8.30. Now, at 10, the first course is not yet on the tables, and a lady has her digestion to think of. The hostess is furious, and so am I—furious because I didn't think of it first.

Endless chatter, clinking glasses, then suddenly, at midnight, a group puts out to sea in a chugging motor boat. In it is Gertrude Sanford, of Amsterdam, New York, and Addis-Ababa, Abyssinia.

In no time her expedition has vanished beyond the impenetrable curtain of darkness that falls just outside the range of the dinner party's winking lamps. But a few minutes later a searchlight from the shore picks it up, and there she is, riding a surf board—the pale gleam of her silken gown somehow heightening the immense isolation of that tiny, defiant, Luciferian figure picked out of the universal blackness, a rebel finding in the strange, mutinous craft with which she rides the midnight waters a more magic carpet than ever her grandpa's looms turned out in Amsterdam.

As the passing comet streaks out to sea, there is a very rustle of appreciation, of enjoyment, of relish, of envy, from the startled fringe of watchers on the shore. Myself, being at once faithless and incorrigibly reportorial, somehow find time to note that among those watchers none is so lovely as Irene Castle, standing on a high rock like a blue and silver figurehead on some gallant galleon. Does she know, I wonder, that she can put on a little summer something and still make every other woman within range seem dowdy? Probably. Then why that furrow of discontent? Ah, yes, it is not she, but someone else, out on that surf board.

Someone is singing. Grace Moore, perhaps. No, that exquisite voice is momentarily stilled—a large body of prima donna, entirely surrounded by beautiful young men. No, this time the voice issues from the vast, virile bulk of Elsa Maxwell, which is crushing a nearby rock. In her fine, unabashed baritone, she is singing snatches of songs she doesn't quite know, but somehow always coming out on top.

"Here am I, with all my breeches burned—"

Thus her voice assaults the night. A bitter young woman whispers a running fire of musical criticism in my ear.

"That," she remarks sourly, "must have been the largest conflagration since the Chicago fire."

And so on, and so on. Have I given you any notion of what Antibes is like? Do you think you would find it pleasant? Or perhaps just a trifle exhausting?

Anyway. I must run now. I am taking the next train to Vermont.

AN AMERICAN MUSEUM
OF MODERN ART

ALFRED H. BARR JR.

FROM NOVEMBER 1929

For many years, certainly since the riotous, epoch-making Armory Exhibition of 1913, an increasing number of people have thought and talked about and set their hearts upon a museum of modern art in New York. Urgent editorials have been written, excellent dinners eaten, and fulminating speeches delivered, but until this autumn no positive, large-visioned effort has been made to bring about a public institution which might give New York a consistently adequate idea of modern art. Tentative experiments have been tried such as the extreme leftward exhibitions of the heroic Société Anonyme, the Whitney Studio Club, and the Gallery of Contemporary Art at Washington Square College. But these, worthy as they are, have lacked scale and resources and the capacity for growth.

The Metropolitan Museum, New York's single important public art gallery, has only at times been persuaded to touch, a little gingerly, the less controversial phases of modern art. This reluctant policy has induced facile critics to call—or cat-call—the Metropolitan a mausoleum. Apparently they forget those remarkable achievements which at times have put the Metropolitan ahead of other great museums. Long before the Louvre or any other European gallery had recognized Manet's existence as an artist the Metropolitan had acquired two of his paintings. Before the

Luxembourg could tolerate the post-impressionists, indeed while Paris was still debating over Claude Monet's art, the Metropolitan had purchased a Cézanne. But these bold steps were taken, alas, long ago, before the war. Since then the inadequate French exhibition of 1921, the Bellows Memorial Exhibition, and the recent "modernistic" decorators' show have been the only events at the Metropolitan which might be called modem.

Meanwhile, museums throughout Europe and America have left New York far behind. Little German industrial towns such as Halle and Erfurt, Essen and Mannheim, Russian cities such as Witebsk and Kharkov, have galleries devoted primarily to modern art. Tourists who visit Utrecht or Novgorod, Bremen, Strasbourg, Prague, Hanover, in search of the quaint and picturesque are surprised to discover rooms in public museums which are alive with an emphatically contemporary atmosphere.

And in our own country are Worcester with its Gauguins and Dufresnes, Detroit with its Matisses and Chiricos and its splendid modern German collection. Brooklyn, without the means to purchase extensively, has given temporary space most courageously and generously for all phases of modem art from impressionism to *sur-réalisme*. The Los Angeles Museum, through the Preston Harrison gift, confronts its citizens with Dufy's wit, Picasso's abstractions, Derain's power. Columbus, with Ferdinand Howald's encouragement, prides itself on its Demuths and Marins.

More enviable still to the poor New Yorker are the Birch-Bartlett and Martin Ryerson rooms in the Chicago Art Institute. Here are magnificent Van Goghs, Seurat's *La Grande Jatte*, Cézanne's greatest still-life, works of the first rank by Toulouse-Lautrec, Henri Rousseau, Segonzac, Utrillo, Picasso, Lhôte and others.

Yet even more pertinently important are the modern collections of New York's peers—the great "world-cities". Berlin, Paris, London, Moscow, Amsterdam, Munich, while they force us to most uncomfortable comparisons, also offer us valuable suggestions. The Louvre, the National Gallery at Trafalgar Square, the Rijksmuseum, the Kaiser Friedrich Museum, these, like the Metropolitan, are great historical museums, national collections of supreme importance. But they differ in one essential from New York's institution: they do not even pretend to any interest in modern art. Their function is to preserve the past rather than to explain the present. But in addition to these shrines of the traditional there are in all of these cities separate institutions with distinct organization, staff and buildings, which are given over specifically to modern art.

Berlin has its *National-Galerie* in the former Crown Prince's Palace where the abstract impressionists, Kandinsky and Klee, and the cubists, Picasso and Feininger, prove their victory over popular contempt. Moscow has three or four museums of modern art both native and "western". In the latter, housed in the Tchukine and Morosov Palaces, may be seen the greatest collection of modern French painting in the world, including, one may remark in passing, twenty Cézannes, sixteen Gauguins, nine Rousseaus, thirty-five Matisses, a dozen Derains and fifty-five Picassos. Even in placid, conservative Munich, one can leave the *Alte Pinakothek* to visit the *Neue Staats-Galerie* where, among a half-dozen Van Goghs, is the most famous of his *Sunflowers*.

Another and equally fine version of the *Sunflowers* has found a permanent home in an even more surprising place, the Tate Gallery of London—surprising, that is, to Americans who tend to consider the Tate sacred to the memory of Turner, Watts and Sir Frank Dicksee, R. A. Yet one may leave the Pre-Raphaelites, pass through a magnificent room of Daumier, Manet, Degas, and Renoir, into a shrine where hangs one of the greatest modern paintings, Seurat's *La Baignade*, surrounded by first-rate Cézannes, Matisses, Bonnards, Utrillos.

But of all these stimulating modern galleries, the oldest, the most famous and for us the most significant is the Luxembourg, for it was founded in order to solve a problem very similar to that which confronts

New York. Neither the Louvre nor the Metropolitan can afford to take a chance of being wrong. But the Luxembourg does not pretend to confer any final sanction upon its painting and sculpture, which is, all of it, tentatively exhibited. If the work of art survives time's criticism, it may go, ten years after the artist's death, into the Louvre or it may be discarded as unworthy of remaining permanently public property. But during this process of trial and error, or critical selection, even those works which may prove of transitory importance remain constantly visible to the generation which created them and admires them. It is then a principle of acknowledged fallibility upon which the Luxembourg is founded, though unfortunately it has been hampered by politic timidities and inadequate financial support, so that it has not always been able to realize the latitude of taste which the principle permits.

It is, nevertheless, with an *ideal* Luxembourg in mind that seven enthusiastic and influential American men and women have organized themselves into a committee which, during the past few months, has made remarkable progress toward the foundation of a Museum of Modern Art.

The committee, fully realizing the difficulties of their project, have decided that for the first two years the new museum should function as a series of the finest possible loan exhibitions.

These loan exhibitions will be held on the twelfth floor of the Heckscher Building, on Fifth Avenue and Fifty-seventh Street, where the new galleries will be opened early in November.

The exhibitions will cover a wide range of modern activity. American art will of course be emphasized, together with French, from which most modern art throughout Europe and America derives. But painting and sculpture from Germany, England, Mexico, Russia, and other countries will also be included. The work of *living* men will form the majority of exhibitions but will not exclude occasional homage to the past.

Fifty years ago one of the greatest of all French painters died, Honoré Daumier. Long neglected, and even now too little known, he will be honoured by a memorial exhibition.

The first, and perhaps, intrinsically, the most important exhibition at the new museum will be devoted to four of the founders of that great period of European Art, which began about 1875. Cézanne and Seurat, Van Gogh and Gauguin, are great springs at which hundreds of subsequent and lesser men have drunk. Cézanne and Gauguin died about 1905, Van Gogh and Seurat as long ago as 1890. The first three are known the world over; their work has borne the brunt and reaped the glory of that remarkable revolution ineptly labeled Post-Impressionism. The fourth, Georges Seurat, has suffered even longer neglect having at first been pigeon-holed with faint praise for his invention of the "pointilliste" or "spot" technique. During the last fifteen years we have begun to recognize his importance as a very great master of composition, disciplined, classical in the essential meaning of the word, [his work possessing an] extraordinary poise and simplicity of vision which are peculiarly his. Today Seurat's seven masterpieces are divided among the museums of Paris, London, Chicago, and The Hague, and the collections of three very foresighted connoisseurs. Of these scant seven, *La Parade*, will hold the place of honor in the first exhibition of The Museum of Modern Art.

> EDITOR'S NOTE: *The seven members of the organizing committee, which is shortly to be considerably augmented, are:*
> *Miss Lizzie Bliss*
> *Mrs. W. Murray Crane*
> *Mr. Paul J. Sachs*
> *Mrs. Cornelius J. Sullivan*
> *Mr. Frank Crowninshield, Secretary [Editor of* Vanity Fair]
> *Mrs. John D. Rockefeller, Jr., Treasurer*
> *Mr. A. Conger Goodyear, Chairman*

THE EXTREMELY MOVING PICTURES

THOMAS MANN

FROM DECEMBER 1929

I have sometimes thought in my capacity as a literary man of making a precise statement of my views about motion pictures, but that must be reserved for more leisurely days. To-day I will say only this much: during the last few years my interest in this modern form of expression has become a real obsession, in fact it has even assumed the character of a gay passion.

I frequently go to motion picture theatres and for hours I do not tire of these spectacles spiced with music. I enjoy equally travel and animal pictures; the living newspapers called "news reels" interest me; occasionally, some tricky bit of comedy or other amuses me or a gripping bit of knavery intrigues me; I become absorbed in a touching love story, when the actors are convincing, good to look upon, and agreeable personalities; film actors may be vain, but they are seldom unnatural. So far as the story is concerned, even if it be silly in the extreme, it nearly always has other values to offset the poverty or sentimentality of the plot. Its details and incidents are so real, so true to life, that the human element, in a hundred single flashes, triumphs over the childish incredibility of the story as a whole.

I spoke of a "form of expression", for—if you'll pardon me—I believe that motion pictures have little to do with art, and I consider it a mistaken idea to approach them with criteria taken from the sphere of art. This is the critical attitude adopted by those humanistic, conservatively attuned souls, who then contemptuously and sadly turn away from the motion picture as from a low and wildly democratic mob entertainment.

For my part, I am contemptuous of the films too, but I love them. They are not art, they are life and actuality. Their effect in their ever-moving silence is crudely sensational in comparison to the intellectual effect of art, but it is real. It is the effect which life and actuality have on the passive observer, assuaged by the comfort of his surroundings and the attendant emotional encouragement supplied by the music. Just tell me why people always cry at the moving pictures, or rather bawl like servant girls? I went to see the opening of *The Big Parade* not long ago. Olaf Gulbranson, the caricaturist, was there too. I met him in the lobby. That jolly, muscular Norseman was bathed in tears; "I haven't dried myself yet," he said, excusing himself. Side by side we stood there for a long time with moist eyes, sniffling like children. Is that the state of emotion in which one takes leave of a work of art, turns one's back on a painting, puts down a book, or departs from the theatre? It's true, old gentlemen weep, when *O alte Burschenherrlichkeit* is sung in *Old Heidelberg,* but they are not moved to tears by Shakespeare, Kleist, or Hauptmann. Art is of a colder sphere, say what you will. It belongs to the world of intellect and high interpretation; the world of style, the world of letters, of creations of the most intricate and exalted kinds; the objective world, the world of understanding ("For it comes from understanding," says Goethe). Art is significant, aristocratic, chaste, and sensitive. Its vibrations, passing through the medium of the creator, are finely tempered; in the presence of art one moves carefully, conscious of its majesty. How different is the screen! Here we watch two lovers, ravishingly good-looking young people. They are in a real garden with waving grass, parting forever to an accompaniment of the most ingratiating music obtainable. Who could resist so definite an onslaught upon the emotions? Who wouldn't let the insistent tears flow on? For this material has passed through no medium. It lies at first hand—a warm and hearty hand. It works like onions and garlic. My tears trickle in the darkness; in dignified secrecy I flick them off with my first finger on my cheek.

For the rest and in particular, motion pictures have nothing to do with the drama. They tell the stories in pictures; the visible presence of the characters does not prevent their spirit, their best effects, from being epic; and if the motion pictures touch poetry at any point, it is here in their actuality. They are much too real to be theatre.

Stage settings are calculated on the basis of an intellectual illusion: you see what you are supposed to be thinking about. Beholding the lush and soothing scenery of the screen, you think about only what you see. Neither have the human figures of the picture the bodily presence and reality of the interpreters of dramatic rôles. They are living shadows, and so they will always remain, static and unchangeable, like the characters in a story book. Even the voice which has come to the screen by way of the talking pictures, is essentially mechanical.

As an author, I have not had that fabulous luck with the motion picture magnates that one reads about every day in the newspapers and magazines. They made a picture of my novel, *Buddenbrooks*—it was not very satisfactory to those who liked the book, however. . . . But I have tasted blood. And—although I refrain from making a definite statement—it is not impossible that I may become, one of these days, a member of that gilded group, writers for the motion pictures, who (I have heard) live so delightfully in jewelled boudoirs and think only in the superlative. I have in mind now a story of mine which should find a happy home in Hollywood, since it abounds in charm, and has as one of its leading rôles that of a lovable dog.

But whether or not we, as authors, share personally in the triumph of the motion pictures we cannot—we dare not—quarrel with them; they are too permanent, too specialized, too securely moulded to their own triumphant pattern. It would be as reasonable to criticize the tides of the sea, or to belittle Mount Everest because it is not heaven.

I should like—as I observed at the beginning of this article—to examine more thoroughly my feelings about the motion pictures, and to disclose them more fully. I should like to do this, and—in a more leisurely moment—I shall. But there is no time now, for I am on my way to see a new film.

1930s

A STOCK MARKET POST-MORTEM

DAVID CORT

FROM JANUARY 1930

What distinguished the recent collapse of the stock market from other American panics, multiplying the total hysteria but deadening the individual shock, was that it was a thoroughly democratic affair: everybody was in it. All the disgrace in a bourgeois country of being bankrupted was eliminated by the fact that almost everybody else was being bankrupted simultaneously. Other panics have been professional: a movement in stock values, supported in the main by professional traders, to correspond with an imminent or indicated shift in the nation's industrial status. Thus, the recessions after the Civil War, at the opening of the World War, at the beginning of the twentieth century.

But this latest show, in addition to being everyman's party, had nothing whatever to do with any industrial condition, commodity or inventory inflation, war or politics. It was, so far as the eye can yet see, an event all by itself, with no beginning and only a middle and end, an event suspended in mid-air and admirably suited to observation and rationalization to prove anything at all.

It was all Wall Street; but since, in this instance, Wall Street was coincident with Main Street, it was super-Wall Street, nightmare Wall Street. Thus it is public property, and incidentally the property of every cracker-barrel philosopher, with or without a theory.

Oddly enough, the newspapers under-played it, even though they gave it streamer headlines day after day. They were compelled to under-play it. If they had reproduced starkly the utter bottomlessness of the thing, anything might have happened. They withheld mention of many of the small houses that failed, of the hundreds of undistinguished sui-cides. It was an economic obligation that they should understate, that they should insert the qualifying word of hope and good cheer. On days when twelve million and sixteen million shares were being sold for whatever they would bring, to the quite conclusive ruin of butcher and baker, rich man and poor man, the papers sensibly concluded that it was not a time for realism. They naturally reported it in superlatives, as it deserved, but in such a way that hardly anyone realized that they were superlatives of tragedy. Instead, screaming laughter was the keynote. It became suddenly very respectable, even smart, to have been cleaned out in Wall Street. It was the joke of a month, of two, and its point dulled very gradually. The strange delight of the puff to one's self-esteem conveyed by appearing (in-directly, of course) in headlines on the front page, served as a paralyzing drug to the humble. "STOCKS BREAK ON HUGE SELLING RUSH" somehow meant me and you and you, it was infinitely more personal than reparations or lobbying or elections. For that little hour we were intensely and thrillingly living. It was all like a children's party on a roller-coaster. Wheee! Here we go! Hold on everybody! The uncertain intoxication of moving rapidly through space without any power under heaven to control the vehicle dulled for a while any accurate realization of exactly what was happening.

It was a longer ride down than anyone had expected. Bump after anti-climactic bump shook off the few grim survivors. Everyone was pretty bored with it long before it was over. At last realism had its day. By word of mouth went the rumours of the failures and the suicides. Half the people you knew were penniless and beginning all over again. It was no joke, no joke at all, all that money gone—pouf! and what to use for money in the unmagical morning? The luxury and semi-luxury industries had laid off thousands of workers. Millions in contracts had been cancelled. The jewelers, the dressmakers, the fur houses, the steamship companies, suffered the worst immediate penalty. Men who a month before had been in retirement with comfortable fortunes were out looking for jobs. The tailor on the corner had had to fire his assistant, but the butcher was dead.

It is easy to be cynical and to say that if you win in the stock market you are investing, but if you lose you are gambling. Yet that is very closely the popular philosophy. The amateur trader in buying stocks on margin does not do it in the same spirit that he plays poker or bets on a horse, that is, he does not take into equal consideration the two possibilities that he may lose his money as well as that he may double it. He believes that he is using his business head to make money and that if he has a good business head he will win. He does not admit that pure chance is the controlling factor. He does not admit it, that is to say, unless his stock goes down. In that case he lays it to bad luck, not to poor judgment. But if it goes up, that is good judgment. Although it sounds silly and perverse, the credo is simple enough and it has an integrity of its own. But during the past years in the United States it has been augmented by another premise. In such a great and prosperous country the small speculator has felt that he is, in a sense, underwriting America's prosperity when he buys ten shares of so-and-so on margin. He has conceived of himself as riding along with his country on a wave of unlimited prosperity.

This sensation of being a part of a well-to-do and comfortable society is what has logically led to the extreme conservatism of the American people, their extreme shyness of change. And this conservatism was demonstrated with the most astounding completeness throughout the stock market crash. In any other country in any other time so many ruined men, so many suddenly unemployed, would have become a danger, at least an embarrassment, to the country. But such a possibility is effectually checked in the United States by the fact that the average man has an enormous respect for the industrial structure that has given him so many gifts. This is translated into a thoroughly undemocratic awe of the lords of industry, far more binding than the awe of a medieval serf for his monarch because it is more intellectual. The captain of industry is not, in fact, a man at all: he is an invisible symbol, a force operating omnipotently down through a vast impersonal hierarchy. This is no place, however, for a study of American industry, surely a strange and unparalleled phenomenon, except for the notation of this awe in which the "small man" holds the "big man", an awe which is one of the most valuable bulwarks of our civilization. It has served its turn again without a ripple of effort, in preventing this convulsion of the small man's purse from assuming serious sociological or political significance, except as this may be led down controlled channels.

For the class affected in this event is probably the most important body of citizens in any country: the ambitious, comfortably placed, industrious and responsible small brains and small talent of America, the non-commissioned and minor commissioned officers of the industrial army, and their wives. For many of these the most important financial event of their lives will always remain the 1929 Wall Street panic. Conclusions of some kind they must manufacture and nourish for the sake of their self-respect, but what they will be I do not know.

For they have seen some very peculiar sights. They have watched, among others, the common stock of the United States Steel Corporation, one of the strongest and wealthiest companies anywhere in the world, tumble over 100 points from 260; Westing-house Manufacturing from almost 300 to 100; General Electric break in two from over 400 to under 170; Montgomery Ward from 156 to 49; Continental Can from 92 to 40. The gilt-edged stocks of the world crumpled in value at a time of uninterrupted and in some cases mounting prosperity; and after the assurances of the president and leading industrialists to the effect that business was "sound", conditions "healthy", had been published, they continued to crumple. The banks bought, the big financiers announced that they were buying, and still they sagged.

During that time, wealth as represented by confidence in the securities of American industry had absolutely vanished. In that sense (and a unique sense it is, too) the United States of America went through a bloodless revolution. It ran true to the standard form of revolutions in being based on disillusion and desperation. It was an attack in the strictest

sense on the foundations of society. And the revolutionaries were ultimately suppressed: they were bankrupted. By the very act of their revolt
(merely that of selling their holdings at any price) they were made powerless. As too, with all other revolutions, their loyalty was rejected, they were
literally forced into revolt. But like the skeletons of dead coral that pile one
on another and in a mass anonymity make their totality felt, so the total
of this despairing selling raised its head for a terrible hour above the
smooth surface of American prosperity and optimism.

But, whatever the beginnings, the end involved the reversal, perhaps
the destruction, of several principles inherent in the current American
social hierarchy. America is a capitalistic country, but it is unique among
capitalistic countries in that the rewards and the responsibilities of its
industries have been more and more widely distributed among the small
investors. The "big fellows" may retain the key positions but they have
made at least a pretense of deferring to the wishes of the thousand small
stockholders. The 1929 panic to a large degree eliminated these small
people and returned the vast majority of ownership to the professional
capitalists and traders. This development alone is absorbingly interesting
from the sociological point of view, but there is another and perhaps more
vital consequence of the catastrophe. From the beginning of time, in all
forms of society, humanity has reposed its faith in the absolute necessity
of conservatism. But part of the secret by which America has so magnificently exploited its industrial pre-eminence in the world today has resided
in its lack of conservatism in the financial (not the social) sense. The
American method has been to use capital two or three times over simultaneously, to keep the ball always in the air, to make capital dynamic, not
static.

But the 1929 panic constituted a perfect contradiction of America's
belief in the instruments of its prosperity. It was a complete *volte-face*.

But on whose part? Those who recanted, who sold out and are bankrupt, have already been forgotten. Wall Street wants fresh money, fresh
optimists. During the hysteria the small investors were left to make of it
what they could. No concrete official endorsement of their former belief

was anywhere forthcoming. The Morgan gesture was only a gesture. The market was permitted to seek its own level. The stadium of rich, nasty old men, the shell-backed tortoises, mixed with their tears the salty I-told-you-sos.

The "small people" demonstrated again that, together, they can do anything, but in this instance they only ruined one another.

A PORTRAIT OF JOAN CRAWFORD

DOUGLAS FAIRBANKS JR. (HER THEN-HUSBAND)

FROM JULY 1930

Joan Fairbanks (is my bosom swelling) née Crawford is one of the few people in the film colony who does not change her manner at the close of the working day. If she is any different then, it is only an instinctive nervous let-down after the tension to which she subjects herself during her work. She has the most remarkable power of concentration of anyone I have ever known. Under any circumstance this tremendous faculty is at her very finger tips. She is consumed with an overwhelming ambition.

I sincerely doubt if she has the faintest idea where her ambition is to carry her, but that does not worry her at all.

She is always prepared for any emergency. She has a great capacity for study. If she feels that she is not up to standard in a certain line she will go to any extreme to master it. Although she has a great desire to write, it is the one ambition in which she lacks the self confidence that is evident in her other undertakings.

In her spare time, when there is such a time, she covers herself in yarn, threads and needles and proceeds to sew curtains and make various types of rugs. *Entre nous*, they are quite good.

She is not easily influenced, and must be thoroughly convinced before she will waver in her opinion on any point. She must always feel herself moving forward, and when anything tends to arrest that progress she sulks mentally. She will stand by a belief with Trojan ferocity. She has temperament without being temperamental. She demands the things to which she knows she has the right, and will ask for no more until she knows with all sincerity she is worthy of it. This is particularly true in her professional life. When she meets with disappointment she has a tendency toward bitterness rather than remorse, which no doubt, is a throwback from an acute memory of less happy days.

She is extremely sensitive to surroundings and instantly conscious of any discord. When she is depressed she falls into an all-consuming depth of melancholy out of which it is practically impossible to recover her. At these times she has long crying spells. When it is over she is like a flower that has had a sprinkling of rain and then blossoms out in brighter colors. She is extraordinarily nervous. She is frightened out of her wits to be left alone in the dark. She has a secret desire to eat everything with a spoon as a small child would.

She has seen life in its less fortunate aspects, yet remains thoroughly unsophisticated at heart; however, she likes to be thought sophisticated. Like many people who have had little happiness in their own childhood, she has a tremendous sympathy for children. She loves to play like a child and adores dolls. She takes a great interest in clothes and all things feminine yet has the analytical mind of a man. She is an excellent business woman but a poor trader.

She is intolerant of people's weaknesses. If someone does her a wrong she is slow in forgetting it but when she does there is no doubt of her attitude. It is difficult for her to hide her feelings and she is embarrassingly honest in her opinions.

She wears her fingernails at an abnormal length. She is forever devising new ways to fix her hair. She loves to cook. She is thoughtful to a point of extravagance. She never drinks but smokes like a cowboy on his last cigarette. She is sensitive about her lower teeth being crooked. She has a deadly fear of all doctors. She takes a pardonable pride in the strides that she has made in her chosen field yet she is never satisfied with her work. Jealousy is not in her makeup but she resents those who have become successful without serving the same trying apprenticeship that she herself experienced.

She loves to have a *masseuse* give her a treatment and she could spend hours every day having her head scratched. She walks pigeon-toed. Her temper, in its threatening stages, is alarming but actually it is harmless. She has a passion for antique furniture. She drinks quantities of coffee and puts away at least eight or ten glasses of water every day. She has a tendency to dramatize any anecdote which she may relate. Music affects her emotionally. She is sentimental to an extreme degree, and is gullible when the most obvious sob stories are told.

There are innumerable things that I might add to what I have already stated but I hope that I have already given a fair picture of her. She is a ten-year-old girl who has put on her mother's dress—and has done it convincingly.

A CLOSE-UP OF COLE PORTER

CHARLES G. SHAW

FROM FEBRUARY 1931

On a farm, near the town of Peru, which lies in the Indiana wheat belt, Cole Porter was born on the ninth of June, 1892. He began to study music at the age of six, originally turning his energies to the violin. At eleven, he composed a waltz, called the *Bobolink Waltz*, which was later published. He is since accountable for *Let's Do It, What Is This Thing Called Love?, You've Got That Thing* and a horde of other popular refrains.

On finishing prep school (Worcester Academy), Cole Porter made a hasty tour of Europe, returning to the U. S. A. in the fall of 1909 to enter Yale as a Freshman with the class of 1913. His best-known student creations—*Bingo* and *Bulldog*—are two of Yale's most popular ditties.

After graduation, he turned to the Harvard Law School—though probably the last man on earth fitted for the law—where he spent two years thumbing tomes on pleas and torts. In 1915, he entered the Music School of Harvard, withdrawing before the end of the term to produce, in collaboration with T. Lawrison Riggs, a musical show entitled *See America First*, which became memorable solely for the one-step: *A Shooting Box in Scotland*. The following two years were spent in New York and France, Cole having enlisted in the Foreign Legion, subsequently transferring to the Fifteenth (French Army) Regiment of Artillery. Shortly after the Armistice, he married Linda Lee Thomas and, returning to America, knocked off the score for Raymond Hitchcock's *Hitchy-koo* whose *Old*

Fashioned Garden sold more than two million copies. For a London revue, known as *Mayfair to Montmartre*, he wrote *The Blue Boy* and a year later, with one Gerald Murphy, fashioned *Within the Quota*, a vehicle for the Swedish Ballet. He has since turned out a *Greenwich Village Follies* score, an *Ambassadeurs* revue, *Paris*, *Wake Up and Dream*, *Fifty Million Frenchmen*, and *The New Yorkers*, serving in each case as both composer and lyricist.

So much for the sketchy outline of Cole Porter's major accomplishments. I would now touch upon a more personal side—a side embracing his idiosyncrasies, likes, aversions, tastes, and habits—in short, his real and innermost self.

He is wholly unable to shave himself, which operation must be performed at an average of twice a day. He never carries a walking stick or gloves and wears a hat as little as possible. Most of his suits are gray and he has a passion for soft shirts with collars attached. He writes entirely with his left hand, at an angle almost upside down. He loves a good dirty limerick.

To continue to write musical shows and, eventually, to die in Venice, is his notion of life's supreme happiness. He attributes his interest in Venice to a picture of the Grand Canal painted on the front-drop of the Peru (Indiana) Opera House, which he was in the habit of visiting as a youth.

He speaks excellent French, fair Italian, and a little Spanish, though he prefers listening to talking. He is the world's worst story teller by long odds. His favorite cigarettes are Old Golds.

His dislikes are many and varied, among the more pronounced being golf, steam-heated rooms, pressed duck, English railway hotels, Belgium, and poetry. He delights, however, in all kinds of scandal and crime news. He is five feet, seven and a half inches tall and weighs a hundred and forty pounds. In America he likes town; in Europe he prefers the country.

He needs only five hours' sleep and, save for an occasional headache, keeps in pretty fair trim.

He is the possessor of a *Croix de Guerre* and belongs to the Racquet and Tennis Club of New York and the Traveller's of Paris. His favourite music is that of Stravinsky, Bach, Mozart, Gershwin, and Rodgers: his favourite lyric writer, P. G. Wodehouse. He almost never goes to concerts.

His hair is straight and black and his eyes are large and brown. He loves having people around him—people of all kinds and ages. He is full of enthusiasms but is constantly changing his plans.

During the writing of a musical show or revue score, he lives with his music, day and night. He is able to concentrate on work in the centre of the liveliest doings, just as he is a fellow of many moods. He has often played for the King and Queen of Spain and the Prince of Wales. His Paris house in the *rue Monsieur*, has a room done entirely in platinum. He is prone to seasickness and takes Mothersill's by the bottleful.

He has studied at the Schola Cantorum in Paris, under the eminent master, Vincent d'Indy. In playing the piano he uses his left hand little—though with great effect. He whistles a fifth higher than he plays.

He averages at least two baths a day and owns sixteen dressing gowns and nine cigarette cases. His favourite *hors d'oeuvre* is a *trenche* of melon eaten simultaneously with a slice of *jambon de Parme*. He is an ardent movie fan but doesn't give a whoop for baseball.

TWILIGHT OF THE ECONOMIC GODS

JAY FRANKLIN

FROM APRIL 1931

One does not have to be an optimist to realize that the great advantage of having a panic is that it compels us to think about our institutions and to overhaul our ideas. In the process, we get rid of a lot of notions which had been regarded as dogma handed down from Jehovah to our economists.

For a fat decade we have been hearing—chiefly from the bankers and business men—that bankers and business men are preeminently qualified to manage world affairs and that politicians and sociologists are either inefficient knaves or dangerous cranks. Prompted by the big bankers, we have dutifully held our noses whenever politics or statesmanship were mentioned and we have leaped to our feet and cheered ourselves hoarse whenever the Federal Reserve has tried a forward pass with the rediscount rate or the National City Bank has assayed a goal from the field. We have been taught to hew to the ticker and let the stocks fall where they may and we have actually been persuaded that banks and money can cure any international ailment from military flatulence down to hardening of the political arteries.

This golden age of bankers is passing, however. Few of the faithful can confidently affirm the immaculate conception of the Federal Reserve System, after the failure of scores of banks in every part of the country, and with its very existence challenged by demagogues and its organization branded as inadequate by Carter Glass, the man who started it. Those who believed in the literal inspiration of the Stock Exchange have already made the supreme sacrifice and are no longer able to testify financially. With more than five million unemployed, the patented air-tight prosperity formulae of high wages and mass production make Ford and Edison look as up-to-the-minute as the Anti-Saloon League.

When we put a great practical economist in the White House and watched him assist in a neolithic tariff and spend $400,000,000 of our money in a futile attempt to keep up the price of wheat and cotton, a whole economic legend died before it could be used for a second term.

We are now witnessing the twilight of the economic gods. The platitudes and glib formulae of the American economic system are pretty nearly as solvent as the Bank of United States. The old theory that the best way to make every one healthy, wealthy and wise is to let the rich get rich and the poor get children is as dead as McKinley. Our whole system is on trial, in our own eyes, for the first time in sixty years. Never again will we take it for granted that a banker must necessarily be right or a reformer necessarily wrong in his approach to public problems.

For bankers are only human. They are all too likely to invest in Coppers at the peak or to try another round of Oils. They are quite as liable to the vice of self-importance as musicians or lawyers, and they are as likely to make mistakes as doctors. Just as doctors think that every ailment requires a prescription and fee, so do bankers insist that every problem can be treated with a bond-issue and a commission.

If our economic leaders had been endowed with more knowledge than is at the disposal of the average intelligent man, they might have had a little more luck in heading off this recent world disaster. As it was, they were unable to do so as they had bound themselves to the insane, if human dogma that nothing had any existence which was not purely financial. There were no racial animosities, no political problems, no diplomatic arrangements or historical traditions, no conflicts of culture or clash of systems: nothing but loans, currencies, trade balances and risks.

As a consequence of this economic effrontery, the bankers were entrusted with world power for a decade and made a complete mess of it and of the world. There are, for example, three major problems which must be settled before the world can regain its economic health. Bankers cannot settle them, because they are political problems, but bankers and economists could have called attention to their existence and demanded their solution by the political forces of society as a prerequisite to prosperity. These problems are not unemployment, deflation and debt—for these are only the symptoms of the failure of economic statesmanship. The failure lies deeper—in politics—in Germany, Russia and China.

The bankers have had two chances to deal with the question of German Reparations—by the Dawes Plan of 1924 and the Young Plan of 1929. The first was the achievement of a Chicago banker, the second of a New York industrial economist. The failure was worse than abysmal, for the bankers preferred to base the financial credit of the entire world on the shaky foundation of Reparations rather than admit their own inadequacy. There is no doubt that the Germans should pay Reparations. They have admitted it repeatedly. There is, on the other hand, still less doubt that their liability to pay ought to be settled by arbitral procedure. Our bankers simply reckoned German capacity to pay, never German liability to pay, and so put international credit at the mercy of a German default or a German moratorium. The Allied claims for payment have never been impartially assessed. They include such absurd categories as civil pension and undoubtedly incorporate inflated valuations and false claims. They have never been properly offset by German claims against the Allies—as with the German-American Mixed Claims Commission—or by a fair accounting for the huge sums delivered by Germany between the Armistice and May 1921. Until Germany's liability has been legally established and Germany's payments legally accounted for, the smooth clauses of the Young Plan, the glittering Bank of International Settlements at Zurich (which the international bankers so humanely proposed as a solution of all these reparations and war-debt problems) will last just so long as Germany is too weak to throw them out. This is the first opportunity which our economic wonder-workers overlooked in their self-appointed mission to save mankind by foreign loans and adulation.

The second failure is even more damning, if somewhat more understandable. Despite the fact that, without Russia, the world is economically lame, our professional economists have attempted to get on without Russia for twelve fateful years. Of course, Russia deserved it. No American can doubt that. Yes, Russia was in the grip of a foul financial heresy and was being run by a group of socialistic adventurers who were breaking all the rules and getting away with it, but our economists failed deplorably, both as a matter of policy and as a matter of judgment, to recognize the existence of Soviet Russia.

In the first place, they made no determined effort to devise any formula for adjusting the methods of the Russian heresy to the unnecessary processes of the capitalistic world. For the sake of a few millions sunk in deplorable anemic Czarist bonds and for the love of a few bales of depreciated rubles, the bankers strenuously oppressed any effort to adjust our society to the Russian experiment. They instituted and maintained a financial and economic blockade against the Soviets. Even to-day they act as though they were conferring an inestimable boon in permitting the Russians to buy our goods. The financiers withheld help from Russia during the most critical period in her ghastly and difficult evolution and thus assured to our society the future enmity of the most incalculable people on the face of the modern globe. Worse still, our economic lords had the folly to attempt to organize our system of production and exchange after the war, without any reference to Russia. Russia was an economic vacuum, they decreed. Bolshevism could produce nothing, and therefore could neither import nor export. The corrupt tree could not bring forth good fruit. Russia had the wrong idea, so how could wheat grow on the steppes, trees be felled in the forest, or coal be brought out of the mines? As a result of this Old Testament line of reasoning, Russian exports, which were resumed in a large way last summer, dropped on our economic system like a brick from a sky-scraper.

Finally, the disorganized condition of China has placed a huge burden upon world trade and has been a drag upon world prosperity for years.

No, one does not need to go muckraking in the mess of our foreign trade or to remove the fig-leaves from our foreign loans to dictators, to bankrupt governments, to any and every agency that enabled an investment banker to get a commission and unload a batch of bonds on the public. One does not need to point out that our business men, far from keeping government out of business, have positively dragged it into business. One does not need to emphasize the Administration's refusal to consider Senator Wagner's intelligent bills for approaching the problem of unemployment. These are all details. When the bankers and their friends, the economists, can prove themselves so wrong as to misjudge the political potentialities of the Germans, the most vital race in Europe, of the Russians, the most portentous people in Asia, and of the Chinese, the most numerous and industrious race in the world; when the financiers leave out of reckoning a full third of the human race, we cannot be expected to have too much respect for them.

The plain fact is that neither our economists nor our bankers have the foggiest notion of where we are going or how we are going to get there. They scold and mock Soviet Russia for her ambitious Five Year Plan, and have no corresponding idea of what is to be our own course in the next three years. They denounce socialism and then applaud the use of half a billion of the tax-payers' money to pay the farmers for producing too much at a loss.

Of course, our economic leaders are not altogether to blame. Just as the world war demonstrated the bankruptcy of politics, so it seemed logical for the world to turn to non-political leaders. Surely, the world felt, they could do no greater harm than the statesmen had done. High finance could be no more dangerous than high diplomacy, and might even prove beneficial. The world was mistaken.

The financiers did make a mess of it. The economists successfully demonstrated their incapacity and the politicians are coming back to power.

For the underlying factor in the present crisis is, that despite their pretensions to omnipotence, bankers and economists must still take their orders from politics. It would never do for the public to guess that the Young Plan was a weak compromise to conceal the existence of irreconcilable political feuds, or that Adolf Hitler is the result, not of international finance, but of the Anglo-French policy of one-way traffic for reparations. It would not be seemly for the banks to admit that they guessed wrong on Russia, that their anti-Russian bluff has been called, and that they are now powerless against the current of anti-Russian political feeling which they themselves did everything to create. It would be highly indecorous for high finance to admit that nothing can be done to restore China to economic order because political forces prevent any clear-cut solution of Chinese anarchy by the Western powers.

Our economic leaders have never had the power which they have claimed for themselves. Economics, in their hands, has been a science which is purely descriptive, like geography. Their "solutions" have simply been sublimated political manœuvers. Their failures have been political failures. For their pretense that they alone could do the job, they are being punished by the obvious fact that the job is still undone. Rather than admit their own fallibility, they have preferred to lay a time-bomb under international credit and to endanger our entire economic system. It is a high price to pay for a political fiasco. Rather than pay it, a few politicians— demagogues, in the first place, like McFadden, to be followed by vocalizers like Borah—are beginning to suspect that the bankers should be made to pay. In every country and in every age, from Rome down to America, a time has come when it becomes necessary for politics to take command and to oust the financiers from a position of privileged and irresponsible power. For politics is greater than economics, if only for the reason that politics includes economics. We are beginning to wonder whether it will not soon be time to remind our economic leaders of the fact that the whole is greater than the parts, and that economic leadership has been weighed and found wanting in the balance of international politics.

BANKS AND THE COLLAPSE OF
MONEY VALUES

J. M. KEYNES

FROM JANUARY 1932

A year ago it was the failure of agriculture, mining, manufacture and transport to make normal profits, and the unemployment and waste of productive resources ensuing on this, which were the leading features of the economic situation. Today, in many parts of the world, it is the serious embarrassment of the banks which is the cause of our gravest concern. The shattering German crisis of July, 1931, which took the world more by surprise than it should, was in its essence a banking crisis, though precipitated, no doubt, by political events and political fears. That the top-heavy position, which ultimately tumbled to the ground, should have been built up at all, was, in my judgment, a sin against the principles of sound banking. One watched its erection with amazement and terror. But the fact which was primarily responsible for bringing it down was a factor for which the individual bankers were not responsible, and which very few people foresaw,—namely, the enormous change in the value of gold money and consequently in the burden of indebtedness that debtors, in all countries on the gold standard, had contracted to pay in terms of gold.

The German crisis was heralded by the Credit Anstalt trouble in Austria. It was brought to a head by the difficulties of the Darmstadter Bank in Berlin. It led to distrust of the London position on account of the heavy advances, out of relation to the liquid resources held against them, which London had made to Berlin. It culminated in Great Britain's suspension of the Gold Standard. Its final *sequela* as I write these lines, is a feverish removal of foreign balances from New York. But all this nervousness, and hysteria and panic, which is making a farce of our currency arrangements and bringing the world's financial machine to a standstill, is only superficially traceable, though it has all happened suddenly, to quite recent events. It has its roots in the slow and steady sapping of the real resources of the banks as a result of the progressive collapse of money values over the past two years. It is to this deep, underlying cause that I wish to direct attention in this article.

Let us begin at the beginning of the argument. There is a multitude of real assets in the world which constitute our capital wealth—buildings, stocks of commodities, goods in course of manufacture and of transport, and so forth. The nominal owners of these assets, however, have not infrequently borrowed *money* in order to become possessed of them. To a corresponding extent the actual owners of wealth have claims, not on real assets, but on money. A considerable part of this "financing" takes place through the banking system, which interposes its guarantee between its depositors who lend it money, and its borrowing customers to whom it loans money wherewith to finance the purchase of real assets. The interposition of this veil of money between the real asset and the wealth owner is a specially marked characteristic of the modern world. Partly as a result of the increasing confidence felt in recent years in the leading banking systems, the practice has grown to formidable dimensions. The bank-deposits of all kinds in the United States, for example, stand in round figures at $50,000,000,000; those of Great Britain at £2,000,000,000. In addition to this there is the great mass of bonded and mortgage indebtedness held by individuals.

All this is familiar enough in general terms. We are also familiar with the idea that a change in the value of money can gravely upset the relative positions of those who possess claims to money and those who owe money. For, of course, a fall in prices, which is the same thing as a rise in the value of claims on money, means that real wealth is transferred from the debtor in favour of the creditor, so that a larger proportion of the real asset is represented by the claims of the depositor, and a smaller proportion belongs to the nominal owner of the asset who has borrowed in order to buy it. This, we all know, is one of the reasons why changes in prices are upsetting.

But it is not to this familiar feature of falling prices that I draw attention. It is to a further development which we can ordinarily afford to neglect but which leaps to importance when the change in the value of money is *very large*,—when it exceeds a more or less determinate amount.

M odest fluctuations in the value of money, such as those which we have frequently experienced in the past, do not vitally concern the banks which have interposed their guarantee between the depositor and the debtor. For the banks allow beforehand for some measure of fluctuation in the value both of particular assets and of real assets in general, by requiring from the borrower what is conveniently called a "margin". That is to say, they will only lend him money up to a certain proportion of the value of the asset which is the "security" offered by the borrower to the lender. Experience has led to the fixing of conventional percentages for the "margin" as being reasonably safe in all ordinary circumstances. The amount will, of course, vary in different cases within wide limits. But for marketable assets a "margin" of 20 per cent to 30 per cent is conventionally considered adequate, and a "margin" of as much as 50 per cent as highly conservative. Thus, provided the amount of the downward change in the money-value of assets is well within these conventional figures, the direct interest of the banks is not excessive;—they owe money to their depositors on one side of their balance sheet and are owed it on the other, and it is no vital concern of theirs just what the money is worth. But consider what happens when the downward change in the money-value of assets within a brief period of time *exceeds* the amount of the conventional "margin" over a large part of the assets against which money has been borrowed! The horrible possibilities to the banks are immediately obvious. Fortunately, this is a very rare, indeed a unique, event. For it had never occurred in the modern history of the world prior to the year 1931. There have been large *upward* movements in the money-value of assets in those countries where inflation has proceeded to great lengths. But this, however disastrous in other ways, did nothing to jeopardise the position of the banks; on the contrary it increased the amount of their "margins". There was a large downward movement in the slump of 1921, but that was from an exceptionally high level of values which had ruled for only a few months or weeks, so that only a small proportion of the banks' loans had been based on such values and these values had not lasted long enough to be trusted. *Never* before has there been such a worldwide collapse over almost the whole field of the money-values of real assets as we have ex-perienced in the last two years. And, finally, during the last few months— so recently that the bankers themselves have, as yet, scarcely appreciated it—it has come to exceed in very many cases the amount of the conven-tional "margins". In the language of the market the "margins" have run off. So long indeed as a bank is in a position to wait quietly for better times and to ignore meanwhile the fact that the security against many of its loans is no longer as good as it was when the loans were first made, noth-ing appears on the surface and there is no cause for panic. Nevertheless, even at this stage the underlying position is likely to have a very adverse effect on new business. For the banks, being aware that many of their advances are in fact "frozen" and involve a larger latent risk than they would voluntarily carry, become particularly anxious that the remainder of their assets should be as liquid and as free from risk as it is possible to make them. This reacts in all sorts of silent and unobserved ways on new enterprise. For it means that the banks are less willing than they would normally be to finance any project which may involve a lock-up of their resources.

Now in estimating the quantitative importance of the factor to which I am calling attention, we have to consider what has been happening to the prices of various types of property. There are, first of all, the principal

raw materials and food stuffs of international commerce. These are of
great importance to the banks, because the stocks of these commodities,
whether in warehouse or in transit or embodied in half-finished or unsold
manufactured articles, are very largely financed through the banks. In the
last eighteen months the prices of these commodities have fallen *on the
average* by about 25 per cent. But this is an average, and banks cannot
average the security of one customer with that of another. Many individual commodities of the greatest commercial importance have fallen in
price by 40 to 50 per cent or even more.

Next come the common shares of the great companies and corpora-
tions which are the market leaders in the Stock Exchanges of the world.
In most countries the average fall amounts to 40 to 50 per cent; and, this
again, is an average which means that individual shares, even amongst
those which would have been considered of good quality two years ago,
have fallen enormously more. Then there are the bonds and the fixed
interest securities. Those of the very highest grade have, indeed, risen
slightly, or, at the worst, not fallen by more than 5 per cent, which has
been of material assistance in some quarters. But many other fixed interest
securities, which, while not of the highest grade, were, and are, good securities, have fallen from 10 to 15 per cent or more; whilst foreign government bonds have, as is well known, suffered prodigious falls. These
declines, even where they are more moderate, may be scarcely less serious, because such bonds (though not in Great Britain) are often owned
by the banks themselves outright, so that there is no "margin" to protect
them from loss.

The declines in the prices of commodities and of securities have,
broadly speaking, affected most countries alike. When we come to the
next category of property—and one of great quantitative importance—
namely real estate, the facts are more various as between one country and
another. A great element of Stability in Great Britain, and, I believe, in
France also, has been the continued comparative firmness in real estate
values:—no slump has been experienced in this quarter, with the result
that mortgage business is sound and the multitude of loans granted on the

security of real estate are unimpaired. But in many other countries the slump has affected this class of property also; and particularly, perhaps, in the United States, where farm values have suffered a great decline, and also city property of modern construction, much of which would not fetch today more than 60 to 70 per cent of its original cost of construction, and not infrequently much less. This is an immense aggravation of the problem, where it has occurred, both because of the very large sums involved and because such property is ordinarily regarded as relatively free from risk. Thus a situation has been created in the United States, in which the mortgage banks and mortgage and loan associations and other real estate financing institutions are holding a great mass of "frozen" mortgages, the margins on which have been consumed by the fall of real estate values.

Finally, there are the loans and advances which banks have made to their customers for the purposes of their customers' business. These are, in many cases, in the worst condition of all. The security in these cases is primarily the profit, actual and prospective, of the business which is being financed; and in present circumstances for many classes of producers of raw materials, of farmers and of manufacturers, there are no profits and every prospect of insolvencies, if matters do not soon take a turn for the better.

To sum up, there is scarcely any class of property, however useful and important to the welfare of the community, the current money-value of which has not suffered an enormous and scarcely precedented decline. This has happened in a community which is so organised that a veil of money is, as I have said, interposed over a wide field between the actual asset and the wealth owner. The ostensible proprietor of the actual asset has financed it by borrowing money from the actual owner of wealth. Furthermore, it is largely through the banking system that all this has been arranged. That is to say, the banks have, for a consideration, interposed their guarantee. They stand between the real borrower and the real lender. They have given their guarantee to the real lender; and this guarantee is only good if the money value of the asset belonging to the real borrower is worth the money which has been advanced on it.

It is for this reason that a decline in money-values so severe as that which we are now experiencing threatens the solidity of the whole financial structure. Banks and bankers are by nature blind. They have not seen what was coming. Some of them have even welcomed the fall of prices towards what, in their innocence, they have deemed the just and "natural" and inevitable level of pre-war, that is to say, to the level of prices to which their minds became accustomed in their formative years. In the United States some of them employ so-called "economists" who tell us even today that our troubles are due to the fact that the prices of some commodities and some services have not yet fallen enough, regardless of what should be the obvious fact that their cure, if it could be realized, would be a menace to the solvency of their institution. A "sound" banker, alas! is not one who foresees danger and avoids it, but one who, when he is ruined, is ruined in a conventional and orthodox way along with his fellows, so that no one can really blame him.

President Hoover's plans to render some of the banks' better assets more liquid may help to tide over an immediate emergency. But nothing on earth can put the banks in good shape or save them from ultimate default except a general recovery in prices and money-values. For there is a degree of deflation which no bank can stand. Thus over a great part of the world, and not least in the United States, the position of the banks, though partly concealed from the public eye, may be in fact the weakest element in the whole situation. It is obvious that the present trend of events cannot go much further without something breaking. If nothing is done it will be amongst the world's banks that the critical breakages will occur.

Modern capitalism is faced, in my belief, with the choice between finding some way to increase money-values towards their former figure, or seeing widespread insolvencies and defaults and the collapse of a large part of the financial structure;—after which we should all start again, not nearly so much poorer as we should expect, and much more cheerful perhaps, but having suffered a period of waste and disturbance and social injustice, and a general re-arrangement of private fortunes and the ownership of wealth. Individually, many of us would be "ruined", even though collectively we were much as before. But under the pressure of hardship and excitement we might have found out better ways of managing our affairs.

The present signs suggest that the bankers of the world are bent on suicide. At every stage they have been unwilling to adopt a sufficiently drastic remedy. And by now matters have been allowed to go so far that it has become extraordinarily difficult to find any way out. In Great Britain we have gone some way towards solving our own problem by abandoning the Gold Standard, but, unfortunately, we have only made matters worse for countries still adhering to it.

It is necessarily part of the business of a banker to maintain appearances and to profess a conventional respectability which is more than human. Lifelong practices of this kind make them the most romantic and the least realistic of men. It is so much their stock-in-trade that their position should not be questioned, that they do not even question it themselves until it is too late. Like the honest citizens they are, they feel a proper indignation at the perils of the wicked world in which they live,— when the perils mature; but they do not foresee them. A Bankers' Conspiracy! The idea is absurd! I only wish there were one! So if they are saved, it will be, I expect, in their own despite.

THE BABE

PAUL GALLICO

FROM MAY 1932

There is, in all Christendom, no other figure quite like the great, ugly baseball player, christened George Herman Erhardt, who is now known as Babe Ruth; and there is no other nation on the face of the globe better fitted to harbor him, cultivate him, and for that matter, actually bring him into being, than these goofy United States of America.

In France they might call him something like *Le Gros Bébé* but, then, he never could exist in France, because the Gallic temperament is not suited to baseball. The Frenchman could never stomach a close decision around second or home plate without beating someone over the head with a gold headed cane. In Germany, he would be known as *Der Starke Ruth*, and his tremendous and overweening personality would be resented or misunderstood. In England, where nobody would ever call anybody Babe, he would probably he known unhumorously as Georgie Ruth.

The rise, the existence, the *being* of Ruth is purely an American phenomenon, like those other phenomena—crooners, Andy Volstead, the Valentino funeral, million dollar prizefight purses, skyscrapers, peanuts, chewing gum and the freedom of the press. Ruth's nickname, "Babe", is so much a part of our national consciousness that the strange message spelled out in letters six inches high across the top of any afternoon paper, "Babe Conks No. 36" or "Bam Busts Two", is not, as an English or French cryptologist might imagine, a code for "Come home, all is forgiven", but a very simple presentation of the news that Ruth has hit his 36th home run, and that he has made two homers in one game.

Americans called him Babe, because he looks like anything else but and the sports writers re-nicknamed him the Bambino—also for no good reason, as there is no Italian in him—and then characteristically they shortened it to Bam.

The Sultan of Swat, the Colossus of Clout, the Behemoth of Bust, the Bambino and the Slambino, all mean one and the same person, Ruth, a ball player owned by the New York Yankees, whose extraordinary coordination of eye, brain, and muscle, coupled with an enormous frame and the most powerful wrists in the game, enable him to hit more home runs than any other man in the world . . .

Ruth is an American Porthos, a swashbuckler built on gigantic and heroic lines, a great athlete, a Golem-like monster, a huge, vital, vulgar fellow in whose bosom surge all the well-known elementary emotions and whose tear ducts lie close to the surface. He lives—ye gods, how he lives!— wholeheartedly, with complete gusto. He is one of the most completely alive men I have ever known. He loves to eat, to sleep, to royster and horseplay, to drink beer and play cards with companions, to play ball, to play golf, to swear and shout and laugh. Everything about him is big—his frame, his enormous head surmounted by blue-black curly hair, his great blob of a nose spattered generously over his face, his mouth and his hands—only his ankles are strangely slim like a woman's.

He talks in loud tones, he laughs uproariously, his voice is a basso-profundo and rumbles forth from the caverns of his chest like Kilauea. His greeting to all is "Hello kid", and his conversation is ripe, rich and bar-roomy. He talks like a sailor whose every third word is an oath and to whom oaths are so completely idioms of conversation that they are no longer oaths.

Ruth is a beloved figure and the greatest single attraction in the entire world of sport. Dempsey simply isn't in it with him, a statement that will disturb the cult of Dempsey worshippers no end, but the fact is too patent to call for proof. In one baseball season, Ruth draws more people through the turnstiles of the ball-parks than Dempsey has drawn in his lifetime. The Yankees play steadily to fifteen and twenty thousand patrons a day during the week, and over Saturday and Sunday, against opponents high in the League standing, to crowds of sixty and seventy thousand. When Ruth is removed from the line-up for one reason or other, the crowds are cut in half.

The Babe is the only man I have ever known as spectacular in failure as he is in success. His home run is a magnificent thing, a poem of rhythm and timing. The bat meets the ball with a distinctive and peculiar sound all of its own—veterans will say "There she goes," just from the sound, and the ball, a diminishing speck, soars from the inclosures over the top tier of the farthest stands. A strike-out is just as impressive. Ruth is not constituted to do anything unimpressively. When he misses the ball, the force of his swing whirls him around until his legs are twisted like a German pretzel. Sometimes he swings himself clear off his feet. Every miss is its own guarantee of honest effort.

Nobody ever strikes the Babe out with his bat on his shoulder. He takes three healthies at the ball, *andante furioso*, each one more vicious and murderous than the last. Each miss draws a delighted roar from the crowd, or rather a grand and public shudder at the might of this man, and a sigh for what would have happened if he had connected.

The effect of a home run upon an immediate cross-section of any part of the audience is curious and inexplicable. The ball has fled the park. The Babe trots around the base paths with his arms close to his sides, taking little mincing steps on his small feet, and occasionally tipping the peak of his cap to acknowledge the roar of approbation and the patter of applauding hands. Look at your nearest neighbor. You find him acting in a manner that under any other circumstances would call for a spell at Bellevue under close observation. He is grinning from ear to ear, shaking his head from side to side, making strange noises, and thumping the nearest person to him on the back. He is acting like a man who has just been told by the nurse that it's a boy. He looks into his neighbor's face to make sure that there is equal appreciation registered thereon. He lights a fresh cigar and settles back in utter contentment.

There are some men to whom has been given the faculty of living all of their lives in newsprint. They have a natural attraction for headlines. These are very apt to become our heroes. Sometimes, like Lindbergh or Tunney they object to the hot spotlight we turn upon them night and day, upon their private lives, their ills, their triumphs, their personal and domestic problems, an illumination which does not even spare the obstetrical chamber. Then we are liable to be impatient with a modesty which we feel is obtuse and selfish, and which denies satisfaction to our besetting sin—curiosity—not minding our own business.

There has never been any complaint about Ruth's modesty. The only walls he has ever known have been the parallel columns of the newspapers. Even his sins are public and certainly his expiations have been notably so. In 1925 at Asheville, North Carolina, he fell victim to the gluttony that has beset him for years—the gluttony one is liable to find in a poor boy who has never had enough good things to eat and suddenly finds himself with money to eat all he wants. Now gluttony with Ruth is not your stuffy napkin-in-collar, bring-me-a-steak-smothered-in-pork-chops kind. The beginning of the tummyache that was felt around the world was engendered by a wayside collation consisting of nine or ten greasy railroad-station frankfurters mounted on papier-mâché rolls, and washed down with some eight bottles of green, red, and yellow soda pop. Anyway, they shipped him up North on a stretcher, and the whole nation trembled with every turn of the wheels that brought him home. He was tucked into a cot in St. Vincent's Hospital, in grave danger of relinquishing his hold upon his great, mortal body, and hung between life and death for many days—on Page One. Bulletins were issued from the sickroom. Little boys brought nosegays, or congregated outside the high walls of the hospital, and looked up at the window of the room wherein lay the stricken hero. The presses lay in wait with pages of obituaries, and editorials announced the impending catastrophe as a national calamity. Even in England, the penny papers watched at his bedside. That IS fame. He recovered, he convalesced, and the nation sent a great sigh of honest relief up into the ether.

Back in 1922 Babe had a bad year. He was untractable, he drank, he fought with Judge Landis, the high priest of baseball, he abused umpires, he committed the gravest sin in baseball, that of chasing a fan up the stands. Also, he played poor baseball, although he had just signed a contract for five years at $52,000 a year, the largest salary ever paid a player up to that time.

At the annual dinner of the Baseball Writers Association, Ruth met Senator Jimmy Walker. The Senator was a baseball lover and an admirer of the Babe. He told Ruth that he owed it to the boys of the nation to behave himself. Later when Ruth was called upon to speak, he arose, gulped, and then with tears rolling down his enormous face he solemnly promised the kids of America that he would reform. He swore off drinking (in large quantities). He reformed.

The scene, the speech, the promise, the great reformation rang through the headlines. Here was a great and touching thing, usually seen only in the privacy of the parlor, where the prodigal son breaks down and promises that he will sin no more. Ruth became everybody's son. Everybody forgave him. Everybody went out to the ball yard the following year to see how his repentant prodigal was making out. He made out very nicely, hammering out 41 home runs, increasing to 46 the following year, then dropping to 25, due to his shortened playing year (the Great Tummyache), and then increasing his output again until in 1927 he had amassed the amazing total of 60.

The man is a hero out of Horatio Alger or Burt L. Standish. He rose from Rags to Riches. Sink or Swim, Do or Die. He is the prototype of every hackneyed hero of juvenile (and adult) dollar literature come to life. The Alger books used to tell us that a poor boy could eventually triumph over temptation and adversity and acquire wealth and position, but nobody ever knew of anyone who really did.

Ruth came from the slums of Baltimore. He was an orphan. He went to a reform school. At St. Mary's Industrial School in Baltimore, he played baseball. He was a natural athlete. At the age of 20, Jack Dunn, the owner of the famous Baltimore Orioles, took him out of the school on the tip of one of the brothers. Dunn sold Ruth to the Boston Red Sox where his rise to fame was almost instantaneous, curiously enough, as a pitcher and not as a great slugger and outfielder.

Thereafter he began to amass folder after folder of news clippings, and photographs, the surest gauge of success. There are fourteen envelopes stuffed with clippings, and seven folders of pictures, seventeen inches deep in The New York *Daily News* Morgue alone. Run through these clippings and you will find no single item of his life omitted, no matter how trivial, from the appearance of a boil on his neck to the mystery that enshrouded the birth of his daughter by his first wife. (He claimed the child was born in February, whereas his wife declared it had happened in June.) Everything is there, his contract squabbles with his owner, his trials with speed cops and the demon rum, his every physical ailment from chipped ankles to flu, pneumonia and tonsil snatching. You find him in the movies, on the stage, engaged in fights on the ball field, suspended by his manager, barnstorming against Landis's orders and suffering punishment therefor. You witness his grief at the grave of his first wife, his courtship, and his marriage of his second, his yearly struggle with avoirdupois, his casual winter golf games, his lawsuits, his sentimental journeys to the bedsides of sick youngsters.

The Babe has become a member of every family in the country that cares anything about Sport, and a great many that don't. No one goes to see him play ball impersonally. No one can look impersonally upon a public figure about which so much is known. British athletes are presented in the glossy print weeklies wearing blazers and smoking pipes, and that is that. The Frenchman makes a fuss over his athletic hero while he is on the scene, but promptly forgets him between games or matches. The Germans react coldly towards their own world's heavyweight prizefight champion, Schmeling. A professional athlete relegating political and national news to page two in Europe is simply unthinkable. But snoopiness is a national disease with us. We are a nation of gossips and Walter Winchell is our prophet. Snoopiness, our unceasing thirst for information about people in the public eye, and the activity of our press in supplying this information, has built up an orphan boy and a reform school graduate to a high estate where he receives as large a salary as the President of the United States, and far more sustained publicity. It could only occur, we are told, in a democracy, hence we are a democratic nation. It is about the only remaining proof left to us.

BOOTLEGGING FOR JUNIOR

DALTON TRUMBO

FROM JUNE 1932

When an impartial history of the Great Depression is written, it will be set down therein that while bankers squealed hideously for a place at the public trough, their closest competitors for our national income—the bootleggers—asked no favors. On the contrary (the account will continue), they went hopefully forward, conducting their comings, goings and killings with regularity worthy of Hooverian applause. Nor will anyone gainsay the historian's comment that in no instance did a good liquor merchant trade his rugged individualism for a place in the breadline.

In penning this tribute to a struggling industry, the chronicler will not overlook the fact that the panic was felt keenly by many prominent rum sellers. Some of them played the market, others dabbled in real estate, and all of them had an extremely tough time of it convincing the gendarmerie that in view of the general wage decline a copper's mite should be reduced accordingly.

But to a man they maintained a wholesome trust in the old sock as the safest place for emergency cash. Thus, instead of being flat when the crash came, they merely were deflated. With the nest egg in reserve, it is not surprising that a tax-free business requiring only a small investment and numbering its customers by the tens of millions, turned in profits while others ran into debt for red ink. If it lost thousands of clients who formerly purchased by the case for celebration, then it gained millions who now buy in pint lots for consolation.

Moreover, the liquor barons displayed an adaptability woefully lacking among other big-wigs. Sensing that a certain portion of their customers no longer could afford strong liquor, they turned to beer—a product which can be made from last night's garbage and sold for a better price than to-morrow morning's milk. This stroke saved many from disaster, although, fundamentally, whisky is the only drink for a red-blooded American. And so long as $200 invested in its makings can produce a profit in the neigh-borhood of $5,000, the liquor business will pay dividends—such large ones, in truth, that an increasing number of college graduates will cast longing eyes in its direction before going over bodily to the wholesale meat racket.

Indeed, it is a question whether the graduates need the profits of boot-legging more than bootlegging needs the enthusiasm of the graduates. Certainly the affinity of youth for an undeveloped field is nothing new. There is every evidence that the gangsters, having grown rich and powerful from selling booze, are neglecting their original bonanzas for the heady profits of racketeering, extortion and political graft. The field from which they are receding inevitably will be occupied by a New Era Bootlegger, for which position there is no likelier candidate than the col-lege man who finds his pathway to legitimate success swarming with Masters of the Arts and Doctors of Philosophy.

The university-trained bootlegger will understand that a law which does not receive public support morally is no law at all. Thus his con-science will be assuaged. From his under-graduate training he will have developed a Messianic enthusiasm for his product, which, combined with the industry and intelligence necessary for survival in any business, will assure him abundant profits. But above all, he will be honorable—a gentleman in the finest sense—for a business in which a contract is illegal and a lawsuit out of the question requires personal honesty to a degree not comprehended in legitimate undertakings. Naturally, the first to analyze the situation and plunge into the fray will reap the richest reward.

* * *

Since the liquor business is a comparatively young and struggling industry, each center of population has developed its hooch supply independent of every other. Nothing short of a national survey can determine where pickings are choicest. The central and eastern states are dominated by gunmen, and the Solid South by thirsty but moralistic fanatics. From Milwaukee to St. Louis, good brewery beer strangles all competition. The Northwest draws upon Canadian neighbors, and the scattered folk of the Rocky Mountains make excellent potato whisky in their own private gullies. Only the Southwest and its highly publicized metropolis, Los Angeles, remain as inviting territory to the peaceful newcomer.

A numerous, hard-drinking clientele which makes no social distinction against the bootlegger is but one of its advantages. The religio-sex mania which places rape and erotic murder second only to backgammon as a public diversion gives the police little time for liquor-snooping. Moreover, the gang as it is known elsewhere does not exist. Bootleggers are divided into cooperative districts which pay lump tributes to the police. A new dealer is expected cheerfully to share his portion of the bribe money, after which he may buy and sell where he pleases, and at whatever price he considers equitable. Instead of gang warfare, all is peace, harmony and loving-kindness. There is no better place for Young America to learn its alcoholic ABC's.

Patently, the bootlegging profession is neither simple nor safe, else its ranks would be clouded unendurably. Like any other enterprise in which money can be made, it will bear thoughtful—even prayerful—study. The grimy lad who peddles pint bottles for $1.50 a throw is but the lowest of a social order which finds its height among the distillers. Between the two extremes stretches an immense and surprisingly efficient organization.

Alcohol, being the base of everything intoxicating, receives the undivided attention of big-time commercial distillers, who leave to their customers the task of converting it into whisky, gin or scented messes for the ladies such as *crème de menthe* and *liqueur d'abricot*. Hi-proof alcohol made from beet sugar is the most popular grade, although in quality it is preceded by grain and cane sugarhol—to lapse into the vernacular—and followed by moon and lowproof, which are products of cheap stills, cheap materials and generally unethical proprietors.

Stills—pots, professionally—vary in daily capacity from fifty to several hundred gallons, and in type from poison-producing tin affairs to magnificent automatic instruments of burnished copper. The distiller's heaviest expenditure (the combined wages of a cook, helper and truck driver amounting only to $250 each week) is for beet sugar—a commodity which cannot be obtained without considerable finesse, since Federal officers are inordinately interested in heavy sugar consumers. The usual method is to visit a thinly disguised supply house where the transaction is inviolate from public scrutiny. Here the distiller may obtain all the sugar he needs, paying the highest retail price, not in cash, but in alcohol evaluated at its lowest wholesale cost. The supply merchant's percentage of profit must be reckoned by the thousand.

Each distiller deals exclusively with one or two responsible jobbers. Truck-loads of five-gallon cans are delivered on consignment, the jobber paying for the last consignment upon the following delivery—a benign credit system which permeates the industry. The jobber in turn delivers his merchandise to wholesalers, contenting himself with a quick turn-over and not more than 200 per cent profit.

The rôles of the distiller and jobber are somewhat unimportant when compared to that of the wholesaler, for the latter's success or failure is that of the whole system. And as the system depends on the wholesaler, so does that gentleman depend on his Kid. Whether he is fifteen or fifty, the Kid is known by no other name. Even if he had a name it would be unethical to call it out. He receives only $35 a week, plus rent, but he doesn't need to worry about bail or fines, and he is learning a profession which pays even better than the movies. Sympathy for him is wasted utterly.

The Kid lives at the plant—an unostentatious private residence—attending to the mysterious enterprise of transmuting raw alcohol into sound whisky. His most important labors are strictly by formula—three parts of hiproof alcohol, testing 190, and two parts of distilled water, mixed in a charred barrel and treated with the electric needle. This widely misunderstood instrument is a simple, foot-long heating element which carries enough current to keep the contents of the barrel gently bubbling for the required twelve hours. It is a greedy consumer of power, and, since an electric bill of $30 or more soon attracts attention, must be fed from a tapped power line—one of the few genuinely dishonest practices in which a liquor worker is forced to participate.

After the needle's work is done, the liquor has absorbed from the barrel an amber color and a whisky flavor. The barrel itself is turned in on a new, freshly charred one, since a single filling exhausts its aging powers. Booze obtained by this process varies from 110 to 115 proof—still too strong for human consumption—and is diluted until its potency registers between 95 and 100 proof. It is important that the alcoholic voltage be always the same, for speakeasy proprietors are shrewd souls. They test each can with the hydrometer and howl fearfully if it is below par.

Discounting loss from evaporation, three cans of alcohol—fifteen gallons—thus treated blossom into twenty-eight gallons of fair whisky. At $15 each, the original cans have cost $45; yet selling for the rock bottom price of $5 a gallon, they will fetch $140—a cool profit of more than 300 per cent, and one reason why bootleggers' children always have shoes. But the eventual profit does not end here. A hip-pocket bootlegger buying at $5 a gallon will sell it for $12, providing he violates a tenet of his trade and does no cutting on his own account—140 per cent profit. And a speakeasy proprietor selling the same gallon by the drink will take $32 into the till for a profit of 640 per cent.

Obviously, the college man contemplating an assault on the liquor citadel can do no better than to become a Kid. The salary is low, but the experience is priceless. He will learn to recognize good liquor and to know why it is good. He will discover trade secrets denied the ordinary blundering amateur and thus save himself many embarrassing skirmishes with the law. Always providing he is honest, he will be able to inspire that confidence and trust among his fellow workers which must precede a larger success with the drinking public.

Under new guidance, the distiller's art—once an honored and holy calling—might again be raised to its ancient dignity. It is not unreasonable to hope that modern science would be called upon to prepare a new ambrosia, the bouquet of which could be hailed proudly as the epitome of our peculiar and exciting civilization—a liquor of such charm and potency as forever to silence the moans of those who cannot forget. Perhaps the depression with its diminished opportunities for college men is but the means of ushering us into the Golden Age of Bootlegging. If this be true, we have not suffered in vain.

THE JIMMY WALKER ERA

ALVA JOHNSTON

FROM DECEMBER 1932

The resignation of Jimmy Walker ended the office-holder's bull market. The crash overtook business in 1929; it did not catch up with New York politics until 1932. During the three years of the depression, Jimmy Walker compelled the treasury of New York City to function on the old boom and bubble basis, with increased dividends, extras and bonuses for job-holders, politicians and contractors. He boosted his own pay from $25,000 to $40,000 in 1930—gave a part of it to charity, to be sure, but kept on drawing it in full—and increased the city's disbursements by a score or more of millions during each of the panic years. Nobody told him about the depression; he thought Hard Times was the name of a book; Jimmy was the last and greatest of the bulls. He probably fancies that Judge Seabury chased him out of office, but the truth is that Jimmy is a delayed victim of the crash. He led Tammany's Dance of the Tax-payers' Millions three years too long. Tammany succeeded in side-tracking McKee but was forced to recognize that Walker was politically dead. Now Jimmy belongs to the ages.

The Jimmy Walker Era was over the day that his successor used the axe on the city payroll. When Joseph V. McKee cut his own salary, New York had a new sweetheart. When he dismissed an aggressively wasteful department head, he was hailed by the taxpayers as a rescue boat is hailed by the shipwrecked mariner. When McKee performed the sensational civic feat of accepting the lowest bid instead of the highest bid on a printing contract, Jimmy Walker was hissed in the cinema palaces.

Jimmy was not the only politician who was late in hearing of the crash. It took two years after 1929 to convince Herbert Hoover that anything had happened. Franklin D. Roosevelt allowed the cost of running New York State to soar in 1930, 1931 and 1932. In 1931, when litigation was falling off, Roosevelt signed a bill compelling the public to pay $300,000 a year for a dozen new and superfluous judges. Politicians everywhere, and especially politicians in the cities, continued after 1929 to act on the theory that the public was richer than ever. By 1931 many of them had been forced to respond to the changing times, but Jimmy Walker and Tammany Hall continued to cherish the belief that all New Yorkers were plutocrats. As against the rest of the country, New York was a "Lost World" like Conan Doyle's imaginary plateau which escaped all changes and was still inhabited by the tyrannosaurus and the brontosaurus. Politically and governmentally, New York remained in the Age of the Dinosaurs; it was still the home of every type of out-of-date tax-eating monster. Giant carnivores, extinct elsewhere, preyed ravenously on the citizens until Joe McKee came to the rescue.

It was the popularity of Jimmy Walker and the power of Tammany Hall which, for three years, kept the citizens of New York City docile under ruinous taxation. Jimmy was not looked upon as an ordinary elected official; he was a sovereign; New York idolized him as England formerly idolized the dear good little Queen. Jimmy kept the tax-payers quiet through love; Tammany kept them mute through fear. Tammany's grip on New York had become absolute. To grumble and murmur against Tammany was not ordinary political opposition; it was disaffection, sedition, conspiracy. A business man, who talked too freely, might find himself gravely embarrassed. All business men have to violate trick ordinances in any over-regulated modern city; a business man who offends Tammany loses the services of the usual fixers and may find it very expensive to mollify inspectors and open the minds of the inferior tribunals. The idea of turning Tammany out of power by the normal use of the ballot is fantastic; it takes a *coup d'état* to change the government of New York City. Entranced by Walker, enslaved bv Tammany, the New York tax-payer continued to be pitilessly exploited. The real estate of New York City was the last Golconda; it was forced to produce more and more revenue, panic or no panic, until it escaped from the fatal fascination of Walker.

I t is easy to trace the sources of Jimmy's popularity. His personality made its impression on the whole country. Probably no mere city official has ever before captured the interest of the nation as Walker did. It was news from Bangor to San Diego when Jimmy was nipped by a pet alligator in Florida; when the Reverend Dr. Christian F. Reisner announced from his pulpit as an important scoop that Jimmy had gone on the water-wagon; when Jimmy kept the Lord Mayor of Dublin waiting for an hour; when he charged that our State Department had spies dogging him nightly in Paris; when he appeared at the City Hall with a black eye and explained that he had slipped in his bathtub; when he was just grazed by constables who raided a floating casino off Montauk Point. The American and European interest in Jimmy reacted in his favor in New York. Like all provincials, New Yorkers are grateful to anyone who puts their town on the map.

But the great basis of Walker's popularity was his passion for making everybody happy. In spurts he handled the city's business impressively, but his chief task was that of spreading sunshine in the metropolis. New York—at least the New York of the Jimmy Walker Era—demanded that the Mayor be a cornerstone-layer, not an administrator. Jimmy was not the loafer that he has sometimes been painted; he toiled and moiled and sweated and slaved at laying cornerstones, dedicating buildings, receiving celebrities and speaking at luncheons and dinners. He rushed madly about the city to show himself at the quilting parties, husking bees, church sociables and other innocent diversions of his constituents. He popped in on the pageants and feasts of the twenty-four important nationalities of New York City.

It was usually 1 or 2 in the morning before he began to have any free time to himself. Other officials, trotting around to varied functions, conserve their mental energy by declaiming tripe from manuscripts prepared by their secretaries. Jimmy always made his own speeches and was nearly always at the top of his form. He has a sixth sense for catching the mood, the atmosphere, the prevailing sentiment of any gathering and rendering it in felicitous sentences. A B'nai Brith convention would instantly perceive that Jimmy was a Jewish boy at heart; the Liederkranz would gather that he was a Teuton snatched from his cradle in infancy; the Southern Society would see Confederate Generals in his lineage. Jimmy never shirked his welcoming, congratulating and condoling work. When, to give an example, forty-eight boys from forty-eight states, each boy the winner of a Thomas A. Edison scholarship, called at the City Hall, Jimmy tried to improvise a bright line on each state. Some of his lines were good, some were pathetic, but Jimmy is the only man alive who would try to turn out forty-eight split-second wisecracks to please forty-eight boys not yet of voting age. And Jimmy does not turn out his work with the facility of the complacent expert; he always spurs his mind to its highest activity. He has a rare gift of establishing a comradeship between himself and a hearer. Valentino's greatness on the screen was an expression of profound intimacy which gave multitudes of women the illusion that a special bond of sympathy existed between each of them and the cinema star. Walker achieves a similar freemasonry, both with men and women, by impish leers and sly allusions which flatter the hearer into the belief that he and Jimmy Walker understand each other; that they are two kindred souls; that they are two, and the only two members, of a secret mysterious order. Hundred of thousands, if not millions of New Yorkers, firmly believe that they are among Jimmy's closest friends. In fact, men who have never heard Walker except over the radio will say, "Jimmy Walker told me thus and so."

Jimmy could not have achieved his greatness in an earlier decade. In the pre-war and pre-Volstead period, he might have been tolerated, but he would never have been glorified. Less than ten years ago, one of the

sagacious elder statesmen of Tammany, while admitting Walker's bril-
liance and his services to Tammany, asserted that the young fellow had no
future. The aged chieftain's theory was that, to rise in New York politics,
a man must be either Puritanical or cautious. That principle did formerly
prevail, but it lost its force in the last decade. The attempt of reformers to
legislate liberty out had legislated license in. It produced the Jimmy
Walker Era. The depression has now finally ended that era. The idol of
the newer epoch is the forbidding type with wrathful countenance and a
spade beard, with a curtailing, slashing, reprimanding vetoing temper,
and with an eloquence which consists wholly of the word "NO."

Walker was the emblem of the reaction against reformers. As a State
Senator, he gave New York Sunday baseball and Sunday movies. He
defeated the crusade to censor books. He is the one conspicuous politician in America who came out flat-footedly in favor of the return of the
saloon. It was the Walker Act which re-established prize-fighting after the
reformers had abolished it. The long whiskers, the frock coats, the black
gloves, the reversed collars, the sour visages left Albany year after year
joining in the prayer that something serious would speedily happen to
Senator Walker.

Later, as Mayor, Jimmy became the embodiment of New York's, and
to some extent of the nation's, growing dislike of Prohibition and Pur-
itanism. He became the foremost American champion of a man's right to
be himself. His life was an antiseptic against hypocrisy; it was a standing
rebuke to the Anti-Saloon League and the Methodist Board of Temper-
ance, Prohibition and Public Morals; it was holy water to the devils of
intolerance and persecution; it was a whiff of insecticide to snoopers,
sniffers, wowsers, informers, meddlers and all similar canaille.

To dislodge an idol of such rare merit was a difficult proceeding.
Seabury's revelations were enough to sink ten ordinary Mayors, but they
failed to turn sentiment against Walker. The composite mind of New York
worked at racing speed to invent fresh excuses for Jimmy after each fresh
Seabury exposure. It was demonstrated clearly that the former Mayor had
mingled his private finances in strange ways with the finances of interests

seeking important favors from New York City. What of that? It was computed that, taking Seabury's allegations at their face value, fewer than a
million mysterious dollars had found lodgment in Jimmy's iron safe. Is a
great metropolis like New York interested in petty cash items of that sort?
Judge Seabury's well-meant strivings would have been laughed to scorn
except for one circumstance. That circumstance was the revolt of New
York's long overtaxed real estate. It was this which brought sudden unpop-
ularity and peril to Walker. With rents cut in half, with thousands of
buildings in receiverships, with the real estate interests already bleeding
to death from overtaxation, Jimmy wanted $697,000,000 to run New York
for one year. That was the last straw. The Sunday supplements used to
entertain their readers with speculations on whether the weight of the
skyscrapers would not some day push Manhattan Island down into the
ocean; to-day the weight of taxes and mortgages is doing practically that.
Jimmy had painted the town red in more ways than one. The bedrock of
Manhattan rose and mutinied, as the stones of Rome were invited to do
by Mark Antony. It was Mother Earth, not Seabury, that finally shook
Jimmy out of City Hall. Jimmy may come back; if so he will be a very
much altered Jimmy. But, in any case, the old Jimmy Walker Era is over.

WHEN LOVELY WOMEN STOOPED
TO THE FOLLIES

HELEN BROWN NORDEN

FROM FEBRUARY 1933

The editors of *Vanity Fair* have been assured that sometime this spring, if all goes well, there will blaze a new sign on Broadway, whose brilliant lights will form the word FOLLIES—a word which the Tenderloin has imagined banished forever from its demesne. In all probability, this *will* be its last public appearance. In memory of the man who once gave her a job, and who later became her good friend, Peggy Fears Blumenthal will produce a memorial to Florenz Ziegfeld, *The All-Time Follies. [Ziegfeld had died the previous summer.]* Follies performers of another day will flock to the standard: Marilyn Miller, Leon Errol, Fannie Brice and the others. They will do again—for the last time—the numbers which first gave them fame under the Ziegfeld banner—the old songs, the old sketches, the half-forgotten dances. And a bright ghost will kick its gleeful heels about the neon bulbs—a naïve ghost of other days, the spectral symbol of early-century gaiety. Ring—oh bells of memory. Dimly, ghosts, burn back to life . . .

In the year 1907, Klaw and Erlanger turned the roof of their New York Theatre over to a young theatrical manager named Florenz Ziegfeld, and there, on the night of July 8, a new species of creature sprang full-blown into the world and a new class-word was given to the language:—the Follies Girl.

Every once in a while, a nation coins a phrase which grows beyond its original descriptive significance and becomes a symbol of certain integral manifestations of that country's social culture. Rome had its Vestal Virgins and Japan its geisha girls; India flowered forth the soft-eyed temple dancers, and there were witches in Salem. Without going quite so far as to compare the late Mr. Ziegfeld's houris with the Vestal Virgins, it is still possible that in the anthropological sense, they too have given us an example of the phrase historic: a Follies Girl.

Now that the institution of the annual Follies is no longer a part of our national scene; now that there are no more glamour-girls in training for that proud, exciting title of Ex-Glorified—the time has come to pass in review a few of those astonishing personalities whose Ziegfeld background was the starting-point which led them on a fragile, perilous chain to fame or wealth or death—or backward to the dark obscurity once more. From these examples there may come some flickering glint of the curious potency of the Follies trademark.

For the past twenty-five years, this species of feminine phenomenon has existed in America, unique and indigenous. There is no classification in the language which has the particular import, the peculiar, glittering magic of this one phrase. Its nearest counterpart in the modern world was the nimbus attached to the dancers of the Imperial Ballet of Czarist Russia. But the significance of the latter was neither so far-reaching nor so cogent.

Glamorous and already legendary are the image connotations which arise from the mere sound of the word "Follies". Chinchilla and orchids and ropes of pearls. Champagne drunk from red-heeled slippers at Rector's (*If a Table at Rector's Could Talk*—ta-de—dum-dum-dum . . .) and breakfasts at Jack's. The bunny-hug, the turkey-trot, the grizzly-bear (*It's a Bear, It's a Bear, It's a Bear!*), the tickle-toe, the shimmy and the Black Bottom. *I Just Can't Make My Eyes Behave—Swing Me High, Swing Me Low, Dearie.*

So much of America is implicit in the phrase: the lavish display, the mushroom leap to fame and fortune, the quick oblivion. Just as every small American boy could hope to be President, so every American girl from rock-ribbed Maine to the Barbary Coast could dream of eventual apotheosis as a Follies Girl. The Follies were an institution—a training-school—an Alma Mater whose graduates wore the words, "a former Follies Girl," like a bright badge of merit for the rest of their lives; and even in death, that phrase alone, attached to their names, was enough to bring them front-page obituaries. A Follies Girl is always good copy, and the lustre of the name has shone on its bearers in the police courts, in Burke's Peerage, in the Social Register and in Hollywood. Follies graduates made the millionaire-chorus-girl marriage popular in America and injected new blood and beauty into many an otherwise effete old family name. But whether they married millions or whether they went into opera, they brought with them the glamorous heritage of their training-school. Even in death, they were decorative and dramatic.

To the observer of casual glance—and other outlying districts—it may look as if every well known woman of the Twentieth Century were once a Follies Girl. This, of course, is not true. It is only almost true. Let us take a few of the more famed examples and see how they have penetrated into the veins of the world as no other specialized group of women has ever done. As another typical American symbol would say, "Let us look at the record."

THE PATH TO FAME

Back in Evansville, Indiana, at the age of five, Marilyn Miller used to climb on a chair in front of a mirror and practice dancing steps. With her parents, sister and brother, she went on tour as "The Four Columbians". The act played Europe for seven years, until Lee Shubert brought them back to America. Then, as it must to all pretty girls of that era, came the Follies. For years, Marilyn was Ziegfeld's première danseuse. She married, and her husband was killed in an automobile accident. Later, she married Jack Pickford, probably—as she once admitted—because Ziegfeld told her he'd fire her if she did. After their divorce, she went to Hollywood, where she made pictures at the publicized rate of $150,000 a picture, a sum which was not justified by the subsequent box-office receipts. Of late, she has been more or less in the news background, emerging sporadically to affirm or deny her engagement to Don Alvarado—a movie hero, darkly sleek. One of these spurts of publicity occurred recently, when she and Alvarado sailed for Europe on the same boat, causing furious rumors of a secret marriage.

Mary Lewis' father was a Methodist minister in Little Rock, Arkansas. At eight, Mary was singing *I'll Be a Little Sunbeam for Jesus* in her father's Sunday-school. Eleven years later, she ran off with a road-show and was stranded in San Francisco, where she got a job singing in Tait's Cafe. First a chorus girl, then a prima donna, she left Ziegfeld for the concert stage. Then she came East. Her Metropolitan début was in 1929. Critics tossed their verbal violets at her feet and for a while she basked in that sweet sunlight. Last fall, attempting a comeback, she was present at the opening of the supper club of the Ritz-Carlton Hotel in New York and was asked to sing. In the midst of *Carry Me Back to Old Virginny*, a drunk tossed pennies at her feet. Gallantly she smiled, stooped to pick them up, and finished her song. Now she is again at leisure.

Bernard Douras was a South Brooklyn magistrate. He sent his blonde daughter, who had been posing for Howard Chandler Christy, to Ziegfeld with a note of introduction. From then on, she was a Follies feature for three years, under the name of Marion Davies. The rest is unofficial history. Her movie career has been long and flourishing; her establishments lavish; her home-grown orchids the most famed in America; and her reputation as a Hollywood hostess without peer. Last year, the government sued her for $1,000,000 income taxes. They compromised on $825,000.

Ina Claire, whose latest Broadway show is *Biography*, is one of the most famed of the Ziegfeld graduates. At thirteen, she was Ina Fagan of

Washington, doing imitations of Harry Lauder. She was a Follies star in the days when W. C. Fields was presenting his amiable Jewish comedy, long before Montague Glass sold his birthright for a mess of *Potash and Perlmutter*. Her Hollywood interlude—which included marriage and divorce with John Gilbert—the screen's one-time Great Lover—is now a part of the cinematic archives.

Most of the $30,000,000 of Sir Mortimer Davis, plump Canadian tobacco magnate, evaporated two years ago. Rosie Dolly sued him for divorce. But the marriage, with its tales of disinheritance, of parental wrath, of Lucullan splendor on the Riviera, had served its function in the public prints. Rosika and Jancsi Dolly, Hungarian twins, are world-celebrated figures now, but they got their start in the Follies. They are always good newspaper copy, whether they are marrying millionaires, breaking the bank at Monte Carlo, dancing with princes or lending their decorative bare brown backs to the Mediterranean sands. When the Moulin Rouge in Montmartre played up Mistinguette's legs ahead of the twins, they sued for 500,000 francs and got it. They are garlanded with bright legends and are practically a modern saga in themselves.

Dorothy Mackaill of the drooping mouth and Botticelli cheekline came from the music-halls of England to the Ziegfeld offices and the Midnight Follies. Marshall Neilan took her to Hollywood. Lilyan Tashman used to give imitations of Frank Tinney. She came to the Follies from a Brooklyn high school. Billie Dove's lucid features gazed serenely from magazine covers until the 1917 Follies, when she could be seen any night, swinging in a hoop hung from an elaborate artificial tree.

Then there are the others: Fannie Brice, whose great Follies song was *Lovey Joe*; Norma Talmadge, now making personal appearances at picture houses; Gladys Glad, the Bronx Venus who came out of an Elks' carnival to the Follies and now conducts a beauty column on the *Daily Mirror*; Helen Morgan, who just got off the *Showboat* piano; Mae Murray of the bee-stung lips and Prince Mdivani; and Ann Pennington, who was *September Morn* in the Follies of 1913 and is still showing her historic knees in 1933.

THE PATH TO WEALTH

Peggy Hopkins Joyce, a unique American symbol in her own right, apart from the Follies connotation, was a barber's daughter from Norfolk, Virginia, who ran away with a trick bicycle rider when she was fifteen. On the train she met another man. This was Everett Archer, whom she married in Denver. It lasted six months. In Washington, she met, married and divorced young Sherburne Hopkins. Thence to New York, where she met Ziegfeld. She couldn't sing, she couldn't act, and she certainly couldn't dance, but in the Follies of 1917, she blossomed forth as an American beauty. Since then, her matrimonial career—America's eighth largest industry, it has been called—is public record. To have been a Joyce consort is almost as great a badge of distinction as to have been a Follies Girl—and there are almost as many of them. At present, the lady is singularly single and has just returned from the Riviera, where she finished another book, the sequel to *Men, Marriage and Me*—a curious document of Americana and commentary on our cultural structure.

Peggy Fears came from New Orleans, met Noel Francis, a Follies Girl now in the Hollywood ranks, and, through her, became the youngest prima donna in the Follies. She left the stage to marry A. C. Blumenthal ("You can have your city hall, I'll take A. C. Blumenthal")—the real estate and film magnate. At present, Mrs. Blumenthal is the busiest theatrical producer on Broadway in her own name, with *Music in the Air*, one of the few authentic hits of the season; *Party* in the near offing; *The Establishment of Mme. Antonia* on her list; and the *All-Time Follies* in her mind.

Ziegfeld's stately Dolores, the best known showgirl of them all—famed for her peacock walk—is now Mrs. Tudor Wilkinson, holding salons in the Rue St. Honoré in Paris. Ethel Amorita Kelly married Frank Gould. Jessica Brown is Lady Northesk; Justine Johnston, who bore, in company with half her countrywomen, the Alfred Cheney Johnson sobriquet of "most beautiful woman in America", now studies medicine and is the wife of Walter Wanger, formerly one of the bigger cinema magnates; Mary Eaton married Millard Webb, cinema director; and Florence Walton, once the dancing partner of the celebrated Maurice Mouvet, married wealth and lives in Europe, as does Anastasia Reilly of the lovely shoulders. Miss Walton is about to publish her memoirs.

THE PATH TO OBLIVION

Beauty contests recruited many of the latter-day Follies Girls. Such a one was Dorothy Knapp, "The American Venus". A convent girl—as what Follies Girl wasn't?—from Illinois, she came to New York to study art, was featured by Earl Carroll in his 1922 Vanities, and two years later, she was in the Follies. Later years have seen her fame confined to a series of law suits, an esoteric battle at a Beaux Arts ball, a mysteriously battered face.

One of the loveliest faces ever to bloom in the Follies was that of Imogene Wilson, the blonde "Bubbles". She came to New York at fourteen from a Missouri orphanage and entered the Follies via the posing route. Linked with Frank Tinney in what was the scandal of the decade, she went to Germany, changed her name to Mary Nolan and became a motion picture actress. Later, she returned to America and Hollywood. Her particular gift for tragedy followed her there, and she became implicated in a slander suit. Shunted out of pictures, she and her husband opened a dress shop which ended in a series of suits brought by their creditors—and eventual bankruptcy. Recently, Mary did a personal appearance tour of the subway-circuit.

Two other former Follies names have recently made news. Helen Lee Worthing of the cameo profile married a Negro doctor, whom she divorced not long ago and who is now suing her, in turn, to have the divorce set aside and the marriage annulled, instead. And Eva Tanguay, who "didn't care" in the Follies of 1919, was a month or so ago the beneficiary of a charity performance held in Manhattan.

THE PATH TO DEATH

When Ziegfeld brought Anna Held of the convex eyes from Paris, the song which made her the toast of New York was this:

"I'm fond of romps and games, you see,

I wish you'd come and play wiz me.

For I have such a nize leetle way wiz me,

I wish you'd come and play wiz me."

This was considered very provocative. (Remember, it was the "I love my wife, but oh you kid!" era.)

Anna Held was born in Paris, of Polish immigrant parents. At fourteen, she began playing tragic rôles in a Yiddish theatre in London's unsavoury Whitechapel district. Later, she drifted to music-hall shows, where Ziegfeld discovered her. She married him in 1896 and divorced him in 1912. Now she is dead—and so is he—but there are many who still retain the glittering memory of her days—the story of how she chased a runaway horse on her bicycle and rescued a Brooklyn magnate—pure Ziegfeld fiction—and of the times when all downtown New York traffic stood still so that Anna Held could cross the street.

Death came also to other lovely bearers of the Follies brand. Bessie McCoy, the original *Yama Yama* girl, died only a year or so ago. Martha Mansfield was burned to death, and rumor dubbed it suicide. Allyn King jumped out of a window; Lillian Lorraine of *Blue Kitten* fame fell downstairs and broke her back; Helen Walsh burned to death last year in the explosion of Harry Richman's yacht; Olive Thomas found tragedy and death in Paris, at the time she was the wife of Jack Pickford; and Kay Laurel died in Paris, winning for her illegitimate son a substantial inheritance.

There they are—the three-score or more whose names have spelled beauty and the high life. They have swung in flower-wreathed swings out over the bald-headed row: they have draped themselves in "living curtains" against incredible backgrounds of Joseph Urban blue; they have pranced across the stage and kicked their heels to metronome beat. And, later, they have gone on into life—to sing, to dance, to act, to marry or to die. And always there has followed them that significant aura, that ultimate encomium: She was once a Follies Girl.

THE MOLL IN OUR MIDST

STANLEY WALKER

FROM AUGUST 1934

n spite of the rumors of war and revolution, the steel strikes, the Washington investigations, the rout of Tammany, the death of Stavisky, the arrival of Insull, and all those items which have made this a particularly newsy year, a certain creature—female in species, unsavory in background—has persistently tripped and triggered its way into the newspaper headlines.

Last May, when a red-headed gun-girl called Bonnie Parker was shot to pieces in Louisiana, even the most cautious were obliged to admit that there had been a minor *coup d'état* in our underworld. The night-club queen had abdicated, she wasn't news any more; the gunman's moll had climbed into her warm but empty throne.

In the days of yore, there was no such thing as a gunman's moll; the old-time bad man may have had a wife hidden away in some rose-covered cottage—or a paramour living two doors from the saloon, one flight up and ring Doake's bell; but his calling was essentially masculine, and he rode the trail with companions as male as himself. Jesse James, for instance, that home-loving Baptist who invented train robbery—*he* lived a mild, monogamous home-life after his marriage to Zerelda ("Zee" to Jesse) Mimms. Whatever else Zerelda may have been, she was no moll.

t was not until this year that the word "moll" really came into its own. It used to mean a woman pickpocket, or a woman associate of pickpockets;

then it became "gun-moll"; then it lost the "gun-", got involved with the Seventh Commandment, and came to mean the light o' love of any mobster, killer or thief. The word has been public property for some years now, but it was only during the last few months that we realized how public it was. The contemporary criminal, we have learned to our cost, *must* have a girl friend to ride along on his wild escapes, encourage his artistry with the tommy-gun, and make up a rubber at bridge—just between bank robberies.

The great Dillinger was a shining example of this—"Just one woman after another," that was his motto. True, he started his amorous career with a marriage—to Miss Beryl Ethel Hovis, sixteen years old and a home-town girl, who divorced him in 1929. But, once he began to make money by sticking up banks, Dillinger's passion for brunettes got the better of him. Most of the ones he chose came from small Middle-western towns, where there was little chance of their picking up worldly ideas, and they were more loyal to him than their city sisters would have been.

The most charming of them all was Evelyn Frechette, the daughter of an Indian woman and a French-Canadian laborer. She used to make occasional week-end trips to Chicago, and it was probably on one of these that she first met Dillinger. "I just drifted until I met Jack," was the way she put it afterwards. "He gave me love."

She was twenty-three years old when they captured her last April. She had been given the credit for supplying Dillinger with that famous wooden pistol which terrified the woman-managed jail at Crown Point; and among her possessions, in the Chicago flat where she was run to earth, were keys to Hollywood police stations. Nobody could say she wasn't a resourceful girl.

She was boastful and defiant in jail, waiting for her trial. "They won't have me here for long," she said. "If Jack won't get me out of here I can beat the rap when they take me to court. All I did was to go to the man I loved when he needed me. I'll do it every time I can. He is my man."

But Jack didn't come. And she didn't beat the rap. She was found guilty of harboring Dillinger, and sentenced to two years' imprisonment.

Girls like Evelyn take terrible risks, but they are realists for the most part. It is better to have clothes and money to go places, they argue, than to sit in a little town and parry the advances of some cloddish swain, or live hungrily but honestly in a hall bedroom, or wash dishes, or stand behind a counter. Coming, as they nearly always do, from surroundings where there is little but poverty and brutality, they can hardly be blamed for making no distinction between virtue and chores.

When it comes to bounce and kick, no Dillinger woman, not even the Frechette herself, could hold a candle to the late Bonnie Parker, known to admirers as the "Cigar-Smoking Gun-woman of the South West". She and her friend, Clyde Barrow, were very thoroughly killed last May in Louisiana; but while they lasted they made an enterprising team. Bonnie was a redhead, not unattractive in a freakish way, and easily recognizable by her striped sweater, which gave her the look of a slim hornet, an insect with which that female sharpshooter had much in common.

Her background follows a familiar design; she was brought up in that section of Dallas, Texas, which borders on the foul swamps of Trinity River. On her thigh was a tattooed heart with "Roy" in it, a memento of her first love, Roy Harding, who went to prison for murder. Her next squire was Barrow, who had been known in the community since before he was fifteen as an incorrigible liar, a loafer, a cheat, and a thief. She worked with him over ten states, and omitting all their other assorted crimes, they were wanted for twelve murders.

The end came when they were ambushed by a group of officers led by Frank Hamer, former Texas ranger, who has killed sixty-five men, and is probably the finest gunfighter since the days of Wyatt Earp, Bat Masterson, and the other immortals. This time he was taking no chances: he and his men pumped 167 bullets into the car which carried Bonnie and Clyde. Bonnie died with her head between her knees, a machine gun across her lap, and a package of cigarettes in her left hand. She had gone to her death all in red. She had on a red dress, red shoes, a red and white hat; under her clothes, on her thin chest, there lay a crucifix, hanging from around her neck; her fingers glittered with diamond rings, and she wore a costly wrist watch.

She was the literary member of the team. Months before the end she had written a poem called "The Life of Bonnie and Clyde", the last verse of which runs:—

"One day they will go down together,
And they will bury them side by side.
To a few it means grief,
To the law it's relief,

But it's death to Bonnie and Clyde."

All this came true, except the second line, for the mothers of the precious pair refused to allow them to be buried side by side, and Bonnie's body lies in the little Fishtrap Cemetery, a full mile from Clyde's. Thousands of people swarmed to his funeral, while only a handful attended hers: it's still a man's world, say what you will. Her tombstone is to bear this epitaph—"As the flowers are all made sweeter by the sunshine and the dew, so this world is made brighter by the lives of folks like you".

Gunmen, fools that most of them are, forget all the precedents which should warn them against association with women. Their girls may be handsome creatures, devoid of all the more discouraging inhibitions, but each one carries a gallows in her handbag. The average moll is a nuisance when it comes to making a rapid get-away, she talks at the wrong time, and the day may come when, sitting in the witness stand, she will send her Robin Hood to hell. That is what Helen Walsh did.

Helen was the sixteen-year-old sweetheart of Francis (Two-Gun) Crowley, the boy who hated cops because he knew, or thought he knew, that he was the illegitimate son of a former policeman. "Such a nice young man", was Helen's mother's opinion. Helen's mother had given her daughter money, in the hope that she would study interior decorating. Instead of that, Helen went out riding with Two-Gun.

One night, they were happily parked in Black Shirt Lane, North Merrick, Long Island. The only trouble in this paradise was the fact that the police were after Crowley for one thing and another; and when a young patrolman named Hirsch came up, peered into the automobile, and recognized Crowley, he was shot dead. The killer and his girl friend sped away; and then the police began to hunt in earnest.

Crowley took a furnished apartment on West End Avenue, New York City, where he lived uneasily with a woman named Billie Dunne and Rudolph Durninger, a 220-pound oaf of a truckman, who had recently killed a dance hall girl and thrown her out of a car in Yonkers. One day he told the Dunne girl that he was through: "I'm bringing a real girl home with me," he said, "you can go with Durninger." Bad stuff; it led to his capture. The police surrounded the apartment, one hundred strong, and there was a big show, with shooting—something of a Roman holiday for thousands of New York citizens.

The police got Crowley, Helen Walsh, Durninger, and a rare literary fragment or two—the beleaguered Helen had been doing some writing.

As the police were closing in, the frightened little exhibitionist wrote this:

"I bet Legs Diamond dies upon something different from bullets. I'll see you in heaven if there is such a place. Everybody thinks he's hard but he can't be. He (Crowley) cooked my breakfast this morning and washed my pajamas so I could sleep in them. If I should see Vivian Gordon I will ask her who shot her. Love to Mother, Father, and Sister. P.S. Show this to my sister so that she will know I died smiling. Please don't talk about me when I'm gone."

Looking like a schoolgirl, Helen sat in the witness stand, and sent Crowley to the electric chair; she herself went free because of her testimony. Just before he was put to death, Crowley got word that she wanted to see him; she hoped to write an article about his execution, so he heard, for one of the tabloids—worse still, there was a rumor that she had been keeping company with a policeman. "All she wants to do is to sell some stories, or go on the stage, or something," said Two-Gun, bitterly. "The hell with her!"

The Millen brothers—Murton and Irving—with their partner, Abe Faber, were recently convicted of murder in Massachusetts. When the brothers were captured in a New York hotel they had Mrs. Norma Brighton Millen, Murton's bride, along with them. Their capture came about when police found a postcard which Norma had written to her stepmother at Natick, Mass. "Murton and I are staying here. We are buying radio parts."

After the gang's arrest, the Rev. Norman Brighton came to New York to take charge of his daughter. "Ah," he sighed, "if only I knew how to protect her." Ah, indeed, Papa Brighton. Norma was only nineteen, and she enjoyed the publicity; she even talked of going into motion pictures. While she was in jail, as a supposed accessory after the fact to a bank robbery, she complained about the prison garb and kicked because there was no sugar in her coffee; and when she was interviewed, she spoke out in the grand old tradition:

"I loved Murt, because he was so gentle and kind to me. He used to do the dishes every night. We'd have such fun—it was like playing house. He used to put on an apron and make me sit in the kitchen chair and watch him. And he was so generous. He gave me everything I wanted. He used to take me to the big department stores and say, 'Look around, Kitten, you can have anything in this store.'"

Ten years ago, there was much excitement in New York over the original "Bobbed-Hair Bandit"—Celia Cooney. Celia was working in a laundry when she met Edward Cooney and married him, and it didn't take them long to decide that his $30 a week as a mechanic wasn't enough. Besides, there was a baby coming. For a while they practised the technique of holdups in their little furnished room, and then went out to do their stuff in public; she wasn't sure who had the idea first.

Celia was known as a "one-rig woman"—that is, she always wore a seal-skin coat, a gray crêpe de Chine gown, and a pink turban. She was twenty years old and as impudent as they come; she used to write taunting notes to the police and her victims. There was a lot of the primitive woman in her, too—ten days before the baby came, she held a gun in her hand and helped her husband to rob the National Biscuit Company in Brooklyn.

The baby died in Florida just before Celia and Edward were captured there and sent to prison, where Celia consoled herself with all the crime fiction she could lay her hands on. They are out now, and said to be going straight, with the powerful aid of a $12,000 reward which Cooney got from the State because he lost a hand in an accident in the prison factory.

Out in the Bronx, in the summer of 1933, some thugs were attempting to rob Isidor Moroh, a jewellery salesman, when a girl named Betty Schwarz strayed into the line of fire and was killed. Two days later, detectives walked in on Lottie Kreisberger Coll and two companions, Thomas Pace and Joseph Ventre, in a Broadway hotel, and arrested them for the murder of the Schwarz girl. Lottie and her boy friends had their guns with them. She pleaded guilty to manslaughter and was sent to the reformatory for from six to twelve years.

Lottie was of exceptionally tough fibre. Brought here from Germany at the age of two, she was dragged up in the Hell's Kitchen district, and much of her girlhood was spent among the wild roosters of New York's West Side. She married Vincent Coll, the smiling killer, the man who was shot down in a telephone booth just a few hours after Mr. Walter Winchell had predicted something of the sort. Coll wasn't her first; there had been at least one marriage and several alliances before he came into her life, and she was only 24 when he died. Of him she said:

"I would rather have lived with Coll on bread and coffee than with anyone else on millions."

Marion "Kiki" Roberts, born Marion Strasmick and a former bathing contest winner, was a show girl trying to get along when she met Jack "Legs" Diamond in New York's Club Abbey in 1929. He asked for her phone number, and got it; and thereafter, in the many shootings that occurred with that durable racketeer on the receiving end, she was usually somewhere around. When he was finally killed in Albany, he had just left her apartment. Their relations seemed to have caused very little worry to Mrs. Legs, who knew her Legs for a temperamental fellow where women were concerned. Miss Roberts, who is now living in obscurity, once said:

"All my life I have been a good girl. Jack was my first sweetheart."

In December, 1930, two aviators found the bullet-riddled body of Stephen Sweeney, head of a gang of New York speakeasy robbers, lying near the motor parkway at Hicksville, Long Island. He had been taken there in an automobile and killed by his own gang, a leading member of which was his 17-year-old sweetheart, Margaret Murray, a blue-eyed blonde from the West Side of New York. Margaret had worked for a time as a telephone operator but had to quit, she said, because of a "weak heart"—a state of things which she remedied by becoming lookout, counsellor, and pal to a gang of killers. Her father was in an insane asylum.

After the gang had been rounded up, Margaret was turned loose, whereupon she dropped these pearls:

"The gangster has no respect for women. He will beat them up, shoot them as readily as he would a man. But to flirt with another gangster's moll is recognised as the most fatal form of chiseling. It is seldom started and seldom allowed to go far.

"I was Sweeney's sweetheart. Never did any other man in the mob make any advance toward me. The gangster usually has a Jane or two on the side. Inside our mob there were no skirt worries. A gangster's moll can't really be overpaid. When her man is bumped off, is jugged, or goes cold on her, she is plenty out of luck."

There was something silent, something wrong about a certain dingy, plain flat in West 104th Street, New York; and the neighbors grew curious and fearful and called the police in. It was a Sunday in August, 1932.

The police found a grisly layout. A man and a woman lay dead there, side by side. The woman was a platinum blonde, dressed in a white crash suit, white shoes, white stockings, and a close-fitting white knit hat; she was rather pretty, and she only weighed eighty-five pounds.

Her name was Rosemary Sanborn, and there will always be some mystery about her strange life. She never got much publicity, even when she died, but she was different from the others and exceptionally competent in her line. In her way, she was one of the greatest of all blackmailers.

The man was Robert Conroy, alias Harry Leo Davis, Robert M. Carney, Robert Newberry, Robert Perry, and R. K. Howard, gunman and counterfeiter. What had happened was obvious—he had shot her and then himself; but there were no messages, no clues as to why he had decided on this brutal ending. There was plenty of other evidence—a hand printing press, copper plates, photographic paraphernalia, counterfeit notes; but the gem of the collection was a series of photographs, all showing Rosemary in a compromising situation with a man.

The Police Commissioner at that time was Edward P. Mulrooney, and he was one of the first to arrive at the flat. A detective took the photographs, remarking that he had better file them at Police Headquarters. "No," said Mulrooney, "nobody will see these again." And the Commissioner then threw them in the stove and burned them.

The next day he was besieged by various men of note, greatly upset, who wanted to know whether their pictures were in the collection, and who were vastly relieved to learn that Rosemary's little Suckers' Gallery had gone up in flames. Rosemary, it seems, used to work the hotels, even the best ones, and the best trains between New York and Washington, Chicago, and Canada. She was clever, this American Madonna of the Sleeping Cars, and curiously attractive for all that she was scrawny; and detectives say that she was the best two-fisted drinker, man or woman, ever to down a highball. Why did Conroy kill her? What was their life together like? He might at least have written a letter, and she—what a poem *she* could have written!

LITTLE CARUSO

WILLIAM SAROYAN

FROM OCTOBER 1934

Playing cards at Breen's, I suddenly felt his presence in the city, like swift and sweeping excitement, all over Frisco, from the Ferry Building to the Sunset Tunnel, and a half hour later, at midnight, I saw him push through the swinging doors and walk down the length of the bar, in a terrific hurry, the way he always was, and I knew it was the same old fight, between my cousin Mano, a small dark fellow of twenty-two in a neat twelve-dollar suit, wanting to be the greatest tenor of all time, and his incredible and insane impetuosity, his everlasting unrest.

"God Almighty," I said.

"We've got no time to lose," he said. "I have been all over the public library looking for you. Is this where you spend all your time these days? What's come over you, anyway?"

"What's the matter?" I said.

"I got kicked out of the house this morning," he said, "but I'll sing from the stage of the Metropolitan Opera House in New York, if it's the last thing I do. Can I see you alone a minute?"

I got up from the table and walked with him to the door.

"Let's go up the alley," he said. "I want to sing *La Donna E Mobile*."

"Never mind that," I said. "Have you any money for a room tonight?"

"I haven't a nickel," he said, "but wait till you hear me sing. I caught a freight this morning, and I practiced all the way up."

"Don't make it too loud," I said. "They'll run us in for disturbing the peace."

"They wouldn't dare arrest a man with my voice," he said.

He sang the song and made something in me laugh from the beginning of time to the end of it, because he did not sing, he shouted, thrusting himself beyond the limitations of his body, outward, into the night, into the vastness of the universe, the endlessness of time, making a marvelous noise in the city. And it wasn't *La Donna E Mobile*: it was the cry of all of us who are seeking immortality on earth, in our own time, and the only thing I could think was, God Almighty.

"My diction is better than Gigli's," he said. "If Otto Kahn could hear me, I'd be sent to Italy in three minutes."

"I've got a dollar and thirty cents," I said. "I'll get you a room for the night, and I'll see you tomorrow."

I found a clean four-bit room for him in a small hotel on Columbus Avenue, and he said, "The world will remember you as the man who helped the greatest tenor of all time when he was broke and friendless. Leave me a half dozen cigarettes because I can't wait to get going."

I left him half a package of cigarettes, and went home. In the morning I took him a safety razor and a half dozen blades, two pairs of socks, and three clean shirts. Playing carefully, I won enough gambling to keep him going for two weeks. He went to every theatre and night club in town, begging everybody he saw to let him sing *La Donna E Mobile*, but they wouldn't let him do it.

"They don't know who I am," he said, "but I'll show them. I'm getting a boat to Italy because I want to walk in the streets where Caruso walked. Don't you think I look a lot like him?"

He spent a week sitting in the Seamen's Hall on Howard Street, but there were no boats to Italy, so he took the next best thing and got a job as wiper on a boat to Rio.

"Nothing is going to stop me from moving the hearts of people everywhere," he said. "I wrote some letters to Otto Kahn and Deems Taylor and a couple of other people, but I can't wait. This trip to South America is just the thing for me. The answers will come General Delivery," he said. "Hold the letters till I get back."

I went to the General Delivery window of the Post Office for two weeks, and the only letter that came addressed to him was one from a girl back in our home town. She wrote bitterly, saying that she had really loved him once, but that it was all over now because he was not the sort of person to marry and settle down and make a name for himself. I kept the letter a month, and then tore it up.

The day he got back I was in Breen's, and I saw him tear through the swinging doors, looking furious, and the old laugh came up in me again, and I was glad he hadn't fallen off the boat and drowned.

"I can't figure you out," he said. "I've been half way around the world, busting my neck trying to establish myself, and you sit in this ungodly joint playing cards. I met a singing teacher in Rio and he said I would be a sensation in the next three years, but I can't wait. What did Otto Kahn say, anyway? Did Deems Taylor answer my letter?"

I thought I ought to lie and tell him Otto Kahn was interested in his voice, but I couldn't do it. Then I remembered that while he was gone Otto Kahn had died, and I said, "I've got bad news for you, Mano. Otto Kahn passed away while you were in Rio."

"Everything is against me," he said. "Just when I need him most, Otto Kahn dies. For the love of Mike, don't tell me Deems Taylor is dead, too. What did Deems say?"

"Well," I said, "I understand Deems Taylor is traveling in Europe. I think he is going to be away for another year."

"All I need is a decent contact," he said. "I know what I can do, but nobody else does."

He had a little money saved, and he stayed in Frisco until the money was gone. Then, humiliated but angry, he went back to his home town, and during the next six months I received an average of three letters a week from him.

"The power of my voice is increasing every day," he said, "and it won't be long before I can be heard from here to the Rainier Brewery, fourteen blocks away. On a clear day I can do it now, but the wind has got to be with me . . .

"I am going to make boxes for Mouradian this summer. I've got to earn enough money to get to New York this fall because once I get there I will electrify everybody with my singing. If you get down this way, be sure and see me at Mouradian's packing house, in East Bakersfield, because I want you to hear me sing *O Sole Mio*."

Two weeks ago I got fed up with the city and began longing for the valley where I was born, for the hot sun and the vineyards and the clarity of life there, the clarity that is driving the whole race of us all over the world, making us want to do tremendous things. I hitch-hiked from Frisco to Bakersfield and went straight out to Mouradian's packing house. Mano was in a corner, at a bench, standing on a platform because he was too small to work well from the floor, furiously nailing boxes, but not singing.

"You're just the fellow I want to see," he said. "I am disgusted with everything, and the way I feel now, I don't know whether I'll ever be able to sing again because this humiliation is getting to be too much for me. Everybody thinks I am nobody because I am in overalls, nailing boxes. Nobody can tell from the way I act that I am the greatest living tenor on earth, and it's burning me up."

"What you are doing," I said, "is only a means to an end. You'll be in New York this fall and everything will be swell."

"But I can't wait," he said. "I hate this atmosphere. It is destroying everything fine in me."

He didn't stop making boxes, but talked while he brought the hatchet down on the nails, bang bang bang, talking and moving his powerful arm with great rhythm.

Fifty young Filipinos stood in the packing house, packing grapes, talking along in their language while they worked, making a low and steady mumble in the heat.

"Listen to them," said Mano. "My voice will be ruined. Never before in the history of the world has a great artist suffered such humiliation as this. I need to be alone, always, so that I can let my voice grow."

He was very bitter and I didn't know what to tell him.

Then something happened that makes me laugh every time I think of it. One of the Filipino boys was having a little fun, throwing grapes at another Filipino boy who was pasting labels on boxes just beyond where Mano was working. One of the grapes went wild and hit Mano on the neck.

Mano was nailing away nicely, but when the grape hit his neck, the rhythm of his movements came to a sudden and furious stop, and he was mad. He got off the platform and walked around his bench, the hatchet still in his hand, lifted high.

"Who threw that grape?" he said, only it was more than speech, just as his singing was less, and more, than singing. The old insane fury.

All the boys were talking along cheerfully until they heard Mano's voice. Then the whole packing house became very quiet.

"Who threw that God-damn grape!" he said. "I'll bust the head of any bastard who throws a grape at the greatest lyric tenor in the world."

A full minute he stood before them, waiting for one of the boys to say some word, or make some false move. There were fifty of them, but they knew they were in the presence of some mighty and glorious power in man, and they were afraid, and I myself was afraid.

"If I get hit with a grape again," he said, "I'll find out who threw it and I'll bust his head. You don't know who I am, but I know."

He walked back to his bench, stepped onto the platform, and began again to nail. "You see," he said sullenly. "I am humiliated because no one knows who I am."

"Take it easy," I said. "I know who you are. You are the greatest lyric tenor alive, and everybody else will know it the minute you get to New York."

And I'm telling you, I wasn't fooling, either. My cousin Mano *is* the greatest living tenor on earth because he *thinks* he is, and nothing is going to stop him from walking out on the stage of the Metropolitan Opera House in New York and electrifying everybody with the fury of his personality, not even the untimely passing of Otto Kahn, the aloofness of Deems Taylor, or the fact that his voice isn't worth a damn.

TARZAN—APE-MAN INTO INDUSTRY

DARWIN L. TEILHET

FROM JANUARY 1935

In purely material accomplishment, not even an Anthony Adverse or a Ben Hur can compare with Tarzan, acrobat of the jungle. Nor has any author more thoroughly exploited his literary produce than has Mr. Edgar Rice Burroughs of Tarzana, California. Some of his stories are pretty lousy, Mr. Burroughs admits, "but they sell," he says simply. "That's what's important."

They certainly sell. The Tarzan books have been translated into twenty-two languages; they are standard items of Arabian publishers and well thought of among readers of Hindustani; they have been best sellers in England, Sweden, Australia, and Italy. They continue to be so in America. Every two years a new Tarzan volume is scheduled for publication; and before the new saga is bound in cloth covers at two dollars a copy, every yard has first been wholesaled as a serial.

Tarzan, however, is rather more than just a literary figure. He is also a radio act; a film hero; a familiar figure to readers of the comic strips; and one whose name has lent authority to such diverse commodities as gum, garters, and inflated rubber toys. He is, in fact, a property any author would be glad to own.

Mr. Burroughs was not always an author; he became one at the age of thirty-three. He had already been a cavalryman, cowboy, railroad policeman, gold dredger, patent-medicine salesman and vendor of a drunkards' cure-all. He also did something not very profitable with a patent pencil sharpener. Eventually he owned half of the patent-medicine outfit; then he transferred his allegiance to a business counsel service in Chicago.

In 1910, while he was still with the business counsel service, a friend informed him that magazine writers received staggering sums of money. This was apparently the first time that Mr. Burroughs had heard the news; he at once decided to get a piece of this money for himself. He constructed a romance entitled *The Princess of Mars*, which concerns a young man who arrives on the planet Mars and falls in love with a Princess. Although the Princess laid eggs (very well, you read it then), the serial, on its appearance in *All-Story Magazine*, scarcely caused a flutter among that publication's hardened readers.

But Mr. Burroughs was paid for it: $400. This miracle inflicted upon him his one and only spasm of creative vertigo. He spent six months boning up on English history in order to produce a masterpiece called *The Outlaw of Torn*; it was thick with knights, dukes, and Tudor atmosphere; but it was pretty much of a bust financially. This taught him his lesson. Henceforth, he was to waste no time on literary background.

In 1912, Mr. Burroughs sent the editors of the old *All-Story Weekly* the uncompleted manuscript of his third adventure tale, *Tarzan of the Apes*, having for his principal character a young man reared and cherished by the primordial apes of darkest Africa. The editors were so ravished by the original plot idea (Mr. Burroughs swears he never thought of Kipling's *Mowgli*) that they purchased the story and impatiently waited delivery.

For the Tarzan saga the author relied on what he remembered of Stanley's *Darkest Africa*, and when *Darkest Africa* failed him he fell back on a prodigious invention. That saved time. Mr. Burroughs hates to see time or energy go to waste. An efficient and economical man, he was even able to salvage most of that six months' historical research.

This was done by transferring Old England to darkest Africa in the third of his Tarzan series, which revolves around the simple theme of a Tudor colony—which had somehow or other been lost in the jungle four centuries ago, and survived unchanged into the present day. A man who can have his heroine lay eggs on the planet Mars isn't one to be troubled by his readers' feelings when they happen upon a description of sixteenth century knights wandering through Africa in modern times.

By 1913, with three serials marketed, he decided to devote himself entirely to fiction. So he and his family trekked to California. A year later, a publisher was finally discovered who would risk committing *Tarzan of the Apes* to a book. Not that it was much of a risk—America seemed to be filled with nature lovers, who took the mighty Tarzan immediately to their bosoms. The book rocketed through one edition after another, into the astonishing sales figures of three million copies. With his royalties, in 1915, Mr. Burroughs purchased the old Otis estate fifteen miles outside of Los Angeles; gratefully renamed it "Tarzana Ranch"; and, for the next decade, slaved away at his task of author, turning out 24 book-length novels, including six more of the imperishable jungle series.

Meanwhile, Selig Pictures had purchased *The Lad and the Lion* in 1916; National Films, *Tarzan of the Apes*, in 1918, one of the first of the silents to gross over a million dollars: National Films, *Romance of Tarzan*, the same year; Universal, *The Return of Tarzan*, in 1919; Century, *Adventures of Tarzan*, in 1920; and West Brothers, *Son of Tarzan*, in 1922.

Middle-westerners had already started moving west to their vision of Paradise. As they passed by his ranch, Mr. Burroughs began to feel that old urge to strike his pitch and begin selling things to the multitude. He subdivided Tarzana ranch into lots, and soon the pleasant township of Tarzana spread out beneath the sterile blue California sky. In 1923, deciding that book publishers' practice of demanding 65 to 90% of the gross returns from authors' brain-children was too much of a good thing, he organized the Edgar Rice Burroughs Corporation, elected himself president, and proceeded to publish and market his own literary wares and also to consolidate his real estate activities.

* * *

From 1923 to 1929 he sold *Tarzan and the Golden Lion* to F.B.O., *Tarzan the Mighty* and *Tarzan and the Tiger* to Universal; he also sold his Tarzana home to the Tarzana Golf Club, Inc.; obtained a Tarzana post office from the Government; assisted at the inauguration of the Tarzana Chamber of Commerce, which has regularly communed once a week ever since. He also limited himself to four hours a day before a dictaphone, uttering twelve eighty-thousand-word novels. Not one of them received a rejection slip, either from the magazines or from Edgar Rice Burroughs, Inc.

Tarzan the Tiger was released in 1930 during the mournful demise of the silent films. The talking-picture came as no surprise to a gentleman who had already blandly written of the scientific marvels of interplanetary communication and travel. He found a small motion picture company which, delighted with the idea of a Tarzan learning to speak, purchased the sound rights to *Tarzan the Fearless*.

The depression stopped these plans; *Tarzan the Fearless* remained unproduced. But Mr. Burroughs has never been easily discouraged. He went to M.G.M.'s white-headed boy, Mr. Irving Thalberg, with *Tarzan the Ape-man*. When it appeared in 1932, starring Johnny Weissmuller and Maureen O'Sullivan, out of the entire industry only the author and the psychic Mr. Thalberg were prepared for the extraordinary run which followed.

Immediately, Mr. Sol Lesser bought the rights to *Tarzan the Fearless* from the producers who had first obtained them from the trusting Mr. Burroughs. And, despite the acute embarrassment of the author, who had sold M.G.M. a sequel, *Tarzan and His Mate*, Mr. Lesser coldly turned his legal property into a rather muddy serial featuring Mr. Buster Crabbe. For the next half year, millions of nature lovers, to whom practically nothing comes amiss, were nevertheless faintly bewildered by the spectacle of two Tarzans bounding and screaming with equal verve among the branches of large studio trees.

But now all is well. Mr. Burroughs recently disposed of his thirteenth Tarzan scenario. It has been taken by M.G.M. for a third Johnny Weissmuller thriller. . . .

Mr. Burroughs does not care to leave his offices in Tarzana. He is furiously occupied with his various projects. Three years ago, for instance, he placed his eldest son, Mr. Hulbert Burroughs, in charge of a newly formed radio division of Edgar Rice Burroughs, Inc.; contracted with an independent radio producer to make a group of Tarzan records based on the Tarzan stories; arranged for his daughter, Joan, to play "Jane Porter," the delicious heroine of the "Tarzan Radio Act", as it is named; had Mr. James H. Pierce, a former cinema Tarzan who eventually wedded Miss Burroughs, return to service as the radio Tarzan; and, in two years, through the independent radio producer, had sold the "Tarzan Radio Act" to stations in every state of the union.

This would have pleased a man of lesser clay; but Mr. Burroughs was not happy. He likes to keep Tarzan entirely in the family. Just as he did with his books, so he took over the entire radio business. Edgar Rice Burroughs, Inc., announced to the trade: "The elimination of a middleman's profit and overhead allows us to furnish this program at a very reasonable figure, while permitting an increase in the cost of production to insure the best act it is possible to offer."

So far, forty-one sponsors, including such well-known firms as the Signal Oil & Gas Co., Reed Tobacco Co., Royal Baking Powder Co., and the venerable H. J. Heinz Co., have sold merchandise by means of Tarzan records broadcast throughout the United States, Canada and Australia. In all his multitudinous activities Mr. Burroughs may be hell on the middleman, but his two organizations have exuded splendid dividends throughout the depression.

Two years ago Mr. Burroughs had another brilliant idea. He contracted with a national newspaper syndicate to sell Tarzan comic-strips. By August of this year, one hundred and sixty daily papers were using the daily strip, drawn by Mr. Rex Mason from material based on the Tarzan stories; ninety-three Sunday newspapers were publishing a full page in color of Tarzan adventures, drawn by Mr. Harold Foster from original material by a ghost writer, under Mr. Burroughs' supervision.

Back in 1913, Mr. Burroughs had the foresight to register "Tarzan" as a trade mark. To date, he has licensed twenty-eight commodities to use the Tarzan name, the list including such items as Tarzan sweat shirts, Tarzan bread, Tarzan ice-cream cups, candy, masks, card games, rubber inflated toys, sponge balls, celluloid buttons, bats, bathing suits, gum, garters and coffee. Tarzan bill-boards advertise to the devout public that a new commodity has "The Strength of Tarzan". One company received permission to develop a Tarzan club: 125,000 members were enrolled. "Every member a potential salesman", declares a Tarzan broadside; this same document states that any business may receive "an official instruction book for the formation of the Tarzan Clan among boys and girls"—a valuable service which, of course, is not offered free by the Edgar Rice Burroughs, Inc.

From his vast experience, Mr. Burroughs has returned to one of his earlier vocations and again provides merchandising counsel to business men. One of his brochures states: "We have an organization that is prepared to assist in working out merchandising campaigns for sponsors; and as owners of Tarzan copyright and a wide range of Tarzan trade marks, we are in a position to make use of the Tarzan name in many lines".

He continues to write as diligently as when he started. His presses are always hard at work, turning out (1) his Tarzan saga, (2) a Martian epic, (3) a many-volumed account of adventures at the earth's core, (4) a new saga of life on the planet Venus.

This incredible activity seems to have no effect on him. He rides horseback, plays tennis regularly, learned to fly a few months ago, and now has his private plane. He is nearly sixty. He could pass for forty-five. He is brown and bald, stocky, has small, sharp eyes with a curiously genial squint, talks in short, quick sentences like a stock-broker with one eye always cocked at the tape, and allocates his time according to the second hand of a watch. He has sold his Tarzana home long ago. He works at his office in the pleasant Spanish-type building of the Edgar Rice Burroughs Corporation in Tarzana, but lives at Malibu near the motion-picture stars.

Finally, having exploited Tarzan as diligently as would the owner of a tooth-paste or washing-machine factory, he is making certain that his Tarzan saga will continue beyond the span of the founder. He is setting up a Tarzan dynasty.

Mr. Hulbert Burroughs, a young man of twenty-five or so, is already in active charge of Edgar Rice Burroughs, Inc. He is being trained to step into his father's position. Modestly, Hulbert Burroughs admits that he "will carry on with Tarzan".

A few weeks ago, Mr. Burroughs organized a second corporation—Burroughs-Tarzan Enterprises, Inc.—and put Hulbert Rice Burroughs in charge of that, too. Burroughs-Tarzan Enterprises, Inc., will film a new series of Tarzan epics with authentic scenic background. The first will be called *Tarzan in Guatemala*; it will follow M.G.M.'s still untitled Tarzan romance. Although the new Tarzan pictures may eventually be produced in darkest Africa, Mr. Burroughs, Sr., doesn't think he will go. He hasn't ever been there.

THE GRAND GUILLOTINER OF PARIS

JANET FLANNER

FROM MAY 1935

Anatole-Joseph-François Deibler, Grand Guillotiner of France, is one of the few high officials who hasn't been shifted from his job in the recent Parisian political shakeup. He is seventy-two years old, a handsome, humorless, taciturn, well-to-do suburbanite, the third generation in a hereditary dynasty of executioners. Owing to a custom that pre-dates the execution of Louis XVI, he is called Monsieur de Paris. Owing to a custom that post-dates the execution of Marie-Antoinette, *La Veuve* Capet, the guillotine is called The Widow. The aides who assist Monsieur de Paris and The Widow in their fatal work are called The Valets. And while, as elsewhere, the death penalty in France is the property of the State, the guillotine is the private property of the Deibler family and is handed down (with repairs) from father to son.

The current Monsieur de Paris owns two Widows—a heavier machine for executions in Paris, and a lighter, more up-to-date model for use in the provinces. Both are equipped with every humane improvement—wheels on which the knife descends faster than in the old-fashioned soaped grooves, and modern shock-absorbers. But in her general set-up, The Widow hasn't changed since the French Revolution.

In the dim dawn of a city street, the guillotine still looks like a tall and narrow window, set up in the wrong place and giving onto nothing. The wooden side-posts which compose the frame weigh seventy-five kilos each and are one and a half times the width of a man's neck apart. They stand approximately fifteen feet high, and are topped in the crossbar by a trigger-set weight of forty kilos, into which the seven-kilo blade is fixed at the last minute before an execution. The weight and blade are sent rushing down by a turn of the *déclic*—a kind of door-knob set in one of the side-posts and connected by pulleys with overhead springs which sustain the weight. Since it sends a man off on his final journey, this weight is termed the *sac à voyage*, or travelling-bag. The blade itself is obliquely edged, and is made of steel and bronze in Langres, the cutlery center of France. When not in use, it is kept in vaseline; and as a result of such solicitous treatment it lasts for many years, and is never honed.

The guillotines used to be stored in an old barn on the outer boulevards. Now, they are kept nearer at hand in the Prison de la Santé, not far behind the Café du Dôme, in Montparnasse. By French law, executions are theoretically public, taking place at dawn, the legal hour, in deserted streets or town squares. For a Paris beheading, the large Widow is trundled out of the Prison about three hours before dawn, around the corner to the Boulevard Arago, in a little old black van that looks so much like a Punch and Judy wagon that it is nicknamed *le guignol*. This van is horsedrawn on iron-rimmed wheels and is lighted by a swinging petrol lantern.

It takes about an hour to set up the guillotine. Each piece is numbered, and the whole is so perfect, mechanically, that it can be assembled in complete silence without even the blow of a hammer. As Deibler is now an old man, his first Valet superintends the job; but, as chief, and despite his age, Deibler fixes the knife to the *sac à voyage* at the last minute, and hoists them both—a weight of about a hundred pounds—to the crossbeam. Occasionally a trial decapitation is made with a roll of hay, to make sure that everything is working smoothly.

About ninety minutes before dawn, Deibler and his first and second Valets drive back to the Prison for their victim. The prisoner does not know that his last hour has come, until they enter his cell with his lawyer, a priest, and the prison warden, who says, *"Ayez courage."* He is given a glass of rum, and a prayer is said.

The condemned man is then led outside to the *guignol*. He is usually clad in his best trousers, silk socks, and well-shined shoes. His shirt is cut away in back over his shoulders, his neck clipped of hair, and his hands tied tightly behind him—the knot being looped vertically to the looser one which binds his feet. A little later, in the Boulevard Arago, this will make him walk his last few steps toward The Widow with his head high, the proud pose being ironically the easiest at his ending.

As he stumbles out of the *guignol* toward the guillotine, the priest marches in front of him, fantailing his black skirt so as to hide the horrid instrument from the prisoner. The Garde Républicaine, drawn up on horseback in a square around the machine, raise their sabres in a final salute of honor for the soon-dead man. Behind the Garde, the lines of policemen begin to cross themselves. In the background, a crowd of citizen onlookers keeps an intuitive silence, although the vital happening of the execution is invisible to them . . . A murderer is beheaded, and he will be buried, according to law, in an unmarked grave in ground supplied by the State. Monsieur de Paris has done his job.

The Deiblers are one of the two famous executioner families of which France has been proud. Curiously enough, the origin of neither family was French. The Sansons, who chopped their way to fame for six generations from 1664 through the Revolution, and until about 1850, were Italian in origin, and of little character-interest. The Deiblers, who succeeded the Sansons, were German, but the facts of their three generations would make up a Turgenev trilogy.

Joseph Deibler, the clan founder, was a farmer, born in Bavaria in 1783, who drifted to France in the Napoleonic era. In 1820, finding himself penniless, he became Valet at Dijon to Desmouret, chief executioner of Burgundy. Slightly mystical, and with a farmer's imperviousness to butchery, he apparently decided that he had been appointed by God to a perpetual Valetship, since, thirty-three years later, at the age of seventy, he turns up again as Valet to the chief executioner in Algeria, Rasseneux. Rasseneux had no son (as much of a misfortune for an executioner as for a king), but he had one daughter, Zoë. A marriage was made for Zoë and Louis Deibler, Joseph's son and heir. Louis was timid, club-footed, and only thirty years old. But he was obedient and ambitious, and was consequently named second Valet and heir-apparent to Rasseneux, his father-in-law.

Old Joseph Deibler had, therefore, founded what he considered to be the divine Deibler dynasty. As proof of its divinity, God (and Napoleon III) appointed him, five years later, at the age of seventy-five, to be chief headsman of Brittany—or, Monsieur de Rennes, Rennes being the principal city of Brittany. Chief executioners had been city-titled since about 1778, when the seven Sanson brothers—head-choppers all over France—began calling themselves Monsieur de Versailles, Monsieur de Blois, *etc.*, to avoid confusion. As Monsieur de Rennes, Joseph Deibler's Teutonic haughtiness finally flowered; he decapitated his French victims with the scorn of an avenging angel. He despised his neighbors' horror of him—their horror of Louis, now his father's Valet, and their horror of Louis' wife. And he knew he was right when God sent Louis and Zoë a son, Anatole-Joseph-François, Grand High Executioner of All France today.

As successor to his father at Rennes, Louis Deibler was a sinister buffoon. Sensitive about his deformity, and at the same time conscious of his own good education, he suffered beneath the ostracism that was put upon him, his wife, and his children. When he went forth to conduct an execution, he dressed like a morbid scarecrow, in his battered plug hat, disreputable *redingote*, and with the giant umbrella which he used as a cane. What he liked to do was to stay home and model little clay figures of dancing women.

So, for nearly forty years, Louis Deibler limped around France, dealing death with no esoteric conviction that he had been appointed by God. Though a clumsy executioner—he lacked the swift, sure style of his father and his son—he was, to his surprise and all the other provincial headsmen's fury, named Monsieur de Paris in 1871. And at this time, moreover, the economizing Third Republic put an end to all local executionerships, making the office national.

In Paris, Louis Deibler took to playing cards in Auteuil cafés and later to religion, always putting on his gloves to take Communion, where other men took theirs off. In 1898, when executing the "toadstool murderer," Carrara, he suddenly screamed for water, crying, "I am covered with blood!" He had succumbed to the dread-of-blood delusion that frequently seizes butchers and surgeons and is now known as hemophobia. Lady Macbeth had called it "Out, damned spot!"

On New Year's Day of the following year came the Chancellery's appointment of Louis' son, Anatole, as Monsieur de Paris. Louis, though never cut out for the work, had assisted at more than a thousand executions, had performed one hundred and eighty as chief. He died in 1904, bequeathing to his son 400,000 gold francs and the family guillotine.

Anatole Deibler, still the incumbent today, is in no sense an eccentric. He divides his time between cinemas, travel, motoring, trout-fishing at his small country place on the Cher, and rose-gardening at his even smaller Paris home at 39, rue Claude-Terrasse, near the Porte St. Cloud. He has spent his life hoping to be treated as other men are treated, although doing what they are forbidden to do.

After finishing school al the Rennes Lycée, he tried to dodge his fate by working in a Paris department store. He persuaded the State to let him undertake military service, though headsmen's sons had been exempt since 1832. Four years of suffering as the barracks' butt brought him the nickname Chin-Chopper. Embittered, he went to Algiers and took up the family burden, becoming Valet to his old grandfather, Rasseneux. (Executioners are peculiarly long-lived.)

At the age of thirty, Anatole returned to Paris to be his father's Valet. The carpenter who made the guillotines (the Deiblers have sold three to China at seven thousand francs apiece, and one is still operating today in the central prison at Peiping) refused to let his daughter marry the young executioner. In the meanwhile, he had taken up fast bicycle-riding and had joined the Société Vélocepédique d'Auteuil (his name appears on the Société's early programs as a sprint hope). In the tandem events he met his final partner, a petty government employee, Mademoiselle Rosine Rogis. They were married in 1898, the year before Anatole was appointed Monsieur de Paris. One little son was born to the Anatole Deiblers. He lived for only a month, dying, ironically, from the poisonous prescription of a careless chemist. Deibler refused to bring suit. Then a daughter was born, Marcelle, still the apple of her father's eye. When Obrecht, Anatole's second Valet, asked for Marcelle's hand, Madame de Paris said she would rather see her daughter dead than married to an executioner. So Obrecht married a schoolteacher; and today, Marcelle, in her spinster thirties, drives her father around in the family Citroën. She and her mother do the housework. Deiblers can't keep servants.

But despite his ambition to be looked upon as an ordinary French citizen Anatole Deibler is a mystery man to most of France. Few but his neighbors and the criminals he executes know him by sight. Because people are either horrified or fascinated by him, the Deiblers have no friends. They have nothing but business associates. On Sunday nights, second Valet Obrecht drops in to drink a weekly Pernod. On Sunday noons, the Deiblers lunch with the Desfourneaux, who are first, third and fourth Valets. The Desfourneaux are connected by marriage with Madame Deibler's family and are themselves from an older clan of executioners than the Deiblers, but one not so renowned. Léopold Desfourneaux, an uncle, who was also a Deibler Valet, couldn't kill a Sunday chicken for stew and was afraid of spiders.

The Valets can afford to behead only as a side-line, as the job is so ill-paid. Deibler's four Valets receive, respectively, twelve thousand, ten thousand eight hundred, seven thousand two hundred, and six thousand francs, annually. Deibler himself is paid only eighteen thousand francs a year, besides the ten thousand francs for upkeep of The Widow, who needs nothing but cheap vaseline and a little paint.

When Deibler is executing in provincial prisons, the smaller guillotine and *guignol* ride free on a flat car on the same train with him. On one occasion, he lost them for three days, and the two condemned criminals, whom he had travelled a long distance to execute, were pardoned, because the legal hour for their deaths had passed by.

Deibler and his Valets all travel together in a second class compartment, reserved by the Authorities of Justice; the blinds are pulled down, and no one is allowed to disturb the occupants. At the local hotel Deibler registers as F. Boyer, Travelling Man from Arras. One necessary item in his travelling equipment is an alarm clock, since an Albi hotel-keeper once forgot to arouse him in time to perform an execution. He also takes a revolver along with him, as headsmen have been repeatedly shot at when executing anarchists.

After thirty-six years as the only national headsman working in Western Europe, Deibler is tired and cardiac. He tried to resign a few years ago, before the execution of Gourgulov, assassin of President Doumer; his resignation was accepted, on the condition that he pass up the full-pay pension which French executioners have always drawn. He is still working. Executioners, since they have little else that is pleasantly worldly in their lives, like money. Deibler permitted Obrecht, his second Valet, to turn the *déclic* for Gourgulov's head, as a sign of his own retreat and as a mark of his dynastic selection, since he has no son. The oldest Desfourneaux, Anatole's first Valet, is entitled to inherit the job, but he is middle-aged, easy-going, and hates responsibility. Obrecht will probably be appointed the future Monsieur de Paris. . . .

Anatole Deibler's stoical, courageous attitude toward his job has done much to satisfy the French people in regard to their method of capital punishment. It appears to be a sensible, economical, and probably painless guarantee of protection for modern society. Deibler does not think of himself as a divine instrument, but as a lonely cog in a large legal machine. He says that he is set in motion by the jury that votes, by the judge that condemns, and by the President of the Republic who fails to grant a pardon. Like them, he is guiltless of blood. But his neighbors will dine with the jurymen, the judge, and especially with the President. They will not dine with Anatole Deibler.

THE BUMS AT SUNSET

THOMAS WOLFE

FROM OCTOBER 1935

Slowly, singly, with the ambling gait of men who have just fed, and who are faced with no pressure of time and business, the hoboes came from the jungle, descended the few feet of clay embankment that sloped to the road bed, and in an unhurried manner walked down the tracks toward the water tower. The time was the exact moment of sunset, the sun indeed had disappeared from sight, but its last shafts fell remotely, without violence or heat, upon the treetops of the already darkening woods and on the top of the water tower. That light lay there briefly with a strange unearthly detachment, like a delicate and ancient bronze, it was no part of that cool, that delicious darkening of the earth which was already steeping the woods—it was like sorrow and like ecstasy and it faded briefly like a ghost.

Of the five men who had emerged from the "jungle" above the tracks and were now advancing, in a straggling procession, towards the water tower, the oldest was perhaps fifty, but such a ruin of a man, such a shapeless agglomerate of sodden rags, matted hair, and human tissues, that his age was indeterminate. He was like something that has been melted and beaten into the earth by a heavy rain. The youngest was a fresh-skinned country lad with bright wondering eyes: he was perhaps not more than sixteen years old. Of the remaining three, one was a young man not over thirty with a ferret face and very few upper teeth. He walked along gingerly on tender feet that were obviously unaccustomed to the work he was now putting them to: he was a triumph of dirty elegance—he wore a pin striped suit heavily spattered with grease stains and very shiny on the seat: he kept his coat collar turned up and his hands thrust deeply into his trousers pocket—he walked thus with his bony shoulders thrust forward as if, in spite of the day's heat, he was cold. He had a limp cigarette thrust out of the corner of his mouth, and he talked with a bare movement of his lips, and a curious and ugly convulsion of his mouth to the side: everything about him suggested unclean secrecy.

Of the five men, only the remaining two carried on them the authority of genuine vagabondage. One was a small man with a hard seamed face, his eyes were hard and cold as agate, and his thin mouth was twisted slantwise in his face, and was like a scar.

The other man, who might have been in his mid-fifties, had the powerful shambling figure, the seamed brutal face of the professional vagabond. It was a face and figure that had a curious brutal nobility; the battered and pitted face was hewn like a block of granite and on the man was legible the tremendous story of his wanderings—a legend of pounding wheel and thrumming rod, of bloody brawl and brutal shambles, of immense and lonely skies, the savage wildness, the wild, cruel and lonely distance of America.

This man, somehow obviously the leader of the group, walked silently, indifferently, at a powerful shambling step, not looking at the others. Once he paused, thrust a powerful hand into the baggy pocket of his coat, and drew out a cigarette, which he lit with a single motion of his hard cupped hand. Then his face luxuriously contorted as he drew upon the cigarette, he inhaled deeply, letting the smoke trickle slowly out through his nostrils after he had drawn it into the depths of his mighty lungs. It was a powerful and brutal gesture of sensual pleasure that suddenly gave to the act of smoking and to the quality of tobacco all of their primitive and fragrant relish. And it was evident that the man could impart this rare quality to the simplest physical acts of life—to everything he touched—because he had in him somehow the rare qualities of exultancy and joy.

All the time, the boy had been keeping step behind the man, his eyes fixed steadily upon the broad back of the vagabond. Now, as the man stopped, the boy came abreast of him, and also stopped, and for a moment continued to look at the man, a little uncertainly, but with the same expression of steadfast confidence.

The bum, letting the smoke coil slowly from luxurious nostrils, resumed his powerful swinging stride, and for a moment said nothing to the boy. Presently, however, he spoke, roughly, casually, but with a kind of brutal friendliness:

"Where yuh goin' kid?" he said. "To the big town?"

The boy nodded dumbly, seemed about to speak, but said nothing.

"Been there before?" the man asked.

"No," said the boy.

"First time yuh ever rode the rods, huh?"

"Yes," said the boy.

"What's the matter?" the bum said, grinning. "Too many cows to milk down on the farm, huh? Is that it?"

The boy grinned uncertainly for a moment, and then said, "Yes."

"I t'ought so," the bum said, chuckling coarsely, "Jesus! I can tell one of youse fresh country kids a mile off by the way yuh walk . . . Well," he said with a rough blunt friendliness, in a moment, "stick wit me if you're goin' to the Big Town. I'm goin' that way, too."

"Yeah," the little man with the mouth like a scar now broke in, in a rasping voice, and with an ugly jeering laugh:

"Yeah. You stick to Bull, kid. He'll see yuh t'roo. He'll show yuh de— woild. I ain't kiddin' yuh! He'll take yuh up to Lemonade Lake an' all t'roo Breadloaf Valley—won't yuh, Bull? He'll show yuh where de ham trees are and where de toikeys grow on bushes—won't yuh, Bull?" he said with ugly yet fawning insinuation. "You stick to Bull, kid, an' you'll be wearin' poils . . . A-a-a-ah! yuh punk kid!" he now said, with a sudden turn to snarling viciousness.

"Wat t'hell use do yuh t'ink we got for a punk kid like you?—Dat's duh trouble wit dis racket now! . . . We was all right until all dese kids began to come along! . . . Wy t'hell should we be boddered wit him!" he snarled viciously. "Wat t'hell am I supposed to be—a noice maid or sump'n? . . . G'wan, yuh little punk," he snarled viciously, and lifted his fist in a sudden backhand movement, as if to strike the boy. "Scram! We got no use fer yuh! . . G'wan, now. . Get t'hell away from here before I smash yuh one."

The man named Bull turned for a moment and looked silently at the smaller bum.

"Listen, Mug!" he said quietly in a moment. "You leave the kid alone. The kid stays, see?"

"A-a-a-ah!" the other man snarled sullenly. "What is dis anyway?—A—noic'ry, or sump'n?"

"Listen," the other man said, "yuh hoid me, didn't yuh?"

"A-a-ah t'hell wit it!" the little man muttered. "I'm not goin' t' rock duh cradle f'r no punk kid."

"Yuh hoid what I said, didn't yuh?" the man named Bull said in a heavy menacing tone.

"I hoid yuh. Yeah!" the other muttered.

"Well, I don't want to hear no more outa your trap. I said the kid stays—and he stays."

The little man muttered sullenly under his breath, but said no more. Bull continued to scowl heavily at him a moment longer, then turned away and went over and sat down on a handcar which had been pushed up against a tool house on the siding.

"Come over here, kid," he said roughly, as he fumbled in his pocket for another cigarette. The boy walked over to the handcar.

"Got any smokes?" the man said, still fumbling in his pocket. They boy produced a package of cigarettes and offered them to the man. Bull took a cigarette from the package, lighted it with a single movement, between his tough seamed face and his cupped hand, and then dropped the package of cigarettes in his pocket, with the same spacious and powerful gesture.

"T'anks," he said as the acrid smoke began to coil luxuriously from his nostrils. "Sit down, kid."

The boy sat down on the handcar beside the man. For a moment, as Bull smoked, two of the bums looked quietly at each other with sly smiles, and then the young one in the soiled pin-stripe suit shook his head rapidly to himself, and, grinning toothlessly with his thin sunken mouth, mumbled derisively:

"Cheezus!"

Bull said nothing, but sat there smoking, bent forward a little on his knees, as solid as a rock.

It was almost dark; there was still a faint evening light, but already great stars were beginning to flash and blaze in cloudless skies. Somewhere in the wood there was a sound of water. Far off, half-heard and half-suspected, there was a faint dynamic throbbing on the rails. The boy sat there quietly, listening, and said nothing.

GOLDEN SWANK

ALLENE TALMEY

FROM FEBRUARY 1936

Nightclubs these days are rancorously shooting off in so many directions that the wisest gangsters refuse to invest in so shaky a business. No fat-faced Dutch Schultz backs the Rainbow Room at Rockefeller Center. No Owney Madden, small and boney, cuts himself unasked into the profits of the Persian Room at the Plaza. No Larry Fay, with horse-teeth, a big black hat, and a record of forty-six arrests, runs the Weylin Caprice Room. No Johnny Irish complains to his headwaiter that in this damp weather all his bullet holes hurt. Those strings of Prohibition nightclubs, owned by the Fays and the Maddens, are gone. Only occasionally do their lieutenants pop up in hidden financial records.

When they do, they claim that they are present just to protect an old investment. Those gangsters who went into it in the old days took it on as a profitable side racket to their large scale bootlegging, their rum running, their hi-jacking. They never rose out of the business by the stern route of busboy, waiter, captain, owner. It is no racket for a gangster. The policy boys from Harlem, who came to Broadway for a bit, are gone. Big Bill Dwyer, a Madden lad, flopped as a partner of Zelli, and only John Bagiano, who once had a hand in Greenwich Village beer deliveries, is happy with his interest in the Versailles. Most of them are willing to back out gracefully, leaving the field to the hotels, to the Rockefellers, and to two gentlemen, suave relicts of Prohibition. They are John Perona and Sherman Billingsley. Their business talents, devoted for years to a sly mockery of snobbery, now flourish with the *Social Register*. None of the dozens of little speakeasy fellows, who rose to be broken on the rack of grafting agents, had the flair of those two for the right set.

Now in their forties, they are columns of respectability. What diffidence they have can be discerned only in their eyes, the soft blue of Billingsley in the pink cushion of his face, the brown pebbles of Perona in his lean hardness. They walk with matronly dignity, secure in their elegance. Sherman Billingsley's scrubbed Middle Western brightness keeps his Stork Club seething. Over in the dumps by the Third Avenue Elevated, John Perona runs El Morocco, the smartest nightclub of them all.

Society is their game these days. The men with the social sense are the winners. Slowly they have built up an aristocracy of the supper clubs with photographs of their hand-made royalty in the social columns. Perona, of course, is the master. Even Billingsley admitted that, when Perona snagged for El Morocco the courtship of Barbara Hutton by Prince Alexis Mdivani.

His El Morocco at two o'clock on a winter's morning is a dream of a nightclub, smoky, stifling, with an electricity of gayety, starting from no known socket. Tables completely cover the dance floor, artfully arranged by Perona into a lovely cross-section of night club aristocracy. In clumps the débutantes sit, calling out from table to table, laughing their high whinny. In further clumps the kept women flash with diamonds almost as big as those of the society girls. There are always actresses, movie stars, models. Somewhere in the center wanders Perona with his sixth Scotch and Perrier, flashing his white smile, talking in his charming accent, which is neither [Italian] nor the English of Eton-bred Roman Princes. Obviously the jolly play-boy, laughing, gay, he talks in fashionable clichés.

There is little evidence then of the Giovanni Perona, born to a small café-keeper in Turino, Italy, who once batted back and forth on the London-Buenos Aires boats as busboy, steward, deck hand, until he met a big fat-handed fighter, named [Luis Angel] Firpo. When Firpo came to New York for the Sailor Maxted fight, Perona came too. He stayed. By the time Firpo returned for the Dempsey fight, the boy had his own speak-easy on West Forty-Sixth Street, filled with the sporting crowd. Deep in the smoke and the betting, Perona played practical jokes with an eye on the cash box.

A few years later he moved to East Fifty-Third Street, setting up, with the exception of Jack and Charlie's, the most exclusive speakeasy of them all. He called it the Bath Club. With a suddenly developed social sense, he sliced off the top layer of the sporting crowd to take with him. The rest he left behind in the débris of Forty-Sixth. To the Bath Club came a newer, smarter crowd, more débutantes, more writers, more swank ac-tresses. When he moved further East three years ago, he sliced again.

It was not until he had El Morocco about a year that Perona achieved the social rise for which he had been struggling. He staked his all on the blank little boys who were working hard on their reputations as men about town. At eighteen he let them run bills until they would come into their inheritances. Like an Oxford tailor he never duns. For that restraint they let him into their secrets, their loves, and their plans. He is confessor, advisor, and doctor to them. Like an analyst, he allows them to confide endlessly, charging only, however, for food and drink.

Some of them this year organized the Round Table. Every night, about fifteen of them eat at a big table with their President, Bill Plankin-ton, at the head, Perona by his side. These professional Peronites include Erskine Gwynne, Bobby La Branch, James and Woolworth Donahue, Dan and Bob Topping. So far the boys have thought of only three rules: two bottles of *vin ordinaire* on the table, no girls for dinner, no one in Plankinton's seat. The Round Table even has its own private telephone.

The boys are only part of the hundred and fifty regulars, the nightclub-going essence of the Social Register, who stop in every night, sometimes only for a single night cap before going home. On dull nights some four or five hundred come, on good nights eight hundred. After closing time, about five or six in the morning, Perona goes over the checks, seeing who the spenders are. Dinner for four, with cocktails, wine at dinner, and champagne later frequently runs up to sixty or one hundred dollars. Parties of eight often spend three hundred. The wily, who know the place, order his special *Armagnac* at $2.25 a pony.

Mugs never find out about the *Armagnac*. When they slip in by mistake, the headwaiter shuffles them hastily to tables by the kitchen's swinging doors. Waiters bump them, bring one drink at a time, get afflicted by waiters' blind eye. Although Perona has no cover charge, any order less than fifteen dollars for two may have a two dollar cover charge slapped on. If the management just doesn't like the faces, the cover charge may balloon to ten dollars a head. Perona is always too busy to hear complaints from the stuck. Their bleat annoys him.

While John Perona stays carefully in the light, his name popping up in the social chatter columns of the tabloids, his picture frequently in the *Evening Journal*, his brother, Joseph, remains in the background, running the kitchens and the kitchen staffs. A puffy gourmand, with a mouth for wine, Joe Perona knows no celebrities, casts no beamish eyes on the pretty girls. He watches the meat. While John flashes handsomely on a mounting wave of social advancement, Joe remains a highly irascible quartermaster, known lovingly as "Mother Superior."

Oddly enough, most of the money Perona makes in the winter, he squanders in the summer on his Westchester Bath Club in Mamaroneck. From an excess of energy, he constantly adds equipment, a badminton court, a pool, boats, an outdoor dancing floor. In faded blue shorts, and a maroon shirt, he lies every day by the pool, playing interminable games of backgammon, a long lime drink by his side. Surrounding him are the professional Peronites with, in addition, the clown or two he always has around. The butts of his gags, the clowns live on the place with no check ever presented. Of all, Peppino, a jolly tub of a man, is his pet. Unhappily, last year Peppino had a breakdown from the strain of exuberant crowds tossing him into the pool.

Of all the gags Perona ever worked, his most superb was the creation of Frank Busby. So constantly and so casually did Perona mention Frank that all El Morocco soon knew these salient details. Frank Busby had been born in South America. He was kidnapped by gypsies, and then adopted by an Indian Maharajah. Reluctantly Perona admitted that his friend was the richest and handsomest man in the world. "He is coming here," Perona casually said one night, "to buy up General Motors and distribute it to the poor."

On Mondays Perona usually relaxes from his week-end strain by racing down to his two-hundred-and-sixty-acre farm in New Jersey with its rambling Colonial house. There he cooks for himself, rows around on his enormous artificial lake. He keeps three boats there; three more on the Sound. When he drives himself, incidentally, he chooses out of his stable of eight, the Austin; likes to have his chauffeur, Confucius, drive him in the Cadillac. Every other year he goes to Europe, mainly to buy his clothes from Caraceni, the best tailor in Rome. Behind him, he leaves his wife and children to live quietly in a mild Jersey suburb, far from the farm and El Morocco.

Far different is Sherman Billingsley's place. He loves the mugs,—the right mugs, mugs who write, fight, and are in the papers. They are the backbone of his business. They come in delighted squads to the Stork Club, just off Fifth Avenue. Behind its fresh white limestone façade, the Stork Club makes no blunt pretenses. Guests run right into the enormous square bar, where three ripe lushes, like a set piece on a Victorian mantel, drink all night. What no one sees is the watchful man in the balcony, checking on the bartenders through a slit to see that no liquor is snitched.

What everyone, however, does see is Billingsley, and his mild periwinkle eyes, a deep blue flower in his buttonhole, stopping by the tables. He whispers in his soft voice, rasping like a well-oiled saw. With everyone he has a secret joke, a flicker of his eye-lid letting them in on a private lark. Too late, they find, as he moves on, he never told the secret joke. Billingsley relishes the dash of excitement here, the heat of people getting happily and gently drunk. When the pace dies off, he orders a brandy on the house for everyone. Sometimes it takes five or six free brandies a night to keep up. That dash of excitement, of course, brings celebrities. There are always a couple of fight managers, a bruiser or two, actresses, men from the track, movie producers, aviators, newspaper men, and enough society names for a bit of elegance in the society columns.

They are all there to be warmed by the ingenuous jollity of Sherman Billingsley, of Anadarko, Oklahoma, where there were only Indians and Billingsleys. By 1920 he had drug stores in the Bronx and four Bronx blocks of monotony known as Billingsley Terrace. Later he turned real estate broker, with his first negotiation a lease for a brownstone house on West Fifty-Eighth Street. His principals insisted that he come in with them. They were going to open a speakeasy, call it the Stork Club.

That private house became the first of the three Stork Clubs. It zoomed quickly into success. As soon as Billingsley found himself really running the place, he startled the trade by not charging extra for enormous blue bowls of celery, radishes and olives. He banked the bar with exposed bottles in an era when bar tenders just poured out a smoky liquid for any order of Scotch, from bottles under the bar. In Billingsley's place the customers named their brands and saw the liquor poured. He put down the first carpet in a speakeasy, advertised his illegality with a bright red canopy.

At that time Billingsley did not care for swells. He wanted the sports and the newspapermen. It all paid him well. After the Federal men, who smashed up most of his places, smashed up the first Stork Club, he put his profits into other peoples' clubs. He went halves with Tex Guinan, owned the Royal Box with Zelli, had an interest in the Park Avenue, the Zone Club, the Kit Kat Club, and the Club Napoleon.

Billingsley loves to run his places from the front. He arrives about five in the afternoon and stays until closing, doing everything for himself except the buying. That is Mrs. Billingsley's job. When *Sally* was the hit of the year, Mrs. Billingsley danced in its chorus. Now, still pretty, and exceedingly efficient, she buys for kitchen and bar. By now Billingsley has worked out a pretty system of running the place. He keeps a smiling blue eye on the waiters. If he notices one of them pushing, or arguing with the customers, he never reprimands. He sends the man a telegram, aimed to arrive at six in the morning. The telegram advises: "Be Nice to Customers." Waiters rush up constantly with notes. The Billingsley autograph stretches around the world. The only details he does not bother with are those of the checkroom, the outside doormen, the cigarette girls, and the ladies' and men's room attendants. From the concessionaires, to whom he leases those privileges, he receives some twelve thousand dollars a year. His rent, however, is only eight thousand.

Last winter he started out to catch the social crowd, but it was not until Marian Cooley opened her Thursday Nights that he really achieved a touch of elegance. Since then the bloods swarm the place. Just to prove, however, that he was not foolish, he took on Jockey Earl Sande, who, through with riding winners, sang moaning ballads through his nose. That publicity brought in mugs even from Hawaii, who took home with them the memory of Billingsley's chunky charm.

But mugs to Billingsley and Perona are merely the spine of their business, the fat and the fun lie in mass arrangements of Whitneys, Astors and Vanderbilts. Theirs is an almost mystic flair for the nuances, the chiaroscuro, of the *Social Register*.

ACKNOWLEDGMENTS

EDITOR **GRAYDON CARTER**

V.F. BOOKS EDITOR **DAVID FRIEND**

MANAGING EDITOR **CHRIS GARRETT**

ASSOCIATE EDITOR **JACK DELIGTER**

Editorial assistance and guidance was provided by:

John Banta, Elien Blue Becque, Marley Brown, Cat Buckley, Lauren Christensen, Lenora Jane Estes, Mary Alice Miller, Tathiana Monacella, Cullen Murphy, Walter Owen, Sarah Schmidt, and Lucie Shelly.

We gratefully acknowledge our partners at Penguin Random House, including Ann Godoff, Scott Moyers, Ginny Smith Younce, Sofia Groopman, Will Carnes, Darren Haggar, Kathryn Court, and Patrick Nolan.

For archival and business expertise, we appreciate the guidance of Alexandra Bernet, Brian Cross, Christopher P. Donnellan, Julie LaPointe, Amanda Meigher, and Shawn Waldron.

We sincerely thank our colleagues at Sabin, Bermant & Gould; the Wylie Agency; and the Rights and Permissions Department of Condé Nast Publications.

And we are forever indebted to Frank Crowninshield, the editor of *Vanity Fair* from 1914 to 1936, who commissioned most of the pieces included herein.

CONTRIBUTORS

SYYED SHAYKH ACHMED ABDULLAH (1881–1945) was the pseudonym of the Russian-born writer Alexander Nicholayevitch Romanoff. Under his pen name, Romanoff wrote a series of pulp novels, most notably *The Thief of Bagdad*, which was adapted into a popular Douglas Fairbanks feature in 1924.

SHERWOOD ANDERSON (1876–1941) was an American novelist, short story writer, and frequent *Vanity Fair* contributor who influenced writers such as Hemingway, Faulkner, Steinbeck, and Wolfe. V.F. editor Frank Crowninshield once observed: "[Anderson has] shown us that there are no limits to what one may see through the little window of the short story."

DJUNA BARNES (1892–1982) was an American author who ran in modernist circles in Paris and New York. Impressed by Barnes's roman à clef novel *Nightwood*, the eroticist Anaïs Nin once told her, "A woman rarely writes as a woman, as she feels, but you have."

ALFRED H. BARR JR. (1902–1981) was an American art historian and the first director of New York City's Museum of Modern Art. Barr helped introduce the American public to experimental art of many genres, led the critical charge to underscore the importance of Picasso's body of work, and set out to establish what would become one of the world's most significant art collections.

ROBERT C. BENCHLEY (1889–1945) was a regular contributor to *Vanity Fair* before becoming the magazine's managing editor in 1919. A celebrated humorist, Benchley—an Algonquin Round Table regular—was the driving force behind the satirical film *How to Sleep*, which won the 1935 Academy Award for Best Short Subject.

GEORG BRANDES (1842–1927) was a noted Danish critic and scholar who championed the modernist movement in Europe in the late ninteenth and early twentieth centuries. His early support of Friedrich Nietzsche helped solidify the philosopher's reputation.

HEYWOOD BROUN (1888–1939), a member of the Algonquin Round Table, was a journalist and editor who founded the American Newspaper Guild. Writing for the *New York World*, Broun published the first syndicated column to be read by one million people.

THOMAS BURKE (1886–1945) was a British author best known for his story collection *Limehouse Nights*, a series that focused on the realities of life in a London slum. The director D. W. Griffith used some of Burke's tales as the basis for his films *Broken Blossoms* and *Dream Street*.

WALTER CAMP (1859–1925), a sportswriter and coach, helped popularize the new sport of football during the late nineteenth and early twentieth centuries. As a member of the Rules Committee, Camp forever changed the game by instituting a line of scrimmage and a proscribed set of downs, thus earning him the sobriquet "The Father of American Football."

JOHN JAY CHAPMAN (1862–1933) was an American critic and essayist whose work appeared frequently in *Vanity Fair* from 1918 to 1925. Following Chapman's death, the critic Edmund Wilson characterized him as "the best letter-writer that we have ever had in this country."

SAMUEL CHOTZINOFF (1889–1964) was a pianist in his youth before turning to music criticism in the 1920s. His essays on jazz and popular song appeared in *Vanity Fair* until he became the music editor for the *New York World* in 1925. He would go on to serve as the music director of NBC radio and television.

JEAN COCTEAU (1889–1963) was an innovative French poet, novelist, dramatist, and filmmaker who occasionally wrote about the arts for *Vanity Fair*. A confidant of some of the most creative men and women of his generation (Proust and Picasso, among them), Cocteau died of a heart attack after being informed of the death of his friend Edith Piaf.

COLETTE (1873–1954) was a French novelist and performer (full name: Sidonie-Gabrielle Colette) as well as a regular contributor to *Vanity Fair* in the 1920s. Best known for her novel *Gigi* (later adapted into successful Broadway and Hollywood productions), Colette published more than thirty books in her lifetime and, upon her death, became the first woman to be afforded a state funeral in France.

RICHARD CONNELL (1893–1949) was an American fiction writer. Best remembered for his short story "The Most Dangerous Game," Connell also received an Academy Award nomination for Frank Capra's *Meet John Doe*, a film based on Connell's short story "The Reputation."

DAVID CORT (1904–1983) was an American author and columnist who wrote for *Vanity Fair* throughout the Jazz Age. In 1936, Cort joined the newly launched *Life*, where he would help oversee coverage of World War II.

NOËL COWARD (1899–1973) was a playwright (*Private Lives, Design for Living, Present Laughter, Blithe Spirit*), composer, director, actor, and singer. He received his first U.S. paycheck at age twenty-one—from *Vanity Fair*—for a satire on royal love affairs, published here.

E. E. CUMMINGS (1894–1962) was an American modernist poet, essayist, and a frequent *Vanity Fair* contributor until a 1927 falling-out with editor Frank Crowninshield, which ended cummings's relationship with the magazine. In the mid-twentieth century he emerged as one of the country's most popular poets.

CLARENCE DARROW (1857–1938) was an American lawyer and a civil liberties stalwart who gained fame for representing high-profile defendants such as the union leader Eugene Debs; the murderers Leopold and Loeb; and John Scopes, the science teacher charged with violating Tennessee law by introducing students to the concept of evolution.

RANDOLPH DINWIDDIE was an occasional *Vanity Fair* contributor in the 1920s.

THEODORE DREISER (1871–1945) was an American novelist and social activist whose books such as *Sister Carrie* and *An American Tragedy* addressed the brutal realities of urban poverty.

T. S. ELIOT (1888–1965), winner of the Nobel Prize in Literature, wrote some of the most highly regarded poems of the twentieth century, notably, *The Love Song of J. Alfred Prufrock, The Waste Land, The Hollow Men,* and *Four Quartets.*

DOUGLAS FAIRBANKS (1883–1939) was a titan of the silent-film era, starring in hundreds of motion pictures and earning the nickname "The First King of Hollywood." In 1919, he formed the independent movie studio United Artists with his future wife, actress Mary Pickford, actor and filmmaker Charlie Chaplin, and director D. W. Griffith.

DOUGLAS FAIRBANKS JR. (1909–2000) was an American actor and World War II hero. The only son of screen legend (and fellow *Vanity Fair* contributor) Douglas Fairbanks, he managed to make a name for himself by appearing in classics such as *The Dawn Patrol, Gunga Din,* and the original version of *The Prisoner of Zenda.*

F. SCOTT FITZGERALD (1896–1940) was an American writer whose four completed novels are considered by many to be the archetypal literary works of the Jazz Age. Upon publication of *The Great Gatsby* in 1925, the poet T. S. Eliot declared it to be "the first step American fiction has taken since Henry James."

JANET FLANNER (1892–1978) was an American journalist and novelist best known for the "Letter from Paris" column she wrote for the *New Yorker* under the pen name Genêt. Flanner was the third guest on the 1971 *Dick Cavett Show* episode that featured Norman Mailer's notorious on-air confrontation with Gore Vidal.

FORD MADOX FORD (1873–1939) was an English novelist (*The Good Soldier*), critic, and editor of the literary journals the *English Review* and the *Transatlantic Review,* through whose pages he helped champion the work of Jean Rhys, Wyndham Lewis, D. H. Lawrence, Joseph Conrad, and many others.

JAMES L. FORD (1855–1928) was a correspondent for the *Railway Gazette* and a critic for the *New York Herald.* His memoir *Forty-Odd Years in the Literary Shop* chronicled the adventures of a rambunctious journalist in turn-of-the-twentieth-century New York City.

JAY FRANKLIN (1897–1967), real name John Franklin Carter, was an American columnist and speechwriter who was a regular *Vanity Fair* contributor throughout the 1930s. Franklin was a speechwriter for Harry Truman during his successful 1948 campaign for president; the following year, he went to work for Truman's opponent, Governor Thomas Dewey.

PAUL GALLICO (1897–1976) was an American novelist, short story writer, and sportswriter whose prose appeared regularly in *Vanity Fair* during the Depression. Gallico became famous for his firsthand accounts of playing sports with professional athletes (boxing with Jack Dempsey, golfing with Bobby Jones). He was also a founder of New York City's Golden Gloves, the amateur boxing competition.

FREDERICK JAMES GREGG (d. 1928) was a frequent *Vanity Fair* contributor as well as an art critic for the *New York Sun*. In his role as publicity chairman for the momentous 1913 Armory Show, Gregg helped introduce mainstream America to Europe's modern-art masters, from Picasso to Matisse to Duchamp.

LANGSTON HUGHES (1902–1967) was an American poet, fiction writer, lecturer, essayist, editor, and social activist who pioneered jazz poetry and helped spearhead the Harlem Renaissance.

ALDOUS HUXLEY (1894–1963) was a British writer, essayist, and humanist best known for his dystopian novel *Brave New World* and for *The Doors of Perception*, his memoir about his experiences under the influence of hallucinogens. Huxley died on November 22, 1963, the day of President John F. Kennedy's assassination.

MAX JACOB (1876–1944) was a French writer, painter, and critic whose poetry was said to bridge the gap between symbolism and surrealism. He died of pneumonia in France's Drancy internment camp after being apprehended by the Gestapo in 1944.

ALVA JOHNSTON (1888–1950) was an American journalist and sometime *Vanity Fair* contributor. A writer for the *Sacramento Bee*, the *New York Times*, and the *New York Herald*, Johnston won a Pulitzer Prize in 1923 "for his reports of the proceedings of the convention of the American Association for the Advancement of Science."

GEOFFREY KERR (1895–1971), a combat veteran of World War I, was a British screenwriter, playwright, and occasional actor whose career spanned silent films and the talkies.

JOHN MAYNARD KEYNES (1883–1946) was a British economist whose principles of macroeconomics and advocacy of state-sanctioned stimulus measures after World War II made him one of the era's most influential financial theorists. Keynes was also the director of the Bank of England and a member of the Bloomsbury Group.

D. H. LAWRENCE (1885–1930) was an English writer, poet, and essayist who broke new literary ground with novels, such as *Sons and Lovers*, *Women in Love*, and *Lady Chatterley's Lover*. The writer E. M. Forster once labeled him "the greatest imaginative novelist of our generation."

STEPHEN LEACOCK (1869–1944) was a Canadian humorist, essayist, and novelist who contributed more than fifty columns to *Vanity Fair*, often satirizing upper-class mores. Following his death, a Canadian postage stamp was released in his honor and the Leacock Medal for Humour was established, an annual award celebrating Canadian levity in letters.

WALTER LIPPMANN (1889–1974) was an American newsman and intellectual who wrote essays for *Vanity Fair* throughout the 1920s and 1930s. A nationally syndicated columnist, Lippmann is said to have popularized the term "cold war" and earned Pulitzer Prizes for Commentary and for International Reporting.

THOMAS MANN (1875–1955) was a German novelist whose works such as *Buddenbrooks, The Magic Mountain,* and *Death in Venice* placed him at the forefront of mid-twentieth-century European letters. He won the Nobel Prize in Literature in 1929; seven years later the German government revoked his citizenship because of his public criticism of Hitler's regime.

EDNA ST. VINCENT MILLAY (1892–1950) was an American poet and playwright whose verse, according to the poet Richard Wilbur, contained "some of the best sonnets of the century." She won the Pulitzer Prize for Poetry in 1923 and continued to write satirical essays for *Vanity Fair* under the pseudonym Nancy Boyd throughout the twenties.

A. A. MILNE (1882–1956) was a British writer, playwright, and humorist acclaimed for his series of poems and stories about Christopher Robin and Winnie-the-Pooh, which are regarded as classics of children's literature.

HELEN BROWN NORDEN (1908–1982) was an American journalist and critic who contributed to *Vanity Fair* during the 1930s. A mistress of Condé Nast, the publisher of *Vogue* and *Vanity Fair,* Norden created a stir in 1936 when *Esquire* published her article "Latins Are Lousy Lovers."

ANNE O'HAGAN (1869–1934) was an early contributor to *Vanity Fair, Munsey's Magazine,* and the *Century Magazine.* Her writing was marked by its strong social conscience, most memorably, perhaps, for her chapter in *The Sturdy Oak,* a composite novel sold to benefit the suffragette movement.

DOROTHY ROTHSCHILD PARKER (1893–1967) was a staff writer and drama critic for *Vanity Fair* from 1917 to 1920; the magazine ran her first published poem in 1915, when she was twenty-two years old. Known for her lacerating wit, Parker, a mainstay of the Algonquin Round Table, was a poet, humorist, short story writer, civil rights activist, and screenwriter. (She received Oscar nominations for her work on *A Star Is Born* and *Smash-Up: The Story of a Woman.*)

E. M. ROBERTS was an American pilot whose memoir, *A Flying Fighter,* recounted his days as a World War I aviator in Britain's Royal Flying Corps.

BERTRAND RUSSELL (1872–1970) was a British philosopher, social critic, mathematician, and essayist who is considered one of the founders of analytic philosophy. Russell was awarded the Nobel Prize in Literature in 1950 "in recognition of his varied and significant writings in which he champions humanitarian ideals and freedom of thought."

CARL SANDBURG (1878–1967) was an American poet, historian, novelist, and journalist who won three Pulitzer Prizes, the first in 1919 for his poetry collection *Cornhuskers,* the second in 1940 for his four-volume biography, *Abraham Lincoln: The War Years,* and the third in 1951 for *The Complete Poems of Carl Sandburg.* Sandburg, who wrote a biography of *Vanity Fair* photographer Edward Steichen, was married to Steichen's sister Lillian.

WILLIAM SAROYAN (1908–1981) was an Armenian American playwright whose works often explored the immigrant experience in America. Saroyan won the Pulitzer Prize for Drama in 1940 (for his play *The Time of Your Life*) and a 1943 Academy Award for the film based on his novel *The Human Comedy.* A statue of Saroyan stands in Yerevan,

Armenia, where half of his ashes are buried; the other half are interred in Fresno, California.

CHARLES G. SHAW (1892–1974) was an American painter and critic who played a major role in the development of abstract art in America. An occasional contributor to *Vanity Fair* and the *New Yorker* during the Jazz Age, Shaw did not begin painting until he was well into his thirties.

ROBERT E. SHERWOOD (1896–1955), a *Vanity Fair* contributor in the teens, was an American playwright, screenwriter, and a member of the Algonquin Round Table. He had several successful screenplays to his credit (including *Rebecca, The Best Years of Our Lives,* and *The Bishop's Wife*) and served as a speechwriter for President Franklin D. Roosevelt, an experience that helped shape Sherwood's Pulitzer Prize–winning history, *Roosevelt and Hopkins.*

GERTRUDE STEIN (1874–1946), an experimental American poet, novelist, and memoirist, contributed poetry and essays to *Vanity Fair,* her early verse appearing while she volunteered as an ambulance driver during World War I. For nearly four decades, Stein's Paris home served as a salon for some of the greatest literary and artistic minds of the early twentieth century. Stein's memoir of those years, *The Autobiography of Alice B. Toklas,* was a literary and cultural sensation.

HYMAN STRUNSKY a short story writer, contributed essays to *Vanity Fair* in the 1910s.

ARTHUR SYMONS (1865–1945) was a British poet, critic, and a cofounder of the short-lived literary magazine the *Savoy*. Symons's monograph *The Symbolist Movement in Literature* is considered to have greatly influenced the early modernist poets.

ALLENE TALMEY (1903–1986) was the managing editor of *Vanity Fair* before becoming an associate editor and columnist for *Vogue*.

DARWIN L. TEILHET (1904–1964) was an American novelist and screenwriter whose most popular detective novels followed the adventures of one Baron von Kaz. His children's book *The Avion My Uncle Flew*—which he wrote under the pseudonym Cyrus Fisher—received a Newbery Honor in 1947.

DALTON TRUMBO (1905–1976) was an American screenwriter, novelist (*Johnny Got His Gun*), and a member of the Hollywood Ten, the group of movie insiders who, in 1947, refused to testify in front of the House Un-American Activities Committee about alleged Communist infiltration of the motion picture industry. Blacklisted for more than a decade, Trumbo (*Kitty Foyle, Roman Holiday, The Brave One, Spartacus, Exodus, The Sandpiper, Papillon*) was often forced to use a pseudonym, only belatedly receiving recognition for his work.

STANLEY WALKER (1898–1962) was an American journalist and the city editor of the *New York Herald Tribune* from 1928 to 1935. In his memoir *City Editor,* Walker wrote of the ideal newsman: "When he dies, a lot of people are sorry, and some of them remember him for several days."

HUGH WALPOLE (1884–1941) was a New Zealand–born British novelist known for his bestselling *The Herries Chronicle*. He enjoyed great literary and commercial success in his day and worked on the screenplays for the 1930s film versions of *David Copperfield* and *Little Lord Fauntleroy*. The essay published here on W. Somerset Maugham was an homage; Maugham, however, would later muddy Walpole's reputation by using him as a model for the self-absorbed, social-climbing protagonist in his novel *Cakes and Ale*.

WALTER WINCHELL (1897–1972) was an American radio personality and the country's first nationally syndicated gossip columnist. Famously ornery, Winchell earned notoriety for his vicious attacks on those he viewed as rivals. He would later narrate the popular television series *The Untouchables*.

P. G. WODEHOUSE (1881–1975), a frequent columnist and drama critic for *Vanity Fair*, was a humorist, playwright, journalist, novelist, and occasional lyricist. So prolific was Wodehouse during his *V.F.* tenure that he often contributed several pieces per issue, using pseudonyms such as Pelham Grenville, P. Brooke-Haven (after the Long Island town), and C. P. West (for Central Park West). Today, he is best remembered for his prize literary creations: the indelible British duo Bertie Wooster and his valet, Jeeves.

THOMAS WOLFE (1900–1938) was an American novelist who achieved distinction as an epic stylist in works such as *Look Homeward, Angel*, and *Of Time and the River*, both of which focused on life in Asheville, North Carolina. One of his most popular novels, *You Can't Go Home Again*, was published after Wolfe's death, at age thirty-seven, from complications related to tuberculosis.

ALEXANDER WOOLLCOTT (1887–1943) was an American critic, commentator, and actor, as well as a frequent contributor to the *New York Times*, the *New York Herald*, *Vanity Fair*, the *New Yorker*, and other publications. A member of the Algonquin Round Table, and the basis for the character Sheridan Whiteside in the George S. Kauffman–Moss Hart play *The Man Who Came to Dinner*, Woollcott died of a cerebral hemorrhage shortly after suffering a heart attack on live radio.